EARLY JUDAISM

D1296442

JEWISH STUDIES IN THE 21ST CENTURY

Frederick E. Greenspahn is Gimelstob Eminent Scholar of Judaic Studies at Florida Atlantic University. Greenspahn is General Editor of the Jewish Studies in the 21st Century Series, and is the volume editor of the following books in the series:

Early Judaism

New Insights and Scholarship

Edited by
Frederick E. Greenspahn

NEW YORK UNIVERSITY PRESS
New York

NEW YORK UNIVERSITY PRESS
New York
www.nyupress.org

© 2018 by New York University
All rights reserved

References to Internet websites (URLs) were accurate at the time of writing. Neither the author nor New York University Press is responsible for URLs that may have expired or changed since the manuscript was prepared.

Library of Congress Cataloging-in-Publication Data
Names: Greenspahn, Frederick E., 1946– editor.
Title: Early Judaism : new insights and scholarship / edited by Frederick E. Greenspahn.
Description: New York : New York University Press, 2018. | Includes bibliographical references and index.
Identifiers: LCCN 2017037989 | ISBN 978-1-4798-9695-0 (cl : alk. paper) | ISBN 978-1-4798-0990-5 (pb : alk. paper)
Subjects: LCSH: Judaism—History—Post-exilic period, 586 B.C.–210 A.D.
Classification: LCC BM176 .E27 2018 | DDC 296.09/014—dc23
LC record available at https://lccn.loc.gov/2017037989

New York University Press books are printed on acid-free paper, and their binding materials are chosen for strength and durability. We strive to use environmentally responsible suppliers and materials to the greatest extent possible in publishing our books.

Manufactured in the United States of America

10 9 8 7 6 5 4 3 2 1

Also available as an ebook

CONTENTS

Introduction

FREDERICK E. GREENSPAHN

Although Judaism traces its roots to the Hebrew Bible, many of its practices and beliefs differ from those mandated there. Most conspicuously,
the Bible never mentions synagogues or rabbis, prescribing instead a regimen of sacrifices led by priests at sacred shrines, most often in Jerusalem.
Even its depiction of familiar customs often differs from modern-day
practice, as when it requires that the Passover holiday be observed by
slaughtering and eating a lamb (Exod 12:1–10) rather than gathering for a
family meal and reciting the story of the exodus as Jews do today.

The most striking difference between biblical religion and Judaism
is the failure of biblical figures to invoke written authority from sacred
texts. Thus, the prophet Nathan condemns David's adultery with Bath-
sheba (2 Sam 12:1–12) without citing the Ten Commandments' prohibition of such behavior, much as Miriam's criticism of Moses's marriage
to a non-Jew (Numbers 12:1) does not refer to Deuteronomy's prohibition of such unions (7:1–4). Nor is there any evidence that holy books
were read regularly during the biblical period, although a sacred book
(presumably Deuteronomy) was discovered and its teachings enacted
toward the end of the kingdom of Judah.[1] This impression is supported
by documents, from a Jewish colony that existed on the island of Elephantine in the Nile Valley late in the biblical period, that do not appeal
to sacred texts, even when addressing practices covered by biblical law.[2]

Judaism's roots may lie in the Bible, but many of its practices and
beliefs took shape later than the events depicted there. Much of its development occurred in the centuries between the Babylonian exile (586
BCE) and the rise of Christianity, during which time Jews were under
the rule of Greeks and Romans as well as their own Maccabean dynasty.
In other words, Judaism as we know it today emerged well after the period described in the Bible.

Yet Jewish tradition claims otherwise, finding biblical precedent for many of its practices. The Talmud, which is the primary source for Jewish practice, often supports its mandates with texts from the Torah, even though close scrutiny reveals many of those claims to be weak. The Mishnah (the earliest part of the Talmud) itself concedes that some of its laws "float in the air with nothing to support them," while the rabbis sometimes acknowledged that these verses are "merely an *asmakhta*" (lit. "support").[3]

One of the most significant developments during the Second Temple period (520 BCE–70 CE) was the rising importance of sacred texts, which seem not to have played a role for most of the biblical era, even if they were in the process of being written then.[4] That focus on texts began early in the Second Temple period. Ezra is said to have publicly read a holy book to those Judeans who returned from Babylonian exile; and the book of Daniel, which is the last book to have been written in the Jewish Bible, cites Jeremiah as scripture, suggesting that the process of creating a Bible was under way by the second century BCE.[5] Other works from that period, such as the Wisdom of Ben Sira, abound with allusions to sacred books, as do the New Testament and the Mishnah, which were compiled in the first and second Christian centuries. These texts also refer to synagogues, rabbis, and scripture reading, suggesting the changes that had already transpired in the tradition's development toward its contemporary form. Indeed, the Mishnah's description of Passover closely matches the way that the holiday is observed today.[6] It also records discussions about which books were sacred and which not.[7] The New Testament's account of scripture reading in a synagogue visited by Jesus (Luke 4:16–21) is supported by the inscription from a first-century synagogue in Jerusalem, which describes the building as a place "for the reading aloud (*anagōsin*) of the law and the study of the commandments."[8] An early rabbinic code also insists that synagogues be equipped with copies of both the Torah and the Prophets.[9]

In short, the Bible itself and, certainly, its liturgical and legal use appear to be products of the "postbiblical" period, beginning around the sixth-century BCE Babylonian exile. That is not to say that its contents were written then, but that the process of collecting them and treating them as sacred—what scholars call "canonization"—took place after the events described within them.[10] In other words, as the philosopher Yeshayahu Leibowitz put it, "Judaism is not founded on the Bible; the Bible is founded upon Judaism!"[11]

The goal of this book is to present what modern scholars have learned about this early form of Judaism—the time in which Judaism as we know it took shape in the wake of the Second Temple period. Only after the Temple was destroyed did a normative Judaism emerge out of the previous diversity, with the proliferation of synagogues, the standardization of the liturgy, and the coalescence of a more-or-less uniform set of beliefs and practices.

As we will see, at the beginning of this period there were various groups under the large canopy of Jewry, each with its own beliefs and behaviors. That diversity is one of the most striking features of Jewish life during the Second Temple period. Ancient authors such as the first-century philosopher Philo, who lived in Alexandria, Egypt, and Josephus, who compiled a history of the Jews while living in Rome, tell of several competing parties—most famously the Pharisees, Sadducees, Essenes, and Zealots.[12] They also describe a group called Therapeautae, who lived in Egypt and interpreted the Bible allegorically, as did others.[13] There were also Jewish temples in the northern part of what is today Israel as well as in Egypt, despite the biblical restriction of sacrifice to Jerusalem.[14]

The New Testament and rabbinic writings mention several of these groups, while other sources tell of individuals who followed Jewish beliefs and practices without becoming fully Jewish.[15] At this early stage, the rabbis were only one of many competing forms of Judaism rather than the "mainstream" it later became. Scholars have, therefore, reexamined rabbinic writings both to glean what they can about the diversity of ancient Jewish life and also to construct the rabbis' own history, including their eventual rise to normativity.

The resulting picture has been dramatically supported by the discovery and publication of the Dead Sea Scrolls over the past half century. Although the identity of the group that produced them is still a matter of debate, there is no doubt as to their Jewishness. However, as James VanderKam explains in this volume, their beliefs were significantly different from those that came to be normative. The fact that these documents were found in the desert, away from the authorities in Jerusalem, suggests that theirs were not the officially approved practices or beliefs at the time. Indeed, the scrolls themselves describe a confrontation between the community's leadership and the priestly authorities as to when the Day of Atonement (Yom Kippur) should be observed.[16] This community also seems to have followed several books that were not accepted by later Jews.

Some of those documents, which have come to be known as the Apocrypha and pseudepigrapha, are preserved in the Old Testaments of various Christian communities.[17] Martha Himmelfarb's chapter describes the beliefs of one of the groups among which these writings originated, while Erich Gruen draws on inscriptions found at various sites along the Mediterranean that demonstrate that Jewishness was understood very differently then than we might assume. Collectively, these sources confirm that Jewish identity was very fluid in antiquity. Some scholars, therefore, speak of the religion of that period as "Judaisms," while others point to pervasive practices, such as circumcision, purity laws, Sabbath observance, sacred gatherings, and support of the Temple, as evidence of a "common Judaism."[18] However, Seth Schwartz's chapter warns against letting our understanding of that period be colored by contemporary concerns.

Christianity, which began as one of the many forms of ancient Judaism, also took shape during this period. Jesus's earliest followers were all Jews, and as late as the fourth century there were still "Christians" who preferred to worship in synagogues. That phenomenon raises the question of how and when Christianity came to be seen as a separate religion. Adele Reinhartz discusses the different scholarly views of how that split, which is still controversial in some circles, took place.

The Romans' destruction of the Jerusalem Temple in the year 70 CE played a major role leading to the emergence of Judaism as we know it today. Although archaeologists have shown that synagogues already existed before that event, Steven Fine's chapter describes how later synagogues commemorated that now-lost institution in both their architectural design and practice. Many of the rituals that had been conducted at the Temple were also incorporated into daily life, albeit in significantly different ways. Even so central a practice as prayer has a history: in biblical times, it seems to have been largely spontaneous and private.[19] However, the Dead Sea Scrolls demonstrate that by the Second Temple period it had come to be a fixed activity. Communal prayer was later standardized, as outlined in Ruth Langer's chapter, and considered a replacement for Temple sacrifice by the rabbis.

Although scholars continue to debate the rabbis' history and their relationship to the other groups that existed prior to the Second Temple's destruction, it was their views that came to be normative. Elizabeth Shanks Alexander's chapter explores the rabbis' understanding of gender, which informs debates about women's roles in Judaism to the present day, though it may not accurately reflect daily experience. Finally, Christine Hayes describes the various reconstructions that scholars have offered for how rabbinic Judaism achieved mainstream status.

The shift from the diversity of the Second Temple period to the dominance of rabbinic Judaism illuminates the roots of many of the features that characterize Jewish life today. Modern Jews are again remarkably diverse, practicing their religion in ways that extend well beyond familiar categories of Orthodox, Conservative, Reform, and Reconstructionist. There are also competing definitions of what it means to be a Jew—whether it is a nationality, a culture, or a religion (which can, itself, take several different forms). Some communities even think it possible to combine Christian beliefs with Jewish practices. And, of course, the emergence of modern Israel has restored Judaism's geographic center, resulting in the presence of a Jewish nation alongside the diaspora for the first time in two thousand years. At the same time, recent studies, such as those embodied in a 2013 Pew Center report, suggest that long-established Jewish social and community structures are dissolving even as Jewish life and practice become more varied.[20] These developments lead Robert Goldenberg, in this volume's conclusion, to infer that we may be experiencing a reversion to the kind of Jewish reality that existed prior to the year 70.

Exploring Jewish antiquity is, thus, of value for understanding contemporary dynamics, at the same time that it illuminates an important and often misunderstood part of the Jewish past. Our growing knowledge about a long-ago period demonstrates the value of academic research for understanding the present as well as the past—in other words, how things are as well as how they came to be.

Many people contributed to this volume's creation besides the scholars whose research and discoveries fill its pages. Herbert and Elaine Gimelstob's commitment and generosity laid the groundwork for the larger project of which it is a part. Robert Goldenberg and Gregory Sterling provided guidance and insight in its formulation. Heather Coltman, Miriam Dalin, Deena Grant, Erik Larson, Kristen Lindbeck, and Susan Marks supported both its execution and evaluation. Jennifer Hammer guided its formulation. Inbal Mazar made sure that all the pieces fit together so that the plan could become a reality. And, as always, Barbara Pearl provided the intellectual, moral, and physical support that made its realization both possible and rewarding.

NOTES

1 Cf. 2 Kings 22–23.
2 Cf. Bezalel Porten, *Archives from Elephantine: The Life of an Ancient Jewish Military Colony* (Berkeley: University of California Press, 1968).
3 *M. Ḥagigah* 1:8, *t. Ḥagigah* 1:9, *t. Eruvin* 11:23–24, *b. Yoma* 74a.
4 William M. Schniedewind, *How the Bible Became a Book: The Textualization of Ancient Israel* (Cambridge: Cambridge University Press, 2004).
5 Nehemiah 8:1–8; Daniel 9:2.
6 *M. Pesaḥim* 10; cf. Baruch M. Bokser, *The Origins of the Seder: The Passover Rite and Early Rabbinic Judaism* (Berkeley: University of California Press, 1984).
7 E.g., *m. Yadayim* 3:5.
8 John S. Kloppenborg, "Dating Theodotus (*CIJ* II 1404)," *Journal for Jewish Studies* 51 (2000): 243–280.
9 *T. Baba Meṣia* 11:23.
10 Cf. Michael L. Satlow, *How the Bible Became Holy* (New Haven, CT: Yale University Press, 2014).
11 Yeshayahu Leibowitz, "An Interpretation of the Jewish Religion," in *Judaism Crisis Survival: An Anthology of Lectures*, ed. Ann Rose (Paris: World Union of Jewish Students, 1966), p. 33.
12 Josephus, *Jewish Antiquities* 13.v.9 §§171–173 and 18:i.2–6 §§11–25 (Loeb Classical Library [LCL] vol. 7, pp. 310–313 and vol. 9, pp. 8–23), *Jewish War* 2:viii.2–14 §§119–166 (LCL vol. 2. pp. 368–387); Philo, *Every Good Man Is Free* 12 §§75–91 (LCL vol. 9, pp. 54–63), *Hypothetica* 11.1–18 (LCL vol. 9, pp. 436–443).
13 Philo, *On the Contemplative Life* (LCL vol. 9, pp. 113–169), *The Special Laws* III. xxxii §178 (LCL vol. 7, pp. 586–587), *Migration of Abraham* XVI §§89–93 (LCL vol. 4, pp. 182–185), and *Questions and Answers on Genesis* IV §196 (LCL Supp. vol. 1, p. 485).
14 Cf. William W. Hallo and K. Lawson Younger, Jr., *The Context of Scripture* (Leiden: Brill, 2003), vol. 3, pp. 125–132; Josephus, *Jewish War* 1:i.1 §33, 7:x.2 §§421–432, *Antiquities* 11:viii.2–4 §§306–324, 12:ix.7 §§387–388, 13:iii.1–3 §§62–73, and 13:x.4 §285 (LCL vol. 2, pp. 18–19, vol. 3, pp. 622–627, vol. 6, pp. 462–471, vol. 7, pp. 200–203, 256–263, and 370–371).

15 Louis Feldman, "The Omnipresence of the God-Fearers," *Biblical Archaeology Review* 12.5 (September–October 1986): 58–69.

16 1QpHab at 2:15, see Geza Vermes, *The Complete Dead Sea Scrolls in English* (fiftieth anniversary edition, London: Penguin, 2011), p. 515.

17 The books of the Apocrypha are included in Catholic editions of the Bible; for pseudepigrapha, see James Charlesworth, *The Old Testament Pseudepigrapha* (Garden City, NY: Doubleday, 1983–1985); and Richard Bauckham, James Davila, and Alexander Panayotov, *Old Testament Pseudepigrapha: More Noncanonical Scriptures* (Grand Rapids, MI: William B. Eerdmans, 2013). See also Lawrence H. Schiffman, Louis H. Feldman, and James Kugel, *Outside the Bible: Ancient Jewish Writings Related to Scripture* (Philadelphia: Jewish Publication Society, 2013).

18 E. P. Sanders, *Judaism: Practice and Belief, 63 BCE–66 CE* (Philadelphia: Trinity Press International, 1992); E. P. Sanders, "Common Judaism Explored" in *Common Judaism, Explorations in Second-Temple Judaism*, ed. Wayne O. McCready and Adele Reinhartz (Minneapolis, MN: Fortress Press, 2008), pp. 11–23.

19 Moshe Greenberg, *Biblical Prose Prayer as a Window to the Popular Religion of Ancient Israel* (Berkeley: University of California Press, 1983).

20 Pew Research Center, "A Portrait of Jewish Americans" (October 1, 2013), www.pewforum.org (accessed July 13, 2017).

PART I

Early Diversity

1

The Dead Sea Scrolls

JAMES VANDERKAM

The Dead Sea Scrolls have attracted much attention from the public and from a decent-sized cadre of scholars who devote much of their research time to studying these texts. The latter group has produced and continues to produce so many studies that it is difficult even for someone in the field to stay abreast of the results.[1] This chapter examines some key aspects of Scrolls studies that are debated by contemporary scholars and surveys what is being said about them.

This chapter thus takes up three broad topics: (1) the archaeology of Khirbet Qumran (where the Dead Sea Scrolls were discovered); (2) the community associated with the scrolls; and (3) questions regarding the "biblical" scrolls. There are certainly other areas of inquiry that could have been selected, since the scrolls have exercised influence on the study of many areas of early Jewish literature and have stimulated debates in them, but the three discussed here should provide insight into the world of Dead Sea Scrolls scholarship. Before turning to those topics, let me give a quick overview of the subject.[2]

The term "Dead Sea Scrolls" refers to the remains of approximately nine hundred manuscripts. We tend to call them "scrolls," but only a few complete or nearly complete scrolls were discovered; most of the texts are fragmentary remains, often very fragmentary, of once intact scrolls. They have fallen apart due to deterioration caused by moisture, other substances, animals, and the like.

Most of those manuscripts were made of parchment, that is, treated animal hides; a number of them are on papyrus, while one is made of copper. They were found in eleven caves situated near the northwest corner of the Dead Sea. The manuscript-bearing caves were found in 1947 (cave 1), 1952 (caves 2–6), 1955 (caves 7–10), and 1956 (cave 11). The most successful hunters for caves containing written material were Bedouin, Arab natives of the area. In 1947 three of them found the first cave. Bedouin also located most of the others, including caves 4 and 11, which, with cave 1, contained the largest amount of written material. Archaeologists found just a few of the caves, most of which had the modest remains of only a small number of texts.[3]

The caves are located in the vicinity of building ruins at a place called Qumran in Arabic (Khirbet Qumran means "the ruin of Qumran"), where, according to most experts, the group that used the scrolls had carried out their communal life. Archaeological evidence suggests that the site was used from after 100 BCE until 68 or 70 CE, with a short break in occupation around the turn of the eras. The structures are unusual in comparison to other building ruins in the area or elsewhere in Judea (more on that below). Distinctive pottery—long, tall scroll jars—found both in the caves and at the site was a first clue that the scrolls in the caves were associated with the people who used the site.

The scrolls, all of which have been published, contain examples of many categories of Jewish literature.[4] The most famous type is probably the "biblical" scrolls. Of the books in the Hebrew Bible (Protestant Old Testament), all are represented except Esther, with a total of 222 separate copies (including Greek and Aramaic translations). If we include the books in the Catholic Old Testament (that is, the Protestant Old Testament plus Apocrypha), the total is a little higher.

It is worth highlighting that in examining the subject of the Dead Sea Scrolls we are really dealing with two major phenomena: the site of the building ruins (Khirbet Qumran) and the scrolls from the eleven nearby caves. No scroll or scroll fragment has turned up in the building ruins. As we will see, the relationship between the site and the scrolls has been debated, although almost all experts who work in this field agree that the two are related in the sense that the people of the scrolls used the site.

Now let us turn to the three topics listed above.

The Archaeology of Khirbet Qumran

It is often instructive in studying the Dead Sea Scrolls to go back to the earliest published articles and books about them. Here is an example. The first discoveries of manuscripts in a cave took place in 1947 (or at least that is the most likely date); it was not until late that year and early in 1948 that scholars obtained some of them and began to study these amazing finds.[5] Other than the Bedouin and a few of their acquaintances, no one even knew where the cave was until January 1949. At that point the first two archaeologists in the field, Father Roland de Vaux and G. Lankester Harding, excavated the cave and also visited the ruins located more than half a mile away—Khirbet Qumran. The first conclusion de Vaux drew upon briefly visiting the site was that the scrolls in the cave and the nearby site were unrelated.[6] Later, when a distinctive kind of jar (for holding scrolls) found in the cave turned up at the site, a relation between them became much more likely. That likelihood greatly increased as the scrolls and the site were examined in more detail.

Once it became evident that the buildings at the site and the scrolls in the cave were related, archaeologists began more thoroughly investigating the ruins occupying a nearby plateau. The leader of five seasons of excavation (1951 and 1953–1956) was de Vaux, who was affiliated with the École Biblique, a French Dominican school in Jerusalem. He was an experienced archaeologist and, because of his prominent role in excavating the site, in an ideal position to articulate a comprehensive interpretation of data.[7]

De Vaux identified two principal periods of occupation. First, in the eighth to seventh centuries BCE, a small city occupied the site. (It may be the one named Secacah in the Bible, in Josh 15:61.)[8] The ruins of a rectangular building were traced to this phase. Second, after a gap of several centuries there is evidence for renewed occupation when the people associated with the scrolls used the area. De Vaux divided the two centuries that he thought were involved in this second occupation into two phases, the first of which he further subdivided. A brief third phase seems to have followed.

Phase Ia

Few remains survive from this early reoccupation because later construction and destruction removed most of them. On the basis of coins and other artifacts from the next phase, de Vaux concluded that the short phase Ia began not far from 140 BCE.

Phase Ib

De Vaux argued that phase Ib began probably during the reign of the Hasmonean ruler and high priest John Hyrcanus (134–104 BCE). The people who utilized the site added upper stories to the existing structures and expanded the buildings to the west and south. They extended the water system, built an aqueduct that brought water from the hills into the building complex, and coated the entire system with plaster. The remains from phase Ib indicate that the population of the area grew considerably beyond the number there in phase Ia. A fire and an earthquake—they may have happened simultaneously—led to the end of the phase. The Jewish historian Josephus (37–about 100 CE) dates an earthquake in the area to the year 31 BCE, so this marked the end of phase Ib for de Vaux.

Phase II

De Vaux believed that the site was abandoned after the earthquake until the death of King Herod in 4 BCE. Phase II lasted from that time until 68 CE, when Roman troops who were putting down the Jewish revolt in the area (the revolt lasted from 66 to 70) attacked and destroyed the buildings, whose ruins also show evidence of a fire. De Vaux inferred the date of 68 from the fact that eighty-three bronze coins of the second year of the revolt (67 CE) were found at Qumran, but there were only five from the third year (68 CE). Some Roman arrowheads made of iron and belonging to a type known in the first century CE were found at Qumran.

Phase III

Roman soldiers who were stationed at Qumran after the end of phase II built a few barracks, mostly in the southwestern corner of the central building. The coins of this phase extend to about 90 CE, although ones from the Bar Kokhba period (132–135 CE) suggest that rebels used the site at this later time.

De Vaux did not think that the buildings at Qumran were residential in nature. For him it was a community center (for eating, meeting, working) while the people who used the buildings may have lived in less permanent shelters, perhaps even in some of the caves. The furniture and two inkwells found in the room designated locus 30 led de Vaux to conclude that at least some scrolls from the caves were written there.

In the post–de Vaux debate about the Qumran site, there have been experts who largely accept his interpretation while adjusting the chronological limits for the phases of occupation that he hypothesized; others have read the evidence far differently. All look forward to the time when the evidence from the digs at Qumran will be published in full. A short summary of the post–de Vaux discussions follows below.

Jodi Magness's monograph *The Archaeology of Qumran and the Dead Sea Scrolls* is the most widely cited study since de Vaux's book.[9] Building on work by others and her own analysis, she defends the following points regarding the phases distinguished by de Vaux:

1. There was no period corresponding to de Vaux's Ia.
2. De Vaux misdated the beginning of Ib (the large number of coins from the reign of Alexander Jannaeus [103–76 BCE] suggested to him that it had been occupied *by* this time whereas they entail only that the coins could not have come from a time earlier than his reign). Magness thinks that the occupation of Qumran occurred some time between 100 and 50 BCE and that the site was sectarian (Essene) from the beginning (the size and number of the ritual baths are one piece of evidence for her conclusion). That is, there is no indication in the archaeological data suggesting a change of function.
3. The gap in occupation between Ib and II was not nearly as long as de Vaux thought. Magness's argument involves the interpretation of a collection of 561 Tyrian silver coins; she places them in phase I and thinks they show that occupation continued until 9/8 BCE. The earthquake of 31 BCE did not cause Qumran to be abandoned; a fire that broke out decades later did, but only for a short time. Soon (early in the reign of Archelaus [4 BCE–6 CE]) the site was rebuilt to look much as it did before—suggesting that the same people were involved.

Unlike Magness, the Israeli archaeologist Yitzhar Hirschfeld thought that the site did undergo a change in function: in his view, before 37 BCE it was a field fort and road station; after that it became a manor house.[10] It never was a sectarian site, and the buildings at Qumran are unrelated to the scrolls in the caves. The scrolls came from the Jerusalem Temple and were deposited there just before the Roman destruction of Jerusalem (a view defended by others before him).

The French archaeologist J.-B. Humbert thinks Qumran at first was a Hasmonean villa associated with farming in the area.[11] Occupation began during de Vaux's period Ia, and the villa was destroyed in 57 or 31 BCE. After 31 BCE, Essenes (one of the Jewish groups existing at the time) turned the site into a cultic center with an altar on the north side facing Jerusalem. It continued without a break in occupation. Only a small number of "guardians" lived in the buildings; others, the people who worked there, came from elsewhere. The site was destroyed in 68 CE.

One problem with Hirschfeld's suggestion that Qumran was for a time a manor house is that no similar structures are known. His theory does not account for the large cemetery adjacent to the site (more than 1,100 individual graves), and both the numerous, large ritual baths and the cemetery are more consistent with a sectarian interpretation. The idea that the people of the site and the scrolls are unrelated is exceedingly difficult to accept. Humbert's theory encounters the problem of demonstrating a change in function for the buildings, and there is no certainty about sacrifice at Qumran, though it may have occurred.[12]

Magness's views appear to be the best interpretation of the evidence; and she, like de Vaux, thinks the inhabitants of the site were the owners of the scrolls. The site is unique in several ways and does not appear to have been a fort or a manor house.

The Community Associated with the Scrolls

The conclusions drawn from the archaeological data have important implications for the bundle of questions involved in any study of the people who constructed and used the buildings. If, as seems likely, the function of the site did not change substantially over time, with what kind of group are the artifacts most consistent? The evidence points to the conclusion that it was a place for a relatively small population that was concerned with matters of ritual purity, was nonmilitary in nature, and lived with a lot of scrolls nearby.[13]

A standard view is reflected in the work of several of the original team of scholars, who published histories of the community of the scrolls (a subject, incidentally, about which we know surprisingly little).[14] Some shared features of those accounts are that, at some point in the mid- to later second century BCE, a group of Essenes (on them, see below) under priestly leadership left the centers of Jewish society in Judea and went to the wilderness near the shore of the Dead Sea. They were a pro- test group led by someone they called the Teacher of Righteousness; they directed their criticisms against the national leadership and the priests. One important point on which this protest group and their op- ponents differed was the calendar used to date the festivals commanded in the law. The people of the scrolls advocated a solar year lasting 364 days and dated the holidays on the basis of it. They believed the cor- rect calendar could be read from the scriptures and that the authorities did not follow it, preferring the luni-solar one current in their world.[15] The group may also have taken issue with the reigning high priest—one of the Maccabees/Hasmoneans who had recently usurped the position from the Oniad family that had traditionally held the office. The way of life pursued by this self-exiled community is described in the Rule of the Community, one of the Dead Sea Scrolls: an all-male fellowship shared meals and possessions, enforced a strict communal discipline, worshiped together, and studied the ancient scriptures together. With one break, the community remained at Qumran until 68 CE, when, faced with an attack by a Roman legion, the members hid their scrolls in nearby caves.

There are some difficulties with this theory if we accept the conclu- sions reached above in the section about archaeology. The evidence in- dicates that the site of Qumran was built up at some time in the first half of the first century BCE, so that the conditions believed to have sparked an exodus of the community to that place would have to be sought in later historical circumstances than the early Hasmonean period (ca. 160–130 BCE), though admittedly all the underlying issues could have been the same at a later time (other than a recent usurpation of the high priesthood by the Hasmoneans). Another problem is explaining why a relatively small, isolated group had so many scrolls.[16] Even if some two hundred people (this was de Vaux's estimate) used the site of Qumran, about nine hundred scrolls is a lot of texts.[17] And why did these people, who often claimed they were living in the last days, remain in their place of exile for more than a century?

While many students of the scrolls have defended or accepted some variation of the theory outlined above, there have been several rival suggestions. Some of them are connected with what appear to be unlikely readings of the archaeological evidence. So, for example, a few scholars (e.g., Hirschfeld, Humbert) have interpreted the place differently—as a fortress, farm, villa, cultic center, trading depot, or scroll manufacturing or handling site. Some of these theories assume a change in function over time, and some posit no connection between those who used the site and the scrolls in the caves—the scrolls reached the caves in some other way and were not owned and used by the people of the site. This last claim is implausible in view of how close cave 4, which contained a majority of the scrolls, is to the buildings. None of these hypotheses have succeeded in incorporating all the evidence from Khirbet Qumran. Weaknesses in these theories do not entail that the dominant one is correct, but they have not dislodged its basic contours. However, as noted, the dominant view sketched above struggles to account for the large number of scrolls in the caves (more on this below).

If the site did not change in function over time and members of the same group used it throughout its existence, it would be helpful to know who they were. From the very beginning of reflection on the scrolls, there has been a widely accepted view that the people at Qumran were a small subset of the much larger Essene movement.[18] Over the decades there have been other suggestions—they were Pharisees, Sadducees (in some sense) (Pharisees and Sadducees were, with the Essenes, important Jewish groups at this period), or they did not belong to any of the groups known to us. None of these other theories, however, are very likely to be true, while the Essene hypothesis is far more consistent with the evidence.

The arguments for the Essene identification are familiar. First, the beliefs and practices seen in the scrolls match the ancient descriptions of the Essenes better than any other group. Second, Pliny the Elder's location of an Essene settlement north of Engedi (*Natural History* 5.73) is consistent with the location of Qumran. Also, his short description of the Essenes fits nicely with what the scrolls disclose about those who used the site of Qumran.

One of the standard objections to the hypothesis that the people of Qumran were Essenes is that in the scrolls the writers never call themselves Essenes. That is, it is a term we know only from other sources written in Greek and Latin. Against those who raise this objection, I think the writers of the scrolls do designate themselves by the Semitic word that gave rise to the Greek and Latin transcriptions of the name. They refer to themselves as "doers of the Torah," and the participle "doers" (ôsê) is the word that was transcribed as "Essene." This proposal has the advantage that it involves a word actually used by the scrolls writers for themselves—something no other theory about the meaning of "Essene" can claim. The letter *n* of the form, used at times by Josephus (in Greek) and by Pliny the Elder (in Latin), could reflect the Aramaic form of the participle (ending in –în). The first vowel of the word in most of the ancient spellings ("e") could have resulted from an Aramaic-like pronunciation of it in the participle (ā), with the guttural letter *(ayin)* influencing it to sound more like an "e"—perhaps especially to a nonnative speaker.

"Doers of the Torah" is used in the Qumran commentary on the biblical book of Habakkuk (1QpHab 7:10–12) as a group designation. The passage contains an explanation of Hab 2:3b: "If it seems to tarry, wait for it; it will surely come, it will not delay" (NRSV). The delay in God's definitive response to evil was a concern for the people of the community who thought the end was close at hand. The commentary (*pesher*) reads: "Interpreted, this concerns the men of truth who keep [lit. "do"] the Law, whose hands shall not slacken in the service of truth when the final age is prolonged." A little farther along in the same sectarian text, when commenting on Hab 2:4 ("but the righteous live by their faith"), the expositor writes, "Interpreted, this concerns all those who observe [lit. "do"] the Law in the House of Judah, whom God will deliver from the House of Judgement because of their suffering and because of their faith in the Teacher of Righteousness" (8:1–3).[19] There are other references as well.[20]

If we agree that the people of Qumran were Essenes, it would help with the problem of the large number of scrolls, because Essenes were a learned group with a reputation for using and interpreting old texts. But the presence of more than nine hundred manuscripts in the desert of Judah remains an issue. One intriguing and innovative suggestion is the thesis that we should not speak of one scrolls community but of several.[21] It has been known for a long time that two of the constitutional texts among the scrolls, that is, ones that describe and legislate for the life of a community—called the Damascus Document and the Rule of the Community—picture different kinds of communities.[22] The former provides for families among members; the latter does not. This discrepancy has usually been interpreted to reflect the statement of Josephus that there were two kinds of Essenes: those who married and those who did not. The Damascus Document describes the arrangements for those Essenes who married, while the Rule of the Community pictures the celibate kind of Essenes. However, beyond this fundamental distinction, the texts indicate that there were additional related communities scattered in various places. One clue is the reference to "camps." In the Damascus Document (CD 7:6–7) one reads: "And if they live in camps according to the rule of the land, marrying and begetting children, they shall walk according to the Law and according to the statute . . ." The Community Rule seems to point in the same direction: though it speaks of the Community (*ha-yaḥad*), it also mentions various smaller groups in different places: column 6 refers to associations of ten wherever they may live (*mgwryhm*; 6:1–8). The community described in this text—the *yaḥad*—seems to be a larger, umbrella organization encompassing a number of subgroups living in various, perhaps nearby places.

This hypothesis not only makes us broaden our view about the number of people associated with the scrolls and their locations reflected in the texts but also provides an answer to the question about why there were more than nine hundred scrolls in the caves. It is possible that the area of Qumran served as a central hiding place for scrolls held by several like-minded communities in the region. This theory may also allow us to explain in a more convincing way why different versions of the Community Rule—some of which have conflicting practical details such as the penalties for the same infractions—were found in the caves. Perhaps the variant versions of this constitutional document belonged to different groups whose practices were not exactly the same.[23]

Questions regarding the "Biblical" Scrolls

Among the more than nine hundred manuscripts identified by editors of the scrolls, some 222 qualify as copies of works that became parts of the Hebrew Bible.[24] The period in which the "biblical" scrolls were transcribed extends from the third century BCE to the first century CE, with most of them having been copied in the first century BCE or the first century CE. They come from a time many centuries before the earliest representative of the Masoretic Text (the official version of the Hebrew Bible)—they date from ca. 900 CE—and the most ancient codex of the Old Greek translation (fourth century CE). The Qumran copies may well mirror the nature of the texts of scriptural books not only at the small site of Qumran (and perhaps neighboring communities) but also elsewhere in Israel. The reason is that at least some of the scrolls (e.g., the earliest ones) were brought to the place from elsewhere, since they antedate the occupation of Qumran. So, what do these ancient copies of biblical books tell us?

Every book in the Hebrew Bible but one is represented by at least a single fragment among the Dead Sea Scrolls; the missing one is Esther. For some books very little remains (e.g., Chronicles), while for Isaiah one of the copies from cave 1 contains the whole lengthy book.

The Qumran manuscripts illustrate the fact that there was, from copy to copy, a degree of variation in the wording of scriptural texts—as one would expect in an age of hand copying. This is not to say that there was free variation in the wording of these books; but, within pretty narrow limits in most cases, there are noticeable differences from manuscript to manuscript.[25]

Among the scrolls there are hundreds of copies of scriptural books and a lot of evidence in the others that those books were important in various ways. Just how important were those books, or, put another way, did these people already have a Bible? The answer is yes and no. There is some evidence indicating that the group regarded some books as highly authoritative, that is, they treated them as what we would call "biblical."[26]

There are several passages in which writers refer to groups of books as authorities. The most common expression for those collections is "the law and the prophets" and variations on that phrase. There is good reason for thinking these two categories—law and prophets—included many of the works designated by the terms "law" and "prophets" in the later Hebrew canon of scripture. The Community Rule 1:1–3 says of the instructor that he is to teach the community members to "seek God with a whole heart and soul, and to do what is good and right before Him, as

He commanded by the hand of Moses and all His servants the prophets." The words of Moses in the law ("as He commanded by the hand of Moses") and those of the prophets ("all His servants the prophets") come from God.

There is a passage in one of the scrolls, called the "Halakhic Letter" (sometimes designated 4QMMT), that the editors of the text think may refer to all three divisions of the later Jewish canon (law, prophets, writings): "[And] we have [written] to you so that you may study (carefully) the book of Moses and the books of the Prophets and (the writings of) David [and the events of] ages past" (C 9–11).[27] The reconstruction presupposes a questionable placement of a fragment and rests on some dubious readings of letters. As a result, it seems unlikely that this text refers to the three divisions known from the later canon.[28]

I have found it helpful to ask several questions in trying to determine what the writers of the scrolls thought of a book or group of books:

1. Are there multiple copies of the book?
2. Does the work serve as an authority? That is,
   a. are citations from the book accompanied by claims they are from God?
   b. are citations from the book introduced by formulas known to be used for authoritative works?
   c. is there a commentary on it?

The more of these conditions a book meets, the more likely it is that it was considered authoritative, normative, even "biblical."

If we apply the first criterion (multiple copies), the most obvious candidates for importance are Psalms (thirty-six copies), Deuteronomy (thirty), Isaiah (twenty-one), Genesis (nineteen to twenty), Exodus (seventeen or fifteen), Leviticus (thirteen or twelve), Daniel (eight), and perhaps the Twelve Prophets (eight to nine). Conversely, it is unlikely that Chronicles, Esther, Ezra, and Nehemiah were valued as highly at Qumran because there are so few copies of them and there are no indications in other texts that they were influential. Moreover, some works not now in the Hebrew Bible appear in more copies than many books in it: Jubilees (fourteen), Enoch (eleven, but for different parts), the Book of Giants (nine or ten), and the Community Rule (perhaps eleven).

As for the second criterion, there are several scrolls passages stating that the material they quote from a book derives from God. There are some thirteen cases in which this happens (eight in the Damascus Document). For example, in Damascus Document 4:13–14 the writer states: "just as God said by Isaiah the prophet, the son of Amoz, saying" before quoting Isa 24:17. In the same text, the writer had earlier introduced Ezek 44:15 with the words "As God promised them by Ezekiel the prophet, saying" (CD 3:20–4:2). There are similar statements for books in the Pentateuch (e.g., CD 9:7–8; 4Q252 4:2–3; 1QM 11:5–7).

Intriguingly, there are cases in which a text or texts not in the Hebrew Bible receive such treatment. The first Psalms scroll from cave 11 (11QPs^a) contains a collection of psalms, most of which are found in the Psalter as represented in the Masoretic Text. One of its interesting features is that it includes nine units not in the standard Psalter. One of them is actually a prose passage, located at the beginning of the twenty-seventh column and called "David's Compositions" by its modern editor, James Sanders:

> David, son of Jesse, was wise and brilliant like the light of the sun; (he was) a scribe, intelligent and perfect in all his ways before God and men.
>
> YHWH gave him an intelligent and brilliant spirit, and he wrote 3,600 psalms and 364 songs to sing before the altar for the daily perpetual sacrifice, for all the days of the year; and 52 songs for the Sabbath offerings; and 30 songs for the New Moons, for Feast-days and for the Day of Atonement.
>
> In all, the songs which he uttered were 446, and 4 songs to make music on behalf of those stricken (by evil spirits). In all, they were 4,050. All these he uttered through prophecy which was given him from before the Most High.

The number of David's compositions catches attention—4,050, many greater than the 150 poems in the traditional Davidic Psalter. This could be an attempt to give David more publications than his son Solomon's 4,005 (see 1 Kgs 4:32), but all David's poetry was, this text claims, written through divine inspiration ("through prophecy" from God). One would think this designation would entail that it was authoritative or scriptural, so the writer and his group considered as inspired more than just the 150 Psalms now in the Hebrew Bible.

In the scrolls there are instances in which citations from scriptural works are introduced by formulas like "as it is written," "thus it is written." The Rule of the Community (1QS) 5, speaking about separating from bad people, legislates that "no member of the Community shall follow them in matters of doctrine or justice, or eat or drink anything of theirs, or take anything from them except for a price; as it is written, '*Keep away from the man in whose nostrils is breath for wherein is he counted?*'" (5:15–17; the citation is from Isa 2:22). Or, in column 8, it reads: "they shall separate from the habitation of unjust men and shall go into the wilderness to prepare there the way of Him; as it is written, *Prepare in the wilderness the way of . . . , make straight in the desert a path for our God* (Isa 40:3)" (8:13–14). This formula and similar ones introduce citations from Exodus (one), Leviticus (four), Numbers (three), Deuteronomy (five), 2 Samuel (one), Isaiah (nine), Jeremiah (one), Ezekiel (four), Hosea (three), Amos (two), Micah (one), Zechariah (two), Malachi (one), Psalms (two), Proverbs (one), and Daniel (two). Jubilees may be the book so referenced in 4Q228 1 i 9 (cf. CD 16:2–4), and a Levi text is introduced in this way in CD 4:15.

A series of prophetic books were considered so important that special commentaries (called *pesharim*) were written on all or parts of them: Isaiah (six), Hosea (two), Micah (two), Habakkuk (one), Nahum (one), Zephaniah (two), and Psalms (three).[29] Other books that received different kinds of commentaries are Genesis (e.g., 4Q252), Jeremiah, and Ezekiel (for the two prophetic works, see 4Q383–390).

By using the criteria listed above, one can show that many books now in the Bible were considered inspired and, therefore, authoritative in the scrolls communities. It is also possible to show that some not now in the Bible were held in similar regard—especially the writings of Enoch and Jubilees. Whether other Jewish people and groups agreed with this assessment we do not know. The scrolls communities did recognize some works as "biblical," to use a later term, but they also believed that God continued to reveal himself in their time—for example, he told the Teacher of Righteousness the meaning of the ancient prophecies (1QpHab 7:3–5)—and therefore more books could be added to the earlier scriptures even in this late time. We know that the people of Qumran treated some books as scriptural, but we do not know how many they so regarded.

* * *

To summarize, the proper interpretation of the ruins at the site of Qumran continues to be debated, though a widely accepted view today is that a sectarian group used it from some time between 100 and 50 BCE until around 70 CE, with one short gap just before the turn of the eras. As for the community that used the site, there is strong reason to think that it was a subset of the Essene movement. While this group used the site, kindred communities may have existed and may have been responsible for some of the scrolls. Finally, the "biblical" scrolls show that there was some fluidity in the wording of the books that were later incorporated into the Hebrew Bible. A number of these books, with a few that did not become components of the Hebrew Bible, were treated as authoritative works by the people who wrote and used the scrolls.

The Dead Sea Scrolls have made contributions to and inspired renewed debate in areas far beyond those treated here. In fact, it is safe to say that they have left their mark on all the areas discussed in this volume—liturgical studies, the history of Jewish law, apocryphal and pseudepigraphic literature, and early Christianity. The scrolls themselves and the references they make to the views of others exemplify the diversity of beliefs and practices among Jewish groups in this time period. The three topics treated here—archaeology, the community, and the "biblical" scrolls—and others (e.g., law) continue to be the subjects of debate among experts in the scrolls, and there appears to be no letup in the interest they inspire. We can hope that ongoing discussion and analysis will lead to greater insights into these and other aspects of the ever-fascinating Dead Sea Scrolls, the community (or communities) that produced them, and the antecedents for the development of the canonized Bible and rabbinic Judaism.

NOTES

1 The most complete listing is the Orion Center's online Dead Sea Scrolls bibliography (Orion Dead Sea Scrolls Bibliography; the Orion Center for the Study of the Dead Sea Scrolls and Associated Literature; orion.mscc.huji.ac.il; accessed July 13, 2017), which at present contains more than ten thousand items. For a much more ambitious attempt than the present chapter to address debated topics in the study of the scrolls, see *The Oxford Handbook of the Dead Sea Scrolls*, ed. Timothy H. Lim and John J. Collins (Oxford: Oxford University Press, 2010). The editors write that their publication "seeks to probe the main disputed areas in the study of the scrolls. For, indeed, many issues remain in dispute, despite the apparently impres-

sive syntheses at the turn of the millennium. There has been lively debate over the archaeology and history of the site, the nature and identity of the sect, and its relation to the broader world of Second Temple Judaism and to later Jewish and Christian tradition" (pp. 1–2). The issues surveyed briefly in the present chapter are included within Lim and Collins's larger coverage of the scrolls.

2 For lengthier introductions, see Lawrence Schiffman, *Reclaiming the Dead Sea Scrolls* (Philadelphia: Jewish Publication Society, 1994); and James VanderKam and Peter Flint, *The Meaning of the Dead Sea Scrolls* (San Francisco: HarperSanFrancisco, 2002). For a briefer introduction, see James VanderKam, *The Dead Sea Scrolls Today*, 2nd ed. (Grand Rapids, MI: Eerdmans, 2010).

3 See Weston Fields, *The Dead Sea Scrolls: A Full History: Volume One, 1947–1960* (Leiden: Brill, 2009).

4 The texts, the numbers assigned to them, their titles, and the designations for the photographs of them can be consulted in Emanuel Tov, *Revised Lists of the Texts from the Judaean Desert* (Leiden: Brill, 2010).

5 See John C. Trever, *The Untold Story of Qumran* (Westwood, NJ: Revell, 1965), 101–113. More recently, Weston Fields has reexamined the issue in his *The Dead Sea Scrolls: A Full History*, where he writes that the discovery of the first scrolls took place "probably sometime between November 1946 and February 1947" (p. 24).

6 Roland de Vaux, "La grotte des manuscrits hébreux," *Revue Biblique* 56 (1949): 586n2.

7 Although he issued a series of preliminary reports in article form, the fullest statement of his work appears in his *Archaeology and the Dead Sea Scrolls* (Schweich Lectures of the British Academy 1959; Oxford: Oxford University Press, 1973). For a short biography of de Vaux and a list of his publications about the archaeology of Qumran, see Jacques Briend, "De Vaux, Roland," in *Encyclopedia of the Dead Sea Scrolls*, ed. Lawrence Schiffman and James VanderKam, 2 vols. (New York: Oxford University Press, 2000), pp. 202–204.

8 See, for example, Jodi Magness, *The Archaeology of Qumran and the Dead Sea Scrolls* (Grand Rapids, MI: Eerdmans, 2002), p. 25. As she notes, it is mentioned several times in the Copper Scroll from cave 3.

9 De Vaux, *Archaeology and the Dead Sea Scrolls*.

10 Hirschfeld, *Qumran in Context: Reassessing the Archaeological Evidence* (Peabody, MA: Hendrickson, 2004).

11 Humbert, "Some Remarks on the Archaeology of Qumran," in *Qumran: The Site of the Dead Sea Scrolls: Archaeological Interpretations and Debates: Proceedings of a Conference Held at Brown University, November 17–19, 2002*, ed. Katharina Galor, Jean-Baptiste Humbert, and Jürgen Zangenberg (Studies on the Texts of the Desert of Judah 57; Leiden: Brill, 2006), pp. 19–39.

12 Magness argues that there was an altar used for sacrifice at Qumran ("Were Sacrifices Offered at Qumran? The Animal Bone Deposits Reconsidered," *Journal of Ancient Judaism* 7 [2016]: 5–34).

13 There have been several attempts to estimate the population using the site in the different phases of its occupation; they run from as high as four hundred to as low as ten to fifteen. See the survey by VanderKam in *Meaning of the Dead Sea Scrolls*, pp. 51–54.

14 De Vaux, *Archaeology and the Dead Sea Scrolls*, pp. 111–126; Frank M. Cross, *The Ancient Library of Qumran and Modern Biblical Studies* (Garden City, NY: Doubleday, 1958), pp. 80–119 (especially on the early history of the group); Józef Milik, *Ten Years of Discovery in the Wilderness of Judaea* (Studies in Biblical Theology 26; London: SCM, 1959), pp. 44–98.

15 For an overview of the 364-day calendar within the context of the calendrical data in the Hebrew Bible and other Jewish literature, see J. VanderKam, *Calendars in the Dead Sea Scrolls: Measuring Time* (Literature of the Dead Sea Scrolls; London: Routledge, 1998).

16 This is one of the difficulties with the Essene hypothesis raised by Norman Golb, *Who Wrote the Dead Sea Scrolls? The Search for the Secret of Qumran* (New York: Scribner, 1995), e.g., pp. 103–104. Golb is among those who think the site was a fortress.

17 De Vaux, *Archaeology and the Dead Sea Scrolls*, p. 86.

18 Eleazar Sukenik was the first scholar to make this identification (in *The Collection of the Hidden Scrolls in the Possession of the Hebrew University*, ed. Nahman Avigad [Jerusalem: Bialik Institute, 1954], p. 26 [Hebrew]). For a short survey of the issue, see VanderKam, *Dead Sea Scrolls Today*, pp. 97–126.

19 Translations of the scrolls come from Geza Vermes, *The Complete Dead Sea Scrolls in English* (London: Penguin, 2011).

20 For a more detailed presentation of this thesis, see J. VanderKam, "Identity and History of the Community," in *The Dead Sea Scrolls after Fifty Years: A Comprehensive Assessment*, ed. Peter Flint and J. VanderKam, 2 vols. (Leiden: Brill, 1998–1999), vol. 2, pp. 487–533.

21 See Alison Schofield, *From Qumran to the Yaḥad: A New Paradigm of Textual Development for the Community Rule* (Studies on the Texts of the Desert of Judah 77; Leiden: Brill, 2009); and John Collins, *Beyond the Qumran Community: The Sectarian Movement of the Dead Sea Scrolls* (Grand Rapids, MI: Eerdmans, 2010).

22 For accessible treatments of these texts, see Charlotte Hempel, *The Damascus Texts* (Companion to the Qumran Scrolls 1; Sheffield: Sheffield Academic Press, 2000); and Sarianna Metso, *The Serekh Texts* (Companion to the Qumran Scrolls 9, Library of Second Temple Studies 62; London: T & T Clark, 2007).

23 This is one of the points made by Schofield in *From Qumran to the Yaḥad*.

24 Eugene Ulrich has assembled the texts of all the manuscripts in his *The Biblical Qumran Scrolls: Transcriptions and Textual Variants* (Supplements to Vetus Testamentum 134; Leiden: Brill, 2010). For an English translation of the biblical scrolls, see Martin Abegg, Peter Flint, and Eugene Ulrich, *The Dead Sea Scrolls Bible: The Oldest Known Bible Translated for the First Time into English* (San Francisco: HarperSanFrancisco, 1999).

25 For the contributions of the scrolls to the study of the text of scriptural books, see Emanuel Tov, *Textual Criticism of the Hebrew Bible*, 3rd ed. (Minneapolis, MN: Fortress, 2012).

26 For an up-to-date discussion of the issue whether there was a canon of scripture (in the sense of a set list of books) at this time, see Timothy Lim, *The Formation of the Jewish Canon* (Anchor Yale Bible Reference Library; New Haven, CT: Yale University Press, 2013). For a summary of the evidence from the Qumran texts and elsewhere, see J. VanderKam, *The Dead Sea Scrolls and the Bible* (Grand Rapids, MI: Eerdmans, 2012), pp. 49–71.

27 The editors of the text are Elisha Qimron and John Strugnell, *Qumran Cave 4 V Miqṣat Maʿaśe Ha-Torah* (Discoveries in the Judaean Desert 10; Oxford: Clarendon, 1994); see, for example, pp. 111–112, for their comments on this text.

28 On the issue, see Eugene Ulrich, "The Non-Attestation of a Tripartite Canon in 4QMMT," *Catholic Biblical Quarterly* 65 (2003): 202–214.

29 A standard edition and translation of and commentary on these texts is Maurya P. Horgan, *Pesharim: Qumran Interpretations of Biblical Books* (Catholic Biblical Quarterly Monograph Series 8; Washington, DC: Catholic University of America, 1979). See also Timothy H. Lim, *Pesharim* (Companion to the Qumran Scrolls 3; London: Sheffield Academic Press, 2002).

2

Second Temple Literature outside the Canon

MARTHA HIMMELFARB

The Second Temple period (515 BCE–70 CE) was a time of political and cultural transition for the Jews. During its first two centuries the Jews of Palestine lived under Persian rule, and the literature they wrote, or at least the portion that survives, is found in the Bible: for example, the books of the prophets Haggai, Zechariah, and Malachi, and the retelling of Israel's history in the book of Chronicles. The conquest by Alexander the Great in the 330s BCE brought an end to the Persian Empire, and in the remaining four centuries of the Second Temple period the Jews came into close contact with civilizations from outside the Near East: first the Greeks and then the Romans. The impact of Greek culture on the Jews was profound, as can be seen in the Jewish literature composed during the centuries from Alexander to the destruction of the Second Temple (70 CE). Yet while this literature is crucial for understanding the evolution from biblical religion to rabbinic Judaism and, ultimately, to Judaism as we know it today, most of it is unfamiliar, even to those with a traditional Jewish education or a strong interest in Jewish history.

This chapter explains why this is so. Before proceeding, let me note that this discussion will leave out two important corpora of texts from the period under discussion: the works of Philo and Josephus. Philo was a philosopher who lived in the first century CE in Alexandria. For Philo, the Torah of Moses was entirely compatible with the philosophy of Plato, and much of his oeuvre consists of commentaries that read the Torah in light of turn-of-the-era Platonism. Josephus was a somewhat younger contemporary of Philo who was born in Palestine and served as a general in the Jewish revolt against Rome that began in 66 CE and ended with the destruction of the Temple. After surrendering to Vespasian, the Roman general who was soon to become emperor, Josephus devoted himself to writing history, and his works are our most important source for the revolt and indeed for much of the Second Temple period.

In this chapter, I focus on a quite different kind of literature: texts, almost all of unknown authorship, that consciously or unconsciously imitate earlier works viewed as authoritative and ultimately included in the Hebrew Bible. These texts do not constitute a corpus in the sense that the works of single authors such as Philo or Josephus do. It is clear that ancient readers did not understand them to belong to a single category, nor, unfortunately, is there any good modern label that applies to all of them. But with the exception of the book of Daniel, which became part of the Hebrew Bible, all of them belong to one or more of three overlapping groups of texts.

One group consists of works belonging to the Apocrypha, the name that Protestants give to books that appear in the Greek Bible but not in the Hebrew Bible, in some cases because their original language was Greek. The Greek Bible started out as the Bible of diaspora Jews, but it came to be used by Christians as the Old Testament, and during the Reformation, Protestants removed these books from their Bible on the grounds that they did not appear in the Hebrew Bible. Hence the name "Apocrypha," which is Greek for "hidden away."[1] Roman Catholics continue to treat these books as part of the Bible even today.

A second group of texts belongs to a category that scholars call pseudepigrapha, or falsely attributed writings. This label reflects the fact that the authors of the texts in question chose not to write in their own names but to attribute their works to more ancient authorities. As with the Apocrypha, no such category existed in antiquity. Nonetheless, the term is widely used as a convenient way to refer to a large number of the works written during the later part of the Second Temple period.[2] To further complicate matters, some of the works in the Apocrypha are pseudepigraphic; indeed, there are many relatively early biblical works that could properly be called pseudepigrapha.

Finally, several of the texts, including some of the Apocrypha and pseudepigrapha, belong to a corpus that did exist in antiquity: the Dead Sea Scrolls. The scrolls, as discussed in chapter 1, are the library of a small Jewish sect from the turn of the era, which, luckily for us, established a settlement near the Dead Sea, where the desert climate served to preserve portions of its manuscripts. The library, which was discovered in the middle of the twentieth century, includes many previously unknown works as well as the most ancient surviving manuscripts of biblical books and the originals of some Apocrypha and pseudepigrapha previously known only in translation; many of the manuscripts are quite fragmentary.[3]

Now let me offer some examples of the texts themselves, which are representative of the range of genres in which they are written and the types of concerns they express. Please keep in mind that these examples are only a sample of both genres and texts.

One important genre consists of works such as the Wisdom of Joshua ben Sira and the Wisdom of Solomon, which bring the biblical Wisdom tradition, represented by Proverbs, Ecclesiastes, and some of the Psalms, into relationship with Hellenistic culture and recent developments in Jewish thought. Another genre consists of retellings of biblical narratives in response to later concerns, such as the Genesis Apocryphon and the Book of Jubilees. A third genre consists of apocalypses—revelations about the course of history and the end of the world or the secrets of the cosmos and the fate of souls after death. The biblical book of Daniel is the best known of the ancient Jewish apocalypses, but it is only one among a number of such works. Several, such as the Book of the Watchers (1 Enoch 1–36), the Book of Dreams (1 Enoch 83–90), and 2 Enoch, are attributed to the antediluvian patriarch Enoch, who, according to Genesis 5:21–24, never died.

Many works in the corpora under discussion are not the product of a single author but rather compilations of multiple sources, displaying varying degrees of editorial control. Furthermore, even the very partial list of texts just presented confirms the implications of the label "pseudepigrapha": authors writing in their own names, such as Joshua ben Sira, are the exception in the Second Temple period. The usual explanation for the practice of pseudepigraphy is that it was intended to confer authority on a text by attributing it to a great figure of the past, often a figure already associated with works in the genre in question or otherwise appropriate to the new work. Thus, for example, the author of the Wisdom of Solomon ascribed his work to the biblical figure most closely associated with wisdom. So, too, many of the apocalypses, which involve the interpretation of visions, take as their heroes biblical scribes, who are professional interpreters. Ezra and Baruch, the heroes of the apocalypses known as 4 Ezra and 2 Baruch, which respond to the destruction of the Second Temple, both appear in the Bible (in the books of Ezra and Jeremiah, respectively) as scribes, and Enoch is depicted as a scribe in most of the apocalypses in which he figures, although the brief biblical account of his life does not mention such a role. Daniel is depicted in the book that bears his name not precisely as a scribe but as a professional wise man. Furthermore, by putting their predictions in the mouth of an ancient hero, the apocalypses not only give them added authority but also create the opportunity for "prophecies" of events that have already taken place (*vaticinia ex eventu*), the accuracy of which serves to guarantee the accuracy of the genuine predictions in the work.[4]

Jewish literature of the Second Temple period was composed in three languages. In the earlier part of the period, the dominant language was Aramaic, the everyday language of the Jews of Palestine throughout the Second Temple era. From the beginning of the second century BCE on, more authors chose to write in Hebrew, the language of scripture.[5] Throughout the period, Jews living in the communities of the Greco-Roman diaspora wrote in Greek, though it should be noted that we have very little evidence for works written anywhere in the diaspora other than Egypt, the most populous and important of the diaspora communities.

Having now provided some sense of the range of interests and diversity of genres in which Jews wrote during the Second Temple period, I must reiterate that the only Jewish text from the second half of the Second Temple period that reaches us because Jews transmitted it through the millennia is the book of Daniel. Other works in Hebrew and Aramaic have reached us as part of the Dead Sea Scrolls, but unlike Daniel these texts were not copied and recopied by Jews generation after generation. Rather, for almost two millennia they survived away from human eyes, and it is only a happy accident that has made them available to us today.

Apart from Daniel and works preserved among the scrolls, Jewish books of the second part of the Second Temple period come down to us only because Christians chose to transmit them. As already noted, the books of the Apocrypha were part of the Jewish Bible in Greek, which Christians then embraced as their Old Testament. Among them are works written in Hebrew and then translated into Greek, such as the Wisdom of ben Sira and 1 Maccabees, as well as works composed in Greek, such as the Wisdom of Solomon and 2 Maccabees. But over the centuries, as Christians laid claim to the Bible in Greek, Greek-speaking Jews relinquished it in favor of the Hebrew Bible. Thus works that Greek-speaking Jews had once regarded as canonical were no longer in Jewish hands. But most texts of the later Second Temple period never became part of either canon, Hebrew or Greek, and those that have reached us, apart from some fragments preserved in the scrolls, do so because Christians found them sufficiently appealing to translate and transmit alongside the canon in Ethiopic, Slavonic, Latin, Syriac, and other languages. Some of these works were likely composed in Greek, but others were originally written in Aramaic or Hebrew, translated into Greek, and then into the languages in which we now encounter them. It is worth noting that we are also indebted to Christian transmission for the survival of the works of Philo and Josephus, which were written in Greek and apparently lost to Jews at some point in antiquity, but, fortunately for us, not before they had been taken up by Christians.

We turn now to the ways in which our understanding of the literature of the second part of the Second Temple period has grown and improved in the past several decades because of two developments at which I have already hinted. One is the discovery of the Dead Sea Scrolls and their publication, only recently completed, which has expanded the corpus of Aramaic and especially Hebrew texts from the Hellenistic and Roman periods and transformed our picture of the previously known literature in important ways. The other is recognition of the significance of the relatively late Christian contexts in which much of Second Temple literature reaches us. Coincidentally, the year 1976 was a crucial moment for both developments. In that year, Jozef T. Milik published the fragments of 1 Enoch from the Dead Sea Scrolls and Robert A. Kraft read his programmatic paper "The Pseudepigrapha in Christianity" to the Society for New Testament Studies at Duke University.[6]

* * *

First, the scrolls demonstrate definitively something we already knew from references in ancient texts: that there were many works written in the Second Temple period that were not transmitted to us. Sometimes it is not difficult to explain why. It is not surprising that with the disappearance of the sect associated with the scrolls no one copied the works it composed for internal purposes, if indeed anyone outside the sect knew them. But the sect's library also contained many nonsectarian works that the sect viewed favorably enough to include in its library, and many of these works, too, have not reached us through other channels. It is not obvious why the Genesis Apocryphon, to offer just one example, was lost to us, and it is certainly possible that it is simply a matter of chance rather than the result of something about the work that later readers found objectionable. One point that scholars have noted is that the previously unknown pseudepigrapha found among the scrolls draw on a rather different set of heroes than those transmitted to us: prophets such as Jeremiah and Ezekiel, and the descendants of Levi, Qahat, and Amram, for example. Among the pseudepigrapha transmitted to us in Christian languages, Levi himself plays a role, and we have apocalypses with Isaiah and Zechariah as their heroes, although both may be Christian compositions; but, as already noted, scribes—Enoch, Baruch, Ezra, and Daniel—figure particularly prominently.[7] Because of the fragmentary character of many of the new works attested by the scrolls it is difficult to say much about their genres with any confidence, but, to offer just one observation, the scrolls do not appear to contain any previously unknown apocalypses in which revelation comes to the hero in the course of an ascent to heaven. Further study will undoubtedly make it possible to say more about how the previously unknown nonsectarian works among the scrolls compare to ancient Jewish works passed down by Christians.

Here we shall focus not on the previously unknown works but rather on the implications of the evidence of the scrolls for a work already known to us via Christian transmission: the Book of the Watchers, the first of the five works included in the Ethiopic 1 Enoch. These fragments, published by Milik together with the fragments of other Enochic works found among the scrolls, settle once and for all the question of the original language of the Book of the Watchers—Aramaic rather than Hebrew—and they also give us important information about the date of the work. In the mid-twentieth century, before the discovery of the scrolls, the Book of the Watchers was usually placed sometime in the second half of the second century BCE, after the Maccabean revolt. But the relatively objective criteria of paleography, the study of ancient handwriting, allow scholars to place the earliest manuscripts of the Book of the Watchers toward the beginning of the second century BCE, which means that the composition of the work could easily belong to the third century BCE. Paleography also allows us to date the fragments of the Astronomical Book (1 Enoch 72–82), another work contained in 1 Enoch, even earlier, making it the earliest of all apocalypses. But the Astronomical Book, a revelation to Enoch mediated by the angel Uriel, focuses almost exclusively on the paths of the sun and moon and their relationship to each other during the course of a 364-day year, and while some later apocalypses, including the Book of the Watchers, show an interest in astronomical phenomena, the Astronomical Book was far less influential than the Book of the Watchers. Thus the Book of the Watchers is of more interest for our purposes here.

The earlier date for the Book of the Watchers required by the fragments from the scrolls has had a major impact on our understanding of Judaism in the Second Temple period and on the understanding of apocalyptic literature in particular. We will begin with apocalyptic literature before turning to the larger picture. Though R. H. Charles, the great early twentieth-century scholar of the pseudepigrapha, saw parts of 1 Enoch as pre-Maccabean, the consensus of mid-twentieth-century scholarship was that the book of Daniel was the earliest apocalypse.[8] The composition of the apocalyptic section of Daniel can be dated with considerable confidence to the midst of the Maccabean revolt, around 165 BCE. Its subject is Israel's final liberation from its oppressors, which it believed was imminent. This liberation would mark the end of history as we know it and inaugurate a new era in which the wicked would be judged and at least some of the righteous, who had suffered so much under the persecution of Antiochus IV, would attain eternal life.

While in popular usage the term "apocalypse" has come to mean the cataclysmic end of civilization—nuclear apocalypse, environmental apocalypse, and so on—the Greek word behind the English means "uncovering" and thus, by extension, revelation. That is, it refers not to content but to the mode in which the information in the text was received. Yet on the eve of the publication of the Aramaic Enoch fragments, most scholars saw Daniel as the prototypical apocalypse because of its canonical status and its early date and thus understood its concerns as defining the genre. The expectation of the imminent end of the world is indeed central to a number of apocalypses of the Second Temple era and the years immediately following, such as the Book of Dreams, 4 Ezra, 2 Baruch, and the book of Revelation in the New Testament. The fact that Revelation, the other canonical apocalypse from a Christian point of view, shared Daniel's focus on collective eschatology—the fate of all humanity at the end of history—served only to strengthen this understanding.

Scholars also came to see symbolic visions, the central mode of revelation in Daniel, as the characteristic mode of apocalyptic revelation. In biblical prophecy from the period before the destruction of the First Temple the standard form of revelation is direct revelation in which the prophet hears God's word. Only occasionally (Amos 8, Jeremiah 1) do prophets before the destruction report visions that require interpretation. In the era of the Second Temple, such visions become more prominent. Thus, for example, the words of the prophet Zechariah, which make up the first eight chapters of the book that bears his name, consist largely of symbolic visions that an angel interprets for the prophet.[9] The increasing importance of interpretation as a mode of revelation is presumably related to the emergence of written documents at the center of ancient Judaism: first, in 622 BCE, half a century before the destruction of the Second Temple, the Book of Deuteronomy, and then, perhaps in the fifth century BCE, the Torah as a whole.

The importance of interpretation is also evident in chapters 2–6 of the book of Daniel, stories about Daniel and his friends already in circulation at the time the book was composed that the author of Daniel incorporated into his work. These stories depict Daniel as a skilled interpreter of dreams. In the apocalyptic portion of the book, written during the Maccabean revolt, revelation still requires interpretation, but here Daniel is the recipient of visions rather than their interpreter. Two symbolic visions (chapters 7 and 8) are interpreted for him by an angel, and an angel also explains the true meaning of a passage from the book of Jeremiah over which Daniel has been brooding (chapter 9). The final portion of the book (chapters 10–12) consists not of a vision but of an angelic discourse, which recalls the standard mode of revelation to prophets in the period of the First Temple. But the fact that in Daniel the revealer is an angel rather than God himself is an indication of the distance traveled from the prophecy of the First Temple era.

For the apocalypses that share Daniel's interest in the end of history, symbolic visions are the dominant mode of revelation, though by no means the only one. Thus for anyone whose expectations about apocalyptic literature were formed by Daniel, both the form and the content of the Book of the Watchers are somewhat unexpected.[10] The narrative of the Book of the Watchers begins with the story of the descent of the Watchers, a category of angel mentioned also in Daniel, because of their desire for the beautiful daughters of men (1 Enoch 6–11). The narrative recalls the brief and enigmatic story in Genesis 6:1–4 of the descent of the sons of God to marry the daughters of man, and the notice of the descent of the Watchers in the Book of the Watchers (1 Enoch 6:1–2) clearly alludes to the passage in Genesis. Yet the story in the Book of the Watchers can hardly be understood as exegesis of the biblical passage. Rather, the Book of the Watchers appears to provide a glimpse of the tradition behind the passage in Genesis, shaped, to be sure, by the authors' knowledge of the book of Genesis in more or less its present form.

The marriages that ensue after the descent of the Watchers have disastrous consequences. Giants are born from the union of angelic fathers and human mothers, and when it becomes impossible for humanity to supply the hungry giants with adequate sustenance, they proceed to devour human beings (1 Enoch 6–7). In addition, the Watchers reveal a variety of arts and skills to human beings: the manufacture of weapons, jewelry, and cosmetics; spells and other magical procedures; and astronomical knowledge (1 Enoch 8). The account of the revelation of these dangerous forms of knowledge, or at least knowledge inappropriate for humanity, is thoroughly integrated into the narrative of descent for marriage, but it appears to reflect an alternative to the story of the descent of the Watchers to marry women, in which it is not the havoc caused by the giants but the use of arts better left unlearned that leads to chaos and disaster.[11]

When the four chief angels report the suffering unleashed by the Watchers' offspring and their revelations, God commissions them to imprison the Watchers, eliminate their offspring, and cleanse the earth of evil, presumably by means of the flood (1 Enoch 9–11). It is at this point that Enoch makes his appearance. Readers would have recognized him as the antediluvian patriarch notable for the unusual notice of his life in the course of the highly formulaic genealogy of Genesis 5. The genealogy covers the first ten generations of humanity, from Adam to Noah. There are some flourishes in the notices about Adam at the beginning (Genesis 5:3–5) and Lamech at the end (Genesis 5:28–31), but the standard notice runs like this:[12]

> Seth lived 105 years and begot Enosh. Seth lived 807 years after he begot Enosh and begot sons and daughters.

All the days of Seth were 912 years, and he died.

> But for Enoch we read:
>   Enoch lived sixty-five years and begot Methuselah. Enoch walked with God 300 years after he begot Methuselah, and he begot sons and daughters. All the days of Enoch were 365 years. Enoch walked with God and he was not, for God took him.

The precise meaning of Enoch's walking with God and God's taking him can be debated, but the notice certainly suggests that Enoch is particularly close to God. It is also suggestive that the years of Enoch's life span, the shortest of any of the patriarchs according to Genesis 5, correspond to the number of days in a year. The number is particularly interesting because the Astronomical Book, as already noted, offers a revelation that presupposes a 364-day year. Above I suggested that the story of the descent of the Watchers in the Book of the Watchers reflects not exegesis of Genesis 6:1–4 but knowledge of traditions that stand behind the biblical passage. So, too, the figure of Enoch in the Astronomical Book and the Book of the Watchers can hardly be the result of exegesis of Genesis 5:21–24; rather, the picture of Enoch in the apocalypses hints at the traditions that informed the notice of Enoch's life in the passage in Genesis.

As soon as it introduces Enoch, the Book of the Watchers identifies him as a scribe (1 Enoch 12).[13] The first activity in which Enoch engages does not seem to require his professional expertise: he is commissioned by the Watchers who remain in heaven to deliver a message of condemnation to their brethren who descended to earth (1 Enoch 12:3–13:3). But the fallen Watchers presumably have his scribal skills in view when they ask Enoch to draw up a petition on their behalf in response to the message of condemnation. Enoch complies with their request, recites the petition by the waters of Dan until he falls asleep, and then ascends in a dream to God's heavenly abode so that he can deliver the petition (1 Enoch 13:4–14:26). As he passes through structures of fire and ice, Enoch is overcome by fear and awe. Finally he arrives at the door of the chamber in which God is seated on a wheeled throne of cherubim before which angels serve day and night. In other words, God lives in the heavenly equivalent of the earthly temple, and angels serve as priests.

Standing before the divine throne, Enoch hears the rejection of the Watchers' petition from God's own mouth (1 Enoch 15–16). Yet the rejection is apparently not meant as criticism of Enoch's professional skills. Indeed the fact that he has reached God's throne unharmed shows Enoch to be worthy of entering the heavenly temple, just as the angels are, and in the concluding portion of the Book of the Watchers (1 Enoch 17–36) Enoch travels to the ends of the earth in the company of angels, who show him sights unavailable to ordinary human beings, including the punishment of the Watchers, the chambers in which souls of the dead await the last judgment, the Garden of Eden, and the mountain throne of God. The tour, too, is a complex composition, drawing on two or perhaps even three sources. The sights of the tour play something like the role of the symbolic visions in Daniel, with the angelic guides explaining each sight to Enoch, usually in response to his questions. But the sights of the tour are not symbolic; they need to be identified rather than decoded.[14]

Even before the new dating provided by the Dead Sea Scrolls, anyone who read the Book of the Watchers—and many other apocalypses— could see that apocalypses display a range of interests beyond collective eschatology, such as the architecture of the heavenly temple and its liturgy, the fate of souls after death, and natural and astronomical phenomena. It was equally clear that in some apocalypses revelation does not take place through symbolic visions but through the visionary's ascent to heaven or, more often in later apocalypses, the seven heavens, where he sees sights and receives revelations related to the interests just noted. Yet when read through the lens of Daniel, these apocalypses appeared somehow marginal to the genre. By focusing attention on the Book of the Watchers as well as on the Astronomical Book that preceded it and on other ascent apocalypses written in its wake, the Aramaic Enoch fragments led scholars to expand their picture of the apocalypses to take account of what is in fact a very significant portion of the corpus.[15]

Increased attention to the Book of the Watchers has also had an impact on the broader understanding of Judaism in the period before the Maccabean revolt. The Enochic corpus makes it clear that some Jews were not entirely satisfied with the explanation for how evil came into the world and why human beings suffer found in the primeval history of the Torah (Genesis 1–11). This prologue to the emergence of the people of Israel attempts to explain how the ordered world God created, which He sees to be "very good," devolved into the world as we know it; and in incident after incident the cause is human unwillingness to live within the boundaries God has prescribed. Adam and Eve's disobedience (Genesis 2–3), Cain's murder of Abel (Genesis 4), human wrongdoing leading to the flood (Genesis 6), Ham's violation of his father (Genesis 9), the building of the Tower of Babel (Genesis 11)—all recount human transgression of divinely established limits.

Like these incidents, the story of the descent of the sons of God is a story of failure to abide by limits, but in this story it is not human beings who fail to do so but divine beings. Genesis 6:1–4 is less explicit about the negative results of the descent of divine beings to earth than the narrative of the Book of the Watchers, but it does indicate God's displeasure and consequent decision to limit the human life span to 120 years (Genesis 6:3). The placement of this passage just before the Torah's account of the flood could also be read as implying that the violation of the boundaries between human and divine it recounts is one of the factors that made the cleansing of the flood necessary. This story is the lone dissenting voice in the primeval history's otherwise unanimous view that humanity is to blame for the evils of the world as we know it. Presumably it was sufficiently well known that the editors of the primeval history chose to include it, though in very compressed form, despite its lack of fit with the message of the unit as a whole. Or perhaps the lack of fit actually made it an appealing way for the editors to raise the possibility that the mess in which we find ourselves is not entirely the fault of humanity.

Apart from the brief notice of Elijah's departure from earth in a whirlwind (2 Kings 2:11), the narrative of Enoch's ascent to heaven in the Book of the Watchers is the first such account in Jewish literature, and the new dating of the Book of the Watchers has led scholars to pay more attention to the ascent to heaven as a mode of revelation in the Second

Temple period.[16] The wheels of the throne on which Enoch finds God seated echo the wheels of the divine throne on which God appears to Ezekiel in the first chapter of that prophetic book. The wheels are Ezekiel's innovation; the Jerusalem Temple, where the prophets believed God's presence could be found, had just been destroyed, and Ezekiel imagines a wheeled throne to enable God's presence to reach his community in exile in Babylonia, at a great distance from Jerusalem. The throne in the Book of the Watchers, on the other hand, is no longer mobile but fixed in the heavenly temple to which Enoch ascends, despite the fact that by the time the Book of the Watchers was composed, a new temple already stood in Jerusalem. But the implication of Enoch's ascent is that, in contrast to the First Temple, God's presence is not available in the Second Temple. The way to stand in God's presence, according to the Book of the Watchers and later ascent apocalypses, is not to go to Jerusalem but to ascend to heaven, a trip possible only for Enoch and other particularly distinguished human beings.[17]

Scholars are divided on whether the apocalypses reflect a practice of ascent among Jews of the Second Temple era. Some have argued that ascent was widely practiced in antiquity—or, to put it more scientifically, that many people in antiquity believed themselves to have ascended to heaven—and read the ascents in the apocalypses as thinly veiled autobiographical accounts. I cannot accept this view, in large part because there is no evidence in texts of the Second Temple era for rituals designed to produce ascent. Nor do the apocalypses depict their ascents as initiated by the visionary. Centuries later, it is true, *hekhalot* texts, the Jewish mystical corpus from late antiquity, describe rituals to achieve ascent to the divine throne or chariot, as it comes to be called. But these texts are much later than the Second Temple period, and recent scholarship has been skeptical about the practice of ascent even here; indeed one *hekhalot* text suggests that it is possible to attain the benefits of ascent simply by reciting the account in that text.[18]

If the ability to ascend to heaven results not from a ritual that can be imitated but from a divine invitation, the hero's ascent cannot be intended as a model for others to follow. This understanding of ascent fits well with the choice of well-known models of piety as heroes of the ascents.[19] Yet while ordinary human beings might not be worthy of a divine invitation, by showing particularly exemplary human beings taking a place in the realm of the angels, the apocalypses nonetheless make a strong statement about the status of human beings in God's eyes. Indeed, some ascent apocalypses hint that their heroes or even the righteous dead generally are more exalted than the angels.[20] This valuation of human potential is significant because scholars have often emphasized the distance between God and humanity implied by the proliferation of angels in the literature of the Second Temple period and contrasted it unfavorably with the more direct relationship with God characteristic of the period before the exile. It is certainly true that Second Temple texts are less likely than earlier texts to understand God as truly available on earth in the Jerusalem Temple, but I would argue that by filling the enormous physical gulf between God and humanity with angels, the authors of the Second Temple period were not distancing God but bringing Him near. Furthermore, as the Book of the Watchers clearly demonstrates, some of these authors understood the boundaries between the divine realm and the human as highly permeable.[21]

* * *

We saw above that Jews wrote a great deal in the Second Temple period but that, except for Daniel, what they wrote was not transmitted by Jews. Thus, much of the evidence for Second Temple Judaism—including the works of Philo and Josephus—comes to us by way of texts translated, transmitted, and preserved by Christians, and it is important to remember that for most of the years from antiquity to the present transmission did not mean printing but rather copying by hand, a process prone to accidental changes and a tempting opportunity for intentional improvements. Still, until a generation ago, few scholars seemed concerned about taking, to offer just one example, 2 Enoch, a work preserved only in Slavonic with the earliest manuscripts dating to no earlier than the fourteenth century, as evidence for Second Temple Judaism. In fact a good case can be made that 2 Enoch is based on a Jewish work from the turn of the era, though it has clearly undergone considerable development since.[22]

The other development in the study of Second Temple Judaism to emphasize is that scholars have begun to invest time and effort in making the case for—or against—the Jewish origin of works like 2 Enoch. To do so requires them to think seriously about the implications of Christian transmission and to try to understand the role the texts in question played for the Christians who copied and read them. In contrast to the fragments of the Dead Sea Scrolls, which provide definitive answers to certain important questions, such as the original language of a work or its approximate date, the questions raised by the rubric "the pseudepigrapha in Christianity"—the title of the article by Robert Kraft to which I referred above—elude definitive answers virtually by definition. To illustrate this point, we can turn to the text that has probably been more studied from this point of view than any other: the Testaments of the Twelve Patriarchs.

The Testaments is a fascinating work that consists of the words it imagines each of the twelve sons of Jacob addressing to his descendants on his deathbed.[23] Often the patriarch's last words reflect his life as depicted in the narrative of Genesis. Thus, for example, Reuben, who angered Jacob by engaging in sexual relations with Jacob's concubine Bilhah after Rachel's death (Genesis 35:22, 49:4), warns his sons against fornication. But alongside the ethical exhortations, the patriarchs of the Testaments also offer their descendants prophecies of the coming of Christ, a rather surprising feature in a Jewish text. Early in the twentieth century R. H. Charles argued that the prophecies were Christian interpolations into a Jewish composition, which could be removed to reveal the original work.[24] Following Charles, the Testaments was generally read as a Jewish work with some easily detachable Christian additions.[25] The acceptance of Charles's view derived at least in part from scholars' reluctance to relinquish any text from among the relatively small number that constitute the corpus of evidence for Second Temple Judaism, particularly a long and very interesting document such as the Testaments. There may even have been a philo-Semitic aspect to the unwillingness, a desire, at least in English-language scholarship, to avoid the supersessionism of attributing Christian authorship to a text some regarded as Jewish. But whatever the reasons, for the first half of the twentieth century the standard approach to the Testaments was to treat the indisputably Christian elements as additions by a Christian redactor to an originally Jewish work.

But starting in the 1950s the Dutch scholar Marinus de Jonge began to make a powerful case for understanding the Testaments as a Christian work. He first demonstrated that the Christian elements of the Testaments were an integral part of the structure of the work; it was thus impossible to remove them without doing violence to the work as a whole.[26] In the decades that followed, de Jonge developed a compelling argument that the Testaments' picture of the sons of Jacob should be understood in the context of early Christian veneration of the patriarchs as models for pious behavior before the law, an attitude attested in the works of such second-century Christian authorities as Justin Martyr and Irenaeus.[27]

The Testaments contains more explicitly Christian material than almost any other work that has been treated as a Jewish text of the Second Temple period, but while the Testaments may not be typical of the purportedly Jewish works of that period that reach us by way of Christians—indeed, there is no such thing as a typical work—de Jonge's success in situating the Testaments in the context of Christian concerns clearly has important implications for any text transmitted to us by Christians with figures from the Hebrew Bible as its heroes. These implications are the subject of Kraft's "The Pseudepigrapha in Christianity." Kraft insisted that scholars begin to take seriously the fact that most of the pseudepigraphic works they read as evidence for Second Temple Judaism reach us only because Christians found them to be of value. Or, to put it a little differently, whatever their origins, from one point of view these pseudepigrapha are Christian texts—just as the Old Testament is a Christian text even if its Hebrew original is not. That is, Christians almost always find the Hebrew Bible between the same covers as the New Testament and read it as a preface to the New Testament, still of value but subordinate to the newer revelation. Kraft also raises the question of whether Christians wrote texts without referring to Jesus, citing the New Testament, or including other features that would obviously stamp the text as Christian—a not implausible possibility in certain genres—and, if so, how we could then recognize the text in question as Christian.

Like many revolutionary insights, Kraft's observations seemed obvious once he made them, yet they are profoundly subversive of much previous scholarship. While many scholars have simply ignored their challenge, continuing to treat works with heroes drawn from the Hebrew Bible as Jewish until proven otherwise, others have carried forward the project of Kraft's paper, and there is now a considerable body of scholarship asking fundamental questions about a variety of texts beyond the Testaments that were at one time treated unself-consciously as Jewish works of the Second Temple period.[28]

One way to gauge the impact of this new direction in scholarship is to compare the first and second editions of George W. E. Nickelsburg's excellent introduction to the literature of the Second Temple period, *Jewish Literature between the Bible and the Mishnah*. In the first edition in 1981, the book contained a chapter entitled "The Exposition of Israel's Scriptures," which discusses a number of works, including the Life of Adam and Eve, Joseph and Aseneth, and the Testaments of the Twelve Patriarchs.[29] Nickelsburg began the chapter by noting that although the works mentioned in it come to us as transmitted by Christians, they probably "originated in Jewish circles, often in more or less their present form."[30] He treats the Testaments somewhat differently than the other works, labeling the current form as "clearly Christian"; but he nonetheless suggests scenarios for its composition that give it a Jewish core.[31] Nickelsburg's chapter on responses to the destruction of the Second Temple treats the apocalypse 3 Baruch without any indication that it might be anything other than a Jewish composition; both the Greek and the Slavonic versions of the work contain undeniably Christian elements, though the elements in the two versions are different, which suggests that they were added at different times to an originally different work.[32] In the second edition of the book, published in 2005, the chapter previously entitled "The Exposition of Israel's Scriptures" has been renamed "Texts of Disputed Provenance." The work of de Jonge and Kraft is acknowledged in the first note in the chapter, and the discussion of each text now includes considerable attention to the difficulties of determining Jewish or Christian provenance.[33] 3 Baruch has disappeared from the volume altogether; although he says nothing about it, Nickelsburg appears to have decided that it does not belong in a book devoted to Jewish literature.[34]

I applaud the developments reflected in the changes to Nickelsburg's book, but it is also important to note a certain irony. By pointing to the ways in which Christians made use of earlier Jewish traditions and texts and showing how heroes of the Hebrew Bible were central to the self-understanding of some early Christians, de Jonge's study of the Testaments and more recent scholarship on a number of other texts call into question the Jewish provenance of a significant portion of the evidence that scholars have used to build up a picture of a pre-Christian Judaism, primarily in the diaspora, focused largely on ethical concerns with little concern for ritual or ethnic identification, that is, a Judaism that anticipates early Christian concerns.[35] The fact that Christians composed and transmitted pseudepigrapha with heroes from the Hebrew Bible demonstrates their ongoing debt to that Bible and to Jewish traditions associated with it. Yet if many of the texts once considered Jewish works of the Second Temple period turn out to be of Christian provenance, it becomes more difficult to argue for the kind of Judaism that many scholars have seen as the context for the emergence of Christianity—because the works that provided the evidence for that Judaism are now understood as Christian compositions or Jewish compositions thoroughly reworked by Christians.

* * *

It should now be clear why anyone interested in Judaism of the Second Temple period must be deeply grateful that early Christians took an interest in Jewish works of the Hellenistic and early Roman eras and transmitted them into the Middle Ages, sometimes after translating them into languages quite distant from their original Aramaic, Hebrew, or Greek. But I hope it is also clear why we cannot simply assume that every ancient text transmitted by Christians that features a hero drawn from the Hebrew Bible is a Jewish composition. Rather we need to examine each text in its own terms. We need to consider whether the text contains undoubtedly Christian elements and whether those elements are integral to the text's structure, and we also need to consider where the text in question might fit in the context of ancient Christianity, even as we look for any aspects of the text that make better sense in an ancient Jewish setting. And, of course, we need to recognize that the answers to our questions may be quite complicated. Thus, for example, although the Testaments of the Twelve Patriarchs is a Christian composition as de Jonge makes amply clear, there can be no doubt that the author or authors drew on Jewish traditions and, in at least one instance, a Jewish text—the Aramaic Levi Document known from the Cairo Geniza and now attested among the Dead Sea Scrolls. Another document among the scrolls, 4QTNaphtali, provides evidence for the tradition about Bilhah's ancestry in the Testament of Naphtali, which is otherwise unattested in antiquity.[36] But despite its name, there is nothing about the very fragmentary 4QTNaphtali to indicate that it is a testament in form. Indeed, even as we recognize that the scrolls include works on which the Testaments may have drawn, we must also take seriously the absence of any evidence in the scrolls for the testament form.

As their importance for our understanding of both the Book of the Watchers and the Testaments indicates, the Dead Sea Scrolls have made an enormous contribution to our picture of Judaism in the Second Temple period beyond the window they have provided on the life of a small if fascinating sectarian group. As we have seen, access to even fragments of the originals of some of the Jewish works of the Second Temple period, previously known only through the translations transmitted by Christians, has had major implications for our understanding of those works. With further scholarly attention to the fragments of the nonsectarian works among the scrolls that had been entirely unknown, such as 4QTNaphtali, we can surely expect further insight into the Second Temple period.

Jewish texts from the second part of the Second Temple period constitute a remarkably diverse corpus composed in three different languages in various genres, reflecting a wide range of concerns and beliefs and, likely, multiple communities. As the examples of the Book of the Watchers and the Testaments of the Twelve Patriarchs demonstrate, we have in hand new resources, both textual and methodological, for studying those texts. As we continue to exploit the new evidence provided by the scrolls and take a fuller account of the implications of Christian provenance for works previously understood to be Jewish, we will continue to develop and refine our understanding of the growth of Judaism in the Second Temple period, an understanding that will have important implications for the study of early Christianity as well.

NOTES

1 The Apocrypha are available in a variety of English translations, both as a separate section in some editions of Protestant Bibles and as a freestanding volume. The books in question can also be found in Catholic Bible translations as part of the Old Testament, integrated at appropriate points. For a recent discussion of the Greek Bible in its ancient context, see Tessa Rajak, *Translation and Survival: The Greek Bible of the Ancient Jewish Diaspora* (Oxford: Oxford University Press, 2009).

2 Current English-language collections of pseudepigrapha include James H. Charlesworth, *The Old Testament Pseudepigrapha*, 2 vols. (Garden City, NY: Doubleday, 1983–1985); H. F. D. Sparks, *The Apocryphal Old Testament* (Oxford: Clarendon, 1984); and Lawrence H. Schiffman, James L. Kugel, and Louis H. Feldman, eds., *Outside the Bible*, 3 vols. (Philadelphia: Jewish Publication Society, 2013).

3 For a useful English translation of most of the nonbiblical texts in the corpus, see Florentino García Martínez, *The Dead Sea Scrolls Translated: The Qumran Texts in English*, trans. Wilfred G. E. Watson, 2nd ed. (Leiden: Brill, 1996).

4 There is a large literature on the subject of pseudepigraphy in ancient Judaism. See, e.g., Martha Himmelfarb, *Ascent to Heaven in Jewish and Christian Apocalypses* (New York: Oxford University Press, 1993), pp. 95–106 and references there; and Michael E. Stone, *Ancient Judaism: New Visions and Views* (Grand Rapids, MI: Eerdmans, 2011), pp. 109–121. For the concept of discourses associated with particular authoritative figures such as Moses, see Hindy Najman, *Seconding Sinai: The Development of Mosaic Discourse in Second Temple Judaism* (Supplements to the Journal for the Study of Judaism 77; Leiden: Brill, 2003).

5 On the use of Hebrew, see Seth Schwartz, "Language, Power, and Identity in Ancient Palestine," *Past and Present* 148 (1995): 3–47.

6 Jozef T. Milik with the collaboration of Matthew Black, *The Books of Enoch: Aramaic Fragments of Qumran Cave 4* (Oxford: Clarendon, 1976). Kraft's paper was not published until almost two decades later, when it appeared with updated notes in *Tracing the Threads: Studies in the Vitality of Jewish Pseudepigrapha*, ed. John C. Reeves (*SBL* Early Judaism and Its Literature; Atlanta, GA: Scholars Press, 1994), pp. 55–86.

7 See the discussion in Stone, *Ancient Judaism*, pp. 31–58.

8 The single work that did the most to shape the thinking of my generation of English-speaking scholars about apocalyptic literature is John J. Collins, ed., *Apocalypse: The Morphology of a Genre* (*Semeia* 14 [1979]). For a useful history of scholarship, see George W. E. Nickelsburg's 2004 paper for the Society of Biblical Literature's group on Wisdom and Apocalypticism in Early Judaism and Early Christianity, "The Study of Apocalypticism from H. H. Rowley to the Society of Biblical Literature," www.sbl-site.org (accessed December 31, 2014).

9 On the interpretation of visions in the Bible, see Michael Fishbane, *Biblical Interpretation in Ancient Israel* (Oxford: Clarendon, 1985), pp. 447–457; on oracles, pp. 458–499. See also M. Fishbane, "The Qumran Pesher and Traits of Ancient Hermeneutics," *Proceedings of the Sixth World Congress of Jewish Studies* (Jerusalem, 1977), vol. 1, pp. 97–114.

10 There is by now an extensive scholarly literature on the Book of the Watchers and 1 Enoch more generally since the publication of the Qumran Aramaic fragments. For commentary and bibliography, see George W. E. Nickelsburg, *1 Enoch 1: A Commentary on the Book of 1 Enoch, Chapters 1–36; 81–108* (Hermeneia; Minneapolis, MN: Fortress, 2001); and G. W. E. Nickelsburg and James C. VanderKam,

1 Enoch 2: A Commentary on the Book of 1 Enoch, Chapters 37–82 (Hermeneia; Minneapolis, MN: Fortress, 2012). For a convenient translation close to the one contained in the two volumes of commentary just mentioned, see G. W. E. Nickelsburg and J. VanderKam, *1 Enoch: A New Translation* (Minneapolis, MN: Fortress, 2004).

11 On the relationship between these two themes and their integration, see Annette Yoshiko Reed, "Heavenly Ascent, Angelic Descent, and the Transmission of Knowledge in 1 Enoch 6–16," in *Heavenly Realms and Earthly Realities in Late Antique Religions*, ed. Ra'anan S. Boustan and Annette Yoshiko Reed (Cambridge: Cambridge University Press, 2004), pp. 47–66.

12 The translations are mine.

13 On the background to this identification, see Martha Himmelfarb, *A Kingdom of Priests: Ancestry and Merit in Ancient Judaism* (Philadelphia: University of Pennsylvania Press, 2006), pp. 11–18.

14 Martha Himmelfarb, *Tours of Hell: An Apocalyptic Form in Jewish and Christian Literature* (Philadelphia: University of Pennsylvania Press, 1983), pp. 50–60.

15 See Himmelfarb, *Ascent to Heaven*, pp. 3–8.

16 See, e.g., the seminal article of George W. E. Nickelsburg, "Enoch, Levi, and Peter: Recipients of Revelation in Upper Galilee," *Journal of Biblical Literature* 100 (1981): 575–600, especially pp. 576–582; and Himmelfarb, *Ascent to Heaven*, pp. 9–28.

17 For the visionary in the ascent apocalypses more generally, see Himmelfarb, *Ascent to Heaven*, pp. 25, 70–71, 93–94.

18 Martha Himmelfarb, "The Practice of Ascent in the Mediterranean World," in *Death, Ecstasy, and Other Worldly Journeys*, ed. John J. Collins and Michael Fishbane (Albany: State University of New York Press, 1995), pp. 123–137, reprinted in Martha Himmelfarb, *Between Temple and Torah: Essays on Priests, Scribes, and Visionaries in the Second Temple Period and Beyond* (Texts and Studies in Ancient Judaism 151; Tübingen: Mohr Siebeck, 2013), pp. 295–305 and references there; and Himmelfarb, *Ascent to Heaven*, pp. 106–114. The *hekhalot* text in question is *Hekahalot Zuṭarti* (Peter Schäfer with the collaboration of Margarete Schlüter and Hans Georg von Mutius, *Synopse zur Hekhalot-Literatur* [Texte und Studien zum antiken Judentum 2; Tübingen: Mohr (Siebeck), 1981]), §§407–426; the paragraphs urging recitation are §§419 and 423. The first to point out their significance as far as I know was David J. Halperin in his review of the *Synopse*, "A New Edition of the Hekhalot Literature," *Journal of the American Oriental Society* 104 (1984): 549–551.

19 The Apocalypse of Zephaniah is an exception. See Himmelfarb, *Ascent to Heaven*, pp. 51–55.

20 Ibid., pp. 47–71.

21 Martha Himmelfarb, "Revelation and Rapture: The Transformation of the Visionary in the Ascent Apocalypses," in *Mysteries and Revelations: Apocalyptic Studies since the Uppsala Colloquium*, ed. John J. Collins and James H. Charlesworth (Journal for the Study of the Pseudepigrapha Supplements 9; Sheffield: Academic

Press, 1991), pp. 79–90, reprinted in Himmelfarb, *Between Temple and Torah*, pp. 283–293; and Himmelfarb, *Ascent to Heaven*, pp. 69–71.

22 Himmelfarb, *Ascent to Heaven*, pp. 37–39. The Greek of which the Slavonic is presumably a translation has not survived. Some scholars believe that recently discovered Coptic fragments are evidence for a Coptic version of 2 Enoch, but this conclusion is by no means certain. For the view that the Coptic fragments are drawn from 2 Enoch, see Joost L. Hagen, "No Longer 'Slavonic Only': 2 Enoch Attested in Coptic from Nubia," in *New Perspectives on 2 Enoch: No Longer Slavonic Only*, ed. Andrei A. Orlov and Gabriele Boccaccini (Leiden: Brill, 2012), pp. 7–34. For criticism of this position, see Christfried Böttrich, "The Angel of Tartarus and the Supposed Coptic Fragments of 2 Enoch," *Early Christianity* 4 (2013): 509–521.

23 For a translation of the Testaments with commentary, see H. W. Hollander and M. de Jonge, *The Testaments of the Twelve Patriarchs: A Commentary* (Leiden: Brill, 1985).

24 R. H. Charles, *The Testaments of the Twelve Patriarchs Translated from the Editor's Greek Text* (London: Adam and Charles Black, 1908), pp. l–lxv.

25 See the brief discussion in Hollander and de Jonge, *Testaments*, pp. 4–7.

26 Marinus de Jonge, *The Testaments of the Twelve Patriarchs: A Study of Their Text, Composition and Origin* (Assen: van Gorcum, 1953).

27 See especially Marinus de Jonge, "The Pre-Mosaic Servants of God in the Testaments of the Twelve Patriarchs and in the Writings of Justin and Irenaeus," in *Jewish Eschatology, Early Christianity, and the Testaments of the Twelve Patriarchs* (Leiden: Brill, 1991), pp. 263–276. De Jonge has produced an impressive corpus of work arguing for the Christian provenance of the *Testaments*, including other essays in the volume just mentioned and *Pseudepigrapha of the Old Testament as Part of Christian Literature: The Case of the Testaments of the Twelve Patriarchs and the Greek Life of Adam and Eve* (Studia in Veteris Testamenti Pseudepigrapha 18; Leiden: Brill, 2003).

28 In addition to the works mentioned in previous notes, see, e.g., Michael E. Stone, *A History of the Literature of Adam and Eve* (Atlanta, GA: Scholars Press, 1992); David Satran, *Biblical Prophets in Byzantine Palestine: Reassessing the Lives of the Prophets* (Leiden: Brill, 1995); Marinus de Jonge and Johannes Tromp, *The Life of Adam and Eve and Related Literature* (Sheffield: Sheffield Academic Press, 1997); Ross Shepherd Kramer, *When Aseneth Met Joseph: A Late Antique Tale of the Biblical Patriarch and His Egyptian Wife, Reconsidered* (New York: Oxford University Press, 1998); the second issue of *Journal for the Study of Judaism* 32 (2001); and James R. Davila, *The Provenance of the Pseudepigrapha: Jewish, Christian, or Other?* (Leiden: Brill, 2005).

29 George W. E. Nickelsburg, *Jewish Literature between the Bible and the Mishnah: A Historical and Literary Introduction* (Philadelphia: Fortress, 1981), pp. 231–275.

30 Ibid., p. 231. See note 29 above for scholarship that suggests that the Life of Adam and Eve and Joseph and Aseneth are Christian compositions.

31 Ibid., pp. 233–234.

32 For a careful treatment of 3 Baruch that ends up favoring Jewish provenance, see Daniel C. Harlow, *The Greek Apocalypse of Baruch (3 Baruch) in Hellenistic Judaism and Early Christianity* (Leiden: Brill, 1996).

33 G. W. E. Nickelsburg, *Jewish Literature between the Bible and the Mishnah: A Historical and Literary Introduction*, 2nd ed. (Minneapolis, MN: Fortress, 2005), pp. 412n1, 301–344.

34 Harlow, too, has become more open to the possibility of Christian provenance: "The Christianization of Early Jewish Pseudepigrapha: The Case of 3 *Baruch*," *Journal for the Study of Judaism in the Persian, Hellenistic, and Roman Periods* 32 (2001): 416–444.

35 For a reading of diaspora Judaism as precursor to Christianity, see, e.g., John J. Collins, *Between Athens and Jerusalem: Jewish Identity in the Hellenistic Diaspora*, 2nd ed. (Grand Rapids, MI: Eerdmans, 2000).

36 See the discussion in Michael E. Stone, "The Genealogy of Bilhah," *Dead Sea Discoveries* 3 (1996): 20–36.

3

Diaspora and the "Assimilated" Jew

ERICH S. GRUEN

The Jews of antiquity labored for many centuries in the lands of or under the aegis of one foreign power or another: Egyptians, Assyrians, Babylonians, Persians, Greeks, and Romans. Some means of keeping track of their own identity, of maintaining continuity, of holding on to a sense of distinctiveness that connected with the past, whether real or constructed, would seem essential for Jewish self-esteem.

In the Greco-Roman era, the period during which the Second Temple stood in Jerusalem, by and large, Jews lived in circumstances of a relatively benign overlordship. That, however, might only have intensified the problem. Were Jews prepared to be swallowed up by what we now term a "majority culture"? Or did they strive to maintain the special characteristics that defined them? The choice, one might imagine, lay between separatism and assimilation. Some Jews took the path of isolation, perpetuating distinct enclaves for the faith, holding themselves apart, and shunning the broader society. Others preferred the choice of accommodation and compromise, keeping a low profile while buying into the practices, institutions, and mind-set of Greek communities in the Near East and Roman authority generally in the Mediterranean.[1] But did most Jews actually take either of these routes?

To be sure, Jews had the reputation of separatism. Notoriously, they preferred their own company to that of everyone else. A famous prayer sums it up nicely. "Thank you, O Lord, for not making me a slave, for not making me a woman—and for not making me a gentile." Better not to have any truck with the gentiles. Jews developed notoriety for sticking to their own kind, keeping non-Jews at arm's length, and maintaining their own traditions unsullied by contact with others. Pagans noticed this tendency and commented upon it. The Sicilian-Greek historian Diodorus characterized the Jews as the only nation that shunned relationships with other peoples and regarded them all as their enemies.[2] That most formidable of Roman historians, Tacitus, weighed in with a typically caustic comment: Jews show intense loyalty and compassion toward one another, but have fierce hostility toward everybody else; they will not eat with gentiles, they will not sleep with them; there is nothing they will not do with one another, but they will not have intercourse with non-Jews.[3] The satirist Juvenal went so far as to write that the Jews in Rome will not even give directions in the street to anyone who is not circumcised.[4] That may be comic exaggeration, but it testifies to the enduring perception of separatism, even misanthropy.

That perception or that construct, however, hardly fits the facts on the ground. We know that Jews did not, in fact, retreat altogether into isolation, cut themselves off from gentile society, or seclude themselves in ghettoized enclaves. They dwelled in cities all over the Mediterranean from North Africa to Iran, in Greek cities for the most part, like Antioch, Alexandria, Ephesus, Sardis, Delos, and Cyrene. They spoke, read, and wrote Greek; some enrolled in Greek gymnasia, benefited from Hellenic education, and even gained familiarity with Hellenic athletics. A number of them indeed enjoyed civic privileges in certain cities, had access to the larger governing structure, and, in a few instances at least, even served as public officials in those cities.[5] When the Mediterranean came under Roman suzerainty, Jewish communities of some size were to be found in Rome itself, large enough to exercise influence on the political scene.[6] And growing numbers of Jews secured Roman citizenship in scattered parts of the world, St. Paul being only the most obvious example, a citizenship that accorded the key mark of status on the larger stage of the empire.[7] The idea of Jewish separatism needs serious qualification. The involvement of Jews in a broad range of social and civic activities in the cities of the Greco-Roman world can hardly be contested.

The old dichotomy between "Judaism" and "Hellenism" that once prevailed no longer holds sway. That formulation has a long history. Tertullian articulated it most famously in the third century CE: "What has Athens to do with Jerusalem?"[8] But scholarship in the past generation or so has broken down that dichotomy, has emphasized the complexities that marked each of the cultures, and has pointed to the fluidity of these boundaries in the realm of the diaspora. No need to reargue that case.[9]

What about the alternative scenario? Did Jews become fully absorbed in the cultural worlds of Greece and Rome, thus compromising their own integrity? Did increasing numbers convert to the ways of the dominant society? In a word, did they become "assimilated"? This brings up a most intriguing issue, rarely raised or confronted. Scholarship has long discussed the question of what it meant to convert to Judaism in antiquity.[10] How do you go about it, who authorizes it, what do you have to do to accomplish it? If males have to get circumcised, what do females have to do? Those and numerous other questions have been confronted. What is noticeable by contrast is the absence of any discussion of conversion *by* Jews. For a perfectly good reason. There was nothing for them to convert to. There is no such animal as paganism. The term "pagan" remains common and conventional. It is used here as well, merely out of convenience. (At least the term "heathen" has happily fallen out of fashion!) But "pagan" was, of course, simply a label applied by Christians to non-Christians, a pejorative designation signifying "rustic" or "country bumpkin." Jews preferred the phrase *ta ethne*, "the nations," which we normally translate as "gentiles." That, too, however, is problematic. Jews could also apply the term *ethnos* to themselves.[11] There was, in any case, no pagan entity, no pagan religion that converts would be expected to join, no uniform set of beliefs to which they would be expected to subscribe. There could, of course, be a falling away from Jewish practices and rituals. The most notorious instance is Tiberius Julius Alexander, whom we commonly regard as the arch Jewish apostate. He became Roman prefect of Egypt and even prefect of Judea on appointment by the emperor. But there is no reason to believe that he converted to anything. The most that Josephus can say of him is that he did not continue to observe the traditions of his ancestors.[12]

So, if there is nothing to convert to, what is there to assimilate to? Was there something out there that Jews could not partake of without losing their integrity? How does one identify a border that could not be crossed without abandoning one's Jewishness?

For some, the idea of a middle ground has been an attractive alternative. It seems more comfortable to supply the term "acculturation" rather than "assimilation"—which in certain circles today softens the somewhat negative connotations of the latter term.[13] As we have seen, diaspora Jews could and did play a role in the social, political, cultural, and educational institutions of Greco-Roman cities. Applying the term "acculturation" to such engagement in the wider world might be more palatable. But it does not resolve the real question. Where does one draw the line that separates embrace of a broader culture from abandonment of core identity? The most obvious place to locate the boundary would seem to be that of religious institutions, conventions, and practices. Here is where researchers usually draw the line: here the barriers remain solid, the borders hold firm. The religious boundary stands fast. To cross it is to assimilate, to dilute or to undermine the faith. Here is where the diaspora experience posed a real challenge for the Jews: either cling to the ancestral religion of the clan or assimilate to the world of the gentile.

On the face of it, that is the critical dilemma. But is it a genuine dilemma? Did Jews of the Greco-Roman era face that choice? The matter is not so simple. We need to problematize this question and to reconceptualize it. Certain revealing texts—both literary texts produced by creative and imaginative Jews and epigraphic texts that take us closer to the conventions of ordinary life—cast a very different light on the issue.

We begin with a particularly fascinating inscription. A half century ago an article was published with the title "The First Greek Jew."[14] The article studied a newly published inscription from Oropos in central Greece of considerable interest and importance. It was a dedication by a certain Moschos Ioudaios (Moschos the Jew) who is, by a wide margin, the first Jew known to us from the Greek mainland, probably from the first half of the third century BCE. Moschos set up this stele at the altar of the Greek god Amphiarios. The offering commemorated Moschos's emancipation with a formula common to manumission documents known elsewhere in the Greek world, notably at Delphi. But Moschos went beyond the usual conventions. He records a dream sent to him by Amphiarios and by Hygieia, goddess of health, presumably while he slept within the shrine. Those divinities had instructed him to inscribe the emancipation document on the stele and to install it by the altar. The author of the article on this document, the eminent epigrapher David Lewis, drew the perfectly reasonable inference that, as he put it, "Moschos, the first Greek Jew whom we know, was thoroughly assimilated to his Greek environment." And he adds, "It is unlikely that Moschos had much Jewish communal spirit."

Perhaps so. A votive dedication by a Jew to pagan divinities is quite striking. Yet the fact that Moschos identifies himself as Ioudaios is at least equally significant. Might a "thoroughly assimilated Jew" not have repressed his origins? Is "assimilation" an appropriate term at all? The expression continues to appear in works on Jewish-gentile relations generally. For many, it has a somewhat pejorative ring, implying compromise, makeover, or even apostasy in order to get along in the larger society. The negative connotations to a modern ear, however, need not determine the issue. It is the ancient practice that requires interpretation.

Moschos's declaration on the stele that he is acting on the instructions of the *theoi* Amphiarios and Hygieia is unequivocal. But his self-identification as Ioudaios is equally pointed and significant. Some scholars have tried to get around this by claiming that Ioudaios on the inscription is a geographic rather than an ethnic designation. That is, Moschos is a man from Judea, not a Jew.[15] The inference may be driven in large part by the presumption that no Jew would invoke pagan divinities; hence the act needs to be explained away. That approach essentially begs the question. Even if Ioudaios can carry a geographical designation, it does not follow and is most unlikely that Moschos of Judea was a non-Jew.[16] One can hardly evade the conclusion that Moschos openly and proudly declares his Jewish identity. He appealed to the protective agency of the pagan shrine to guarantee the endurance of his new status as freedman. But he did not thereby abandon his own identification with the broader Jewish community. The inscription is powerful testimony that an assertion of Jewishness was perfectly compatible with acknowledging the authority of pagan divinities.

The point gains confirmation from two revealing inscriptions from the temple of Pan at El-Kanais near Edfu in Egypt, probably of the Ptolemaic period. Each delivers praise to "god." The first was dedicated by "Theodotos the Jew" who had been saved from the sea, the second by "Ptolemy the Jew."[17] To be sure, the "god" is not specified. But the dedications, inscribed as they were on the rock face west of the temple of Pan, leave little doubt as to their recipient. Pan is plainly the presiding deity. And Jews would not be likely to reckon Pan, half-man, half-goat, as the equivalent of Yahweh. The first dedicator possesses a name that alludes to divinity; the second is a common Greco-Egyptian name. But both unhesitatingly label themselves as Jews. Expressing gratitude to divinity, a frequent practice among pagans, evidently did not dilute these dedicators' Jewishness. And these are no mere civic conventions; they are religious offerings.

Yet another striking illustration deserves mention: an epigraphic text from still a different part of the Mediterranean and still a different instance of Jewish engagement with gentile observances but from a roughly contemporary time in the Hellenistic era. From Iasos in Caria we possess a list of donors who contributed to the Dionysiac festival in that city around the mid-second century BCE. Among the benefactors the inscription lists two metics (resident aliens) who supplied one hundred drachmas each. One of them is designated as Niketas, son of Jason, from Jerusalem.[18] The nomenclature bears notice: "Jason" is a common name among Hellenistic Jews. To be sure, some scholars find it difficult to swallow the idea that a Jew could have contributed to the support of a festival that honored Dionysus, hence expressing doubt that Niketas was Jewish.[19] But this once again begs the question. Not only is the name "Jason" frequently employed by Jews in this period, but the fact that he comes from Jerusalem pretty well clinches the matter. It is, of course, true that some non-Jews lived in Jerusalem. But to claim that Niketas, son of Jason, was one of those very few would be quite a stretch. No need to explain the evidence away. Jewish contributors to a pagan ceremony in a Greek city that included Jews among its inhabitants should, in fact, cause no surprise. And it should certainly not prompt any presumptions about apostasy or "conversion." There is nothing to suggest any border crossings here.

The fluidity of the Hellenistic era blurred distinctions and undermined barriers. A celebrated passage in the *Letter of Aristeas* has relevance here. This work was composed probably in the second century BCE by a Hellenistic Jewish author fully conversant with the intellectual society of Ptolemaic Alexandria. The narrator, a supposed Greek aristocrat at the court of Ptolemy II, states that the god whom Jews worship, the overseer and creator of all, is the same one worshiped by all, including "us" (i.e., Greeks)—only we call him Zeus and Dis.[20] That statement, put in the mouth of a Greek character by a Jewish author, is a telling one. But we need to understand it properly. The remark does not make a claim for syncretism or an amalgamation of the deities. Nor does it breathe the spirit of some abstract universalism. The god in question here is the Jewish god. "Aristeas" makes that clear in the preceding sentence in which he affirms that God who gave laws to the Jews also serves as protector of Ptolemy himself. In fact, the Jewish High Priest Eleazer later in the treatise insists upon a decided differentiation between Jewish practices and those of idolators.[21] So there is no blending or merging of interchangeable deities, as is often claimed. This, to be sure, is an *interpretatio Judaica*, a Jewish take on the subject. But it is a rather ironic one, for the *interpretatio* comes from the mouth of a Greek character manipulated by a Jewish ventriloquist. And the import of the statement is significant. It expresses the Jewish author's view that his people's monotheistic idea can be ascribed without strain to gentiles as well. In other words, gentile religious conceptualizations can, in some sense, be "assimilated" to Jewish sensibility—rather than the other way around. The text makes no big issue of this, and the matter does not resurface again in the work. The possibility of a congruence of understanding could be taken for granted. That alone is significant. There is no irremediable divide.

Another Jewish text, probably contemporary (or nearly so) with the *Letter of Aristeas*, adds a relevant and intriguing report. The Jewish historian Eupolemos, of whose work *On the Kings of Judea* only fragments survive, rewrote various parts of the Bible, including a noteworthy recasting of Solomon's reign. Among other things, Eupolemos embellished the biblical tradition on Solomon's international connections by inventing an exchange of correspondence between the Israelite king and the rulers of Phoenicia and Egypt. The former exchange demands notice. It builds on the narrative in 1 Kings and 2 Chronicles, which records letters passed between Solomon and Hiram the king of Tyre (whom Eupolemos calls Souron), a friendly collaboration in the building of the Temple in Jerusalem. Eupolemos has Souron not only as lord of Tyre but as ruler of Sidon and all Phoenicia. His compliance with Solomon's requests for building material and assistance in constructing the Temple thus adds to the Judean king's stature.[22] And Solomon was generous in return. Not only did he restore the Phoenician craftsmen to their homeland with extensive pay for service, but he sent to the king nothing less than a golden column which, according to Eupolemos, was set up in the temple of Zeus at Tyre.[23] That is quite an extraordinary gift. An offering to a pagan shrine by Solomon who had just completed a monumental act of piety to Yahweh, the construction of the Temple in Jerusalem, has naturally troubled modern commentators. How to account for such incongruity? Some have tried to explain away the passage as erroneous or to postulate a later addition tacked onto the text.[24] But, although modern scholars may feel puzzled, the ancient author seems not to have found any incongruity at all. Eupolemos saw no inconsistency in presenting Solomon both as dedicated servant of the Lord and as patron of a foreign ruler who honored the cult of Zeus. Here again the concept of syncretism would be inaccurate and misleading. The Jewish historian describes something quite different from a harmonizing of the deities. Souron's assistance made possible Solomon's Temple, the great tribute to Yahweh, and Solomon's reciprocal act of generosity expressed itself in enhancing the shrine of the supreme pagan divinity. Neither felt the slightest compromise in his religious commitment by acknowledging and honoring the god of the other—at least in the presentation of the Jewish author.[25]

There is much more along these lines. A host of imaginative writings flowed from the pens of Hellenistic-Jewish authors. Whether recasting biblical stories, adapting Greek genres, or creating historical novels, they attest to the Jewish construction of links to the non-Jewish world. A few instances will suffice. We focus on those that have some religious resonance.

The most fascinating author in this category is a relatively obscure figure named Artapanos. That at least is the name that has come down to us, a Persian name, perhaps a pseudonym, belonging to a writer known only from a few fragments quoted by Alexander Polyhistor and preserved for us by Eusebius. He composed a work entitled *On the Jews*, in Greek, probably in the second century BCE. The extant fragments consist of two short excerpts from his treatment of Abraham and Joseph, and of a somewhat lengthier discussion of Moses. Artapanos's work reveals a creative, imaginative, and perhaps rather whimsical reinterpretation of the biblical narrative. Of particular relevance here is a striking portion of Artapanos's Moses story in which he takes great liberties with the tradition. In Artapanos's re-creation, the Greeks named Moses Mousaios and made him the teacher of Orpheus, the legendary singer and the father of Hellenic poetry. And the Egyptians for their part called him Hermes because he was able to interpret hieroglyphics.[26] They thus associated him with the Egyptian version of Hermes, Thot, who like Moses possessed the skills of craftsmen and the capacity to interpret sacred writings.[27] By having Greeks and Egyptians make the identifications and the ascriptions, Artapanos gave Moses a central place in both cultures, the amalgam that was Ptolemaic Egypt. For Artapanos there was little in Egyptian society or experience that could not be traced to Moses. The Hebrew hero was responsible for inventing ships and weapons, for hydraulic and building devices, and for the introduction of philosophy. And that was just the start. In the sphere of religion Moses really made his mark—quite outside the religion of the Hebrews. According to Artapanos, he founded the city of Hermopolis, named after him (Hermes) and made the ibis sacred there. His magical rods so impressed the Egyptians that they installed rods in all their temples and associated them with the worship of Isis. His advice on the best oxen to till the land turned out to inspire the consecration of the sacred bull Apis, a central element in Egyptian religion. And, just for good measure, Artapanos tossed in the idea that Moses also introduced Ethiopians to the practice of circumcision.[28]

All of this has proved rather disturbing for modern scholars. That Moses was responsible for Egyptian religious institutions, even for animal worship (while no mention is made of him as giving laws to the Israelites), has put the notion of Artapanos as a Jew beyond the pale. Some conclude that he must have been a polytheist or a henotheist or one who believed in monolatry rather than monotheism, or a syncretist, or a half-Jew, or no Jew at all.[29] But these forced interpretations miss the puckish quality of the work. The idea that the Hebrew lawgiver actually brought Egyptian religious, cultural, and social institutions into being and endorsed, even introduced, animal worship could only invite amusement.[30] And few pagans would be in a position to discern the author's witty twists on and deviations from the standard version in Exodus—let alone to compare them. Artapanos's audience must have been primarily Jewish.

But there is more than jocularity here. The theme, repeated in an ingenious variety of ways, of interconnections between the founder of the Israelite nation and other peoples, cultures, and *religious* institutions pervades the text. The work qualifies as a prime document of cultural integration. But it also serves equally well as an exemplar of Jewish appropriation. Moses as culture hero for both Greeks and Egyptians underscores the priority of Jewish ingenuity. Artapanos's inventive history exemplifies the comfortable self-perception of Jews who could play with the idea that gentile institutions and even religious practices might be accounted for by Jewish authorization.

One more instance of this fitting of a biblical figure into a wider cultural world deserves a brief summary. An extended fragment of a Jewish Hellenistic historian conventionally labeled as "Pseudo-Eupolemos" is relevant here. He rewrote parts of the Abraham story in Genesis and added elements that derived from both Babylonian and Greek legendary material. The initial focus of the fragment is on Babylon, first built by those who survived the Flood, according to Pseudo-Eupolemos. He proceeds then to assign construction of the Tower of Babel to giants who were subsequently scattered over the earth. That report has echoes of Greek myths on the Gigantomachia, here imported to the biblical exegesis. The author next introduces Abraham as discoverer of astrology and master of Chaldean craft. Abraham subsequently imparted his Mesopotamian knowledge to other Near Eastern peoples. He taught the cycles of the sun and moon to Phoenicians and a range of astrological matters to Egyptian priests. The author proceeds to have Abraham recount to the Egyptians a mythical genealogy stemming from Kronos, also known (he says) as Belus (Ba'al) by the Babylonians, one of whose descendants, Canaan, became ancestor of the Phoenicians, another, Kush, the forefather of the Ethiopians, and still another, Mizraim, sired the Egyptians. And, as if that were not enough, Pseudo-Eupolemos adds that the Greeks acknowledge Enoch, the Hebrew mythical figure, as the discoverer of astrology—even though they call him Atlas.[31]

This remarkable genealogical stew defies any sorting out. But Pseudo-Eupolemos has clearly dug about in Babylonian, Israelite, and Greek lore and has swept into its vortex Ethiopians and Egyptians as well, all of it connected somehow with the narrative of Abraham. The Hebrew patriarch stands in the center of this extraordinary concoction. He is both progenitor of Israelites and purveyor of culture, learning, and sacred traditions to other peoples of the Mediterranean, both national hero and world-historical figure. Pseudo-Eupolemos's inventive creation reinforces the idea of overlapping links and reciprocal advantages among the nations. And it conveys the notion that major achievements by Hellenic and Near Eastern nations have their roots in Jewish initiative. This form of cultural appropriation represents a mind-set as distant as possible from the stereotype of Jewish isolation and insulation.

These imaginary scenarios, created by clever Jewish intellectuals, can be evocative and illuminating. But we need to get back to matters on the ground, the epigraphic evidence. The testimony comes in bits and pieces, usually lacking context and supplying only minimal information. But what we have turns out to be reassuringly compatible with and provides tangible counterparts to the fancies of the intellectuals. We have seen already some striking examples of this from the Hellenistic period: the Moschos inscription, the documents from the temple of Pan in Egypt, and the donor list from Iasos. They disclose the ease with which self-identified Jews could associate themselves with pagan divinities and pagan religious institutions. That fluidity continued into the Roman era. The epigraphic evidence becomes considerably fuller, and it is widely scattered both geographically and chronologically. Unfortunately, the texts do not allow for any confident sense of development over time, for the gaps remain much larger than the pockets of evidence. But the crossovers and intertwinings can be illustrated in a number of different ways.

Among the most intriguing are the patronage and benefactions accorded to Jewish synagogues by wealthy donors. Inscriptions record gifts and endowments provided for synagogues by benefactors. The donations might be earmarked for building a courtyard, adding a roof, repairing a structure, or even endowing an entire synagogue. What merits notice here are the synagogue inscriptions that honor the donor by awarding a golden crown or a special seat of honor. These are precisely the sort of reciprocal benefactions and expressions of gratitude that are commonly found in pagan inscriptions. The social conventions long established in the Greek cities of the Hellenistic and Roman worlds of gaining stature for contributions to the community and the honors received in return are here precisely mirrored by Jewish practices.[32] No less intriguing is the fact that a fair proportion of these inscriptions refer to women donors and benefactresses. They demonstrate not only that Jewish women could own property in their own right and that some possessed extensive holdings, but also that they bought into the pagan traditions of exhibiting status through handsome donations and receiving honorific awards in return. And equally interesting is the fact that some of these female benefactresses to synagogues were not Jewish at all. We know of instances in which wealthy pagan women made substantial gifts to Jewish synagogues. In one such case, a notable pagan priestess and high official in a city of Asia Minor, Julia Severa, actually funded an entire synagogue.[33] In short, not only did Jews adopt pagan practices and do so without difficulty or discomfort, but pagans of wealth and standing, men and women alike, could advance and enhance the religious institutions of the Jews. The intertwining of Jewish identity and gentile religious institutions and practices can be illustrated, however fragmentarily, over a stretch of centuries.

Two epitaphs from different parts of the vast Roman world, both probably some time in the second or third centuries CE, deserve mention. In each case the deceased, a woman, carries the ethnic marker of "Iudea," but the gravestone is headed by "D.M.," *dis manibus,* a standard formula in pagan epitaphs, alluding to the divine spirits of the dead. The first comes from Pannonia on the Danube, the second from Cirta in North Africa.[34] Again, efforts have been made to explain away the ostensible anomaly. Perhaps, so it has been suggested, Iudea was a personal name—or perhaps the deceased were converts.[35] But those proposals operate on the assumption that no Jew would employ the formula *dis manibus*—which again simply begs the question. Iudea as a personal name is extremely rare, and, as part of a tripartite name, as in the Cirta epitaph, is virtually unknown.[36] Not that *dis manibus* occurs all that frequently in Jewish inscriptions. But plainly no prohibition prevented Jews from adopting a gentile formula alluding to spirits of the dead and interpreting them in their own fashion.

That Jews could freely acknowledge pagan divinities (whatever they may have thought of them) can be exemplified in manumission documents. The practice is attested already in the Hellenistic period. At Delphi a certain Ioudaios emancipated his slave in standard Hellenic fashion through fictitious sale to Pythian Apollo in the late second or early first century BCE.[37] Ioudaios here is obviously a personal name, but it is hardly likely to have been appropriated by a gentile. He is plainly a Jew at home with this Hellenic institution. Adaptation to Greek practices seems quite comfortable and smooth, and the recourse to Apollo perfectly natural. What bears particular notice is the fact that the Jewish emancipator chose to liberate his slave in a pagan shrine under the aegis of a pagan deity.

The manumission declarations from the Black Sea region show that Jews were fully conversant with forms and procedures familiar from Greek *paramone* (conditional manumission) documents. The transactions themselves took place in Jewish synagogues, but the proceedings regularly followed Hellenic models.[38] One such record warrants special attention. In an inscription from Gorgippia in the Bosporan kingdom, dated explicitly to 41 CE, the emancipator invokes *theos hypsistos* (highest god), commonly employed in Jewish inscriptions, and emancipates his slave in the synagogue (*proseuche*). But he accompanies this with a vow that the liberated slave be under the protection of "Zeus, Earth, and Sun."[39] Evidently the dedicator found no strain or tension between appealing to the Jewish god and calling upon the protection of Zeus, Earth, and Sun—a comfortable application of divine powers as formulated by gentiles.

In a different category, but even more fascinating, is a funerary text from Hierapolis in Phrygia, probably from the early third century CE. Here P. Aelius Glyphon announces two endowments that he will supply for decorating the gravesites on specified occasions annually. The first is a gift to the guild of purple dyers to administer the ceremony each year at Passover. The second is a gift to the association of carpet weavers to distribute the proceeds, half at the celebration of the Kalends and half at the festival of Pentecost (Shavuot).[40] It is quite remarkable that Glyphon, doubtless a Jew, specified two Jewish holidays, Passover and Pentecost, as occasions for commemoration, but also designated the festival of Kalends, a pagan event that celebrated the Roman New Year. It is altogether unnecessary to propose, as some have, that Glyphon was a partial convert to Judaism, a sympathizer, or a "god-fearer" who sought to balance his allegiance in this fashion.[41] Such speculations, of course, depend on the presumption that Glyphon's links to both Jewish and pagan festivals create a problem and that therefore we must resolve the problem. No such problem, however, need have existed. That one of the guilds would honor the gravesite both on a Jewish holiday and on a civic holiday was perfectly acceptable and demands no special explanation.

Also from Hierapolis comes an equally illuminating and very different document, only recently published, from the mid-second century

CE. It belongs to the sarcophagus of a certain Hikesios, "also called Judah," whose accomplishments deserve record. The inscription calls him "most famous victor in sacred contests," and indeed adds "multiple victor."[42] Whether his triumphs came in athletic or in musical contests is unspecified. But that a man who carried the name "Judah" could enter—and win—in numerous "sacred contests," that is, contests consecrated to pagan deities, holds real significance. Not only could Jews take part in gymnasial games, but they advertised their participation proudly in these preeminently pagan competitions.

Two other quite different and quite interesting inscriptions merit notice. They provide striking examples of overlap and interchange. The first, a Phoenician epitaph from the fourth century BCE, gives the Hebrew name of a father and the Phoenician name of his son.[43] Both of them possess names that allude to divinity. The startling fact is that one of the names alludes to Yahweh and the other to Astarte. That is a remarkable form of shared religious and ethnic identity. The second document exhibits the other face of the adaptation that has been discussed here. Pagans could appropriate from Jews, as Jews appropriated from pagans. In a text from Aspendos in Pamphylia, dating from the first or second century CE, we can witness *Jewish* influence even upon a *pagan* dedication. The wording directs itself to a god who is infallible and not made by hand.[44] The document is pagan but the unusual expressions sound decidedly more Jewish than gentile. The resonance could echo from either side.

The second inscription stands in a class by itself. It is a gold amulet discovered very recently in a child's grave in Austria dating probably to the third century CE. This is by about half a millennium the earliest evidence of a Jewish presence within the borders of present-day Austria. The amulet is inscribed with a Hebrew prayer, and not just any Hebrew prayer. It records nothing less than the Shema itself: *Shema Yisrael, Adonai Elohenu, Adonai Echad* ("Hear, O Israel, the Lord is God, the Lord is One"). But, although the prayer is in Hebrew, the lettering is Greek, a Greek transliteration.[45] Thus, in a distant corner of the Roman Empire, across the Danube, Hebrew was still used by Jews, but expressed in Greek script.

To summarize, none of this, of course, implies that Jews had submerged or subordinated their identity to a broader cultural world. Far from it. The large number of synagogues that existed across much of the Roman Empire both before and after the destruction of the Temple in Jerusalem makes that abundantly clear.[46] The epigraphic testimony confirms it. Not only do numerous inscriptions sport decorations with Jewish symbols like the menorah, the shofar, the lulav, and the etrog, but we also have several texts that put biblical quotations on display, including one long quotation from Deuteronomy, written in Hebrew, which comes from Palmyra.[47] The evidence, as we have it, challenges any notion of a *Kulturkampf* or of impenetrable borders between paganism and Judaism. Jews hardly retreated into isolation or separatism. Nor, on the other hand, did they resort to wholesale assimilation. The distinctive identity of the Jews was not undermined by participation in the wider world, even the wider religious world. One finds more traces of reciprocity than of rivalry.

The Greek philosopher Hermippos of Smyrna, an admirer and biographer of Pythagoras, who penned his work in the late third century BCE, made an arresting observation. In his study of Pythagoras, Hermippos had no hesitation in maintaining that the Greek sage incorporated much from the laws of the Jews into his own philosophy.[48] More than two centuries later Philo of Alexandria made a comparable assertion from the reverse direction. As he put it, Moses himself not only learned arithmetic, geometry, music, and hieroglyphics from erudite Egyptians, but progressed through the rest of his curriculum, presumably rhetoric, literature, and philosophy, with Greek masters.[49] So, although Moses's measures may have formed the backdrop for later Greek philosophy, he owed his own education in part to Hellenic teachers. It matters little that these constructs have small purchase on reality. The representations themselves carry real significance for the mutual perceptions of Greeks and Jews. The idea of "assimilation" is simply inapplicable.

The supposed distinction between two cultures gives way to a much more complex intersection. We should look less at artificial boundaries than at overlap and interconnection. A final illustration brings this out amusingly. It comes from the rabbinic tradition and appears in the Mishnah.[50] As the tale has it, Rabbi Gamliel went to Acco, a largely gentile city on the coast of Palestine. There he took a bath in a bathhouse dedicated to Aphrodite and adorned by her statue, no doubt in her most seductive pose. The rabbi was then asked by a puzzled Greek philosopher how he could violate Jewish law by entering the sacred space of a pagan shrine—and one marked by a statue of Aphrodite, of all people. Gamaliel had an answer that one might paraphrase as follows: "Look, I came here to take a bath. They did not build the bathhouse for the statue; they built the statue for the bathhouse. So I did not come into Aphrodite's domain; she came into mine." The rabbi's reasoning may have been a bit sophistical, but it makes a nice point. Greek statuary and Roman baths can be comfortably accommodated even in the society of the rabbis.

Ancient Judaism itself was no monolithic entity. Its diverse sects and multifarious experiences in various parts of the Mediterranean provided a flexibility and a fluidity that enabled it to adjust satisfactorily to pre-dominantly non-Jewish societies without compromising core values of religious identity. Such elasticity readily facilitated border crossings.

The blurring of boundaries receives perhaps its most memorable turn of phrase in the words of the neo-Pythagorean philosopher Numenius of Apamea in the later second century CE. As he put it, "What is Plato, other than Moses speaking good Attic Greek?"[51]

NOTES

1 The valuable study of J. M. G. Barclay, *Jews in the Mediterranean Diaspora from Alexander to Trajan (323 BCE–117 CE)* (Edinburgh: T & T Clark, 1997), pp. 92–98, 103–124, and 320–335, seeks to nuance the concepts, distinguishing assimilation from acculturation and accommodation, and further dividing assimilation into high, medium, and low assimilation. But this form of categorization and subcategorization, while thoughtful and serviceable, suggests a degree of specificity that the evidence cannot sustain. And it involves an imposition of modern classification not readily discernible in the ancient texts.

2 Diodorus Siculus 34/35.1.1–2 (Loeb Classical Library [LCL] vol. 12, pp. 52–53).

3 Tacitus, *Histories* book 5.5.1–2 (LCL vol. 3, pp. 180–183).

4 Juvenal, *Satire* 14.104–105 (LCL pp. 272–273).

5 See the comprehensive survey in E. Schürer, *The History of the Jewish People in the Age of Jesus Christ (175 B.C.–A.D. 135)*, rev. ed., by G. Vermes, F. Millar, and M. Goodman, vol. III.1 (Edinburgh: T & T Clark, 1986), pp. 1–176. A brief overview is in E. S. Gruen, *Diaspora: Jews amidst Greeks and Romans* (Cambridge, MA: Harvard University Press, 2002), pp. 105–132. Two excellent collections of texts may be found in L. H. Feldman and M. Reinhold, *Jewish Life and Thought among Greeks and Romans: Primary Readings* (Minneapolis, MN: Fortress Press, 1996); and M. H. Williams, *The Jews among the Greeks and Romans* (Baltimore, MD: Johns Hopkins University Press, 1998).

6   Cicero, *Pro Flacco* 67–68 (LCL vol. 10, pp. 514–517); Gruen, *Diaspora*, pp. 19–23.

7   See A. N. Sherwin-White, *The Roman Citizenship*, 2nd ed. (Oxford: Oxford University Press, 1973), pp. 225–263; Schürer, *History of the Jewish People*, III.1, pp. 133–134; M. Pucci Ben Zeev, *Jewish Rights in the Roman World* (Tübingen: Mohr Siebeck, 1998), p. 152, with bibliography.

8   Tertullian, *De Praescriptione Hereticorum* 7 (see *The Ante-Nicene Fathers*, ed. Alexander Roberts and James Donaldson [Grand Rapids, MI: Wm. B. Eerdmans, 1962], vol. 3, p. 246).

9   Among the works that stress this point, see M. Hengel, *Judaism and Hellenism: Studies in Their Encounter in Palestine during the Early Hellenistic Period* (London: SCM, 1974), 2 vols.; E. S. Gruen, *Heritage and Hellenism: The Reinvention of Jewish Tradition* (Berkeley: University of California Press, 1998); L. I. Levine, *Judaism and Hellenism in Antiquity* (Seattle: University of Washington Press, 1998); J. Aitken, "Review Essay on Hengel, *Judaism and Hellenism*," *Journal of Biblical Literature* 123 (2004): 329–341; J. J. Collins, "Hellenistic Judaism in Recent Scholarship," in *Jewish Cult and Hellenistic Culture: Essays on the Jewish Encounter with Hellenism and Roman Rule*, ed. J. J. Collins (Leiden: Brill, 2005), pp. 1–20.

10 See, especially, S. J. D. Cohen, *The Beginnings of Jewishness: Boundaries, Varieties, Uncertainties* (Berkeley: University of California Press, 1999), pp. 140–174 with bibliography.

11 See, e.g., Philo, *Legum Allegoria* 3.29 §88 (LCL vol. 1, pp. 360–361); *Deus immutabilis sit* 22 §148 (LCL vol. 3 pp. 84–85); *De Migratione Abrahami* 10 §53 (LCL vol. 4, pp. 160–161); Josephus, *Jewish War* 1.10.1 §196 (LCL vol. 2, pp. 90–91), 2.10.4 §197 (LCL vol. 2, pp. 398–399), 4.4.4 §274 (LCL vol. 3, pp. 238–239); *Antiquities* 8.10.3 §261 (LCL vol. 7, pp. 356–357), 10.9.7 §182 (LCL vol. 8, pp. 258–259), 18.9.9 §378 (LCL vol. 12 pp. 210–211).

12 Josephus, *Antiquities* 20.5.2 §100 (LCL vol. 13, pp. 54–55).

13 See Barclay, *Jews in the Mediterranean Diaspora*, pp. 92–102.

14 D. Lewis, "The First Greek Jew," *Journal of Semitic Studies* 2 (1957): 264–266. The inscription is republished as Ach45 in D. Noy, A. Panayotov, and H. Bloedhorn, *Inscriptiones Judaicae Orientis* I (Tübingen: Mohr Siebeck, 2004).

15 See the bibliography in *Inscriptiones Judaicae Orientis* I, Ach45.

16 This is not the place to engage the current debate on whether *Ioudaios* generally signifies "Judean" or "Jew." Among principal contributions, with differing views, see S. Mason, "Jews, Judaeans, Judaizing, Judaism: Problems of Categorization in Ancient History," *Journal for the Study of Judaism* 38 (2007): 457–512; D. R. Schwartz, " 'Judaean' or 'Jew'? How Should we Translate Ioudaios in Josephus?," in *Jewish Identity in the Greco-Roman World*, ed. J. Frey, D. R. Schwartz, and S. Gripentrog (Leiden: Brill, 2007), pp. 3–27; S. Schwartz, "How Many Judaisms Were There? A Critique of Neusner and Smith on Definition and Mason and Boyarin on Categorization," *Journal of Ancient Judaism* 2 (2011): 208–238; and D. R. Schwartz, *Judeans and Jews: Four Faces of Dichotomy in Ancient Jewish History* (Toronto: University of Toronto Press, 2014), pp. 102–112.

17 W. Horbury and D. Noy, *Jewish Inscriptions of Graeco-Roman Egypt* (Cambridge: Cambridge University Press, 1992), #121–122.

18 W. Ameling, *Inscriptiones Judaicae Orientis* II (Tübingen: Mohr Siebeck, 2004), #21.

19 J. N. Sevenster, *The Roots of Pagan Anti-Semitism in the Ancient World* (Leiden: Brill, 1975), p. 73; Schürer, *History of the Jewish People*, III.1, p. 25.

20 *Letter of Aristeas* 16. For a convenient text and translation of this work, see M. Hadas, *Aristeas to Philocrates (Letter of Aristeas)* (New York: Harper and Brothers, 1951), pp. 100–103.

21 *Letter of Aristeas* 134–143 (ed. Hadas, pp. 154–157).

22 Eupolemos, in Eusebius, *Praeparatio Evangelica* 9.33.1–34.17, trans. E. H. Gifford (Grand Rapids, MI: Baker Book House, 1981), pp. 477–478; see text and translation of Eupolemos in C. R. Holladay, *Fragments from Hellenistic Jewish Authors: Vol. 1: Historians* (Chico, CA: Scholars Press, 1983), pp. 93–135.

23 Eupolemos, in Eusebius, *Praeparatio Evangelica* 9.34.18 (trans. E. H. Gifford), p. 480; Holladay, *Fragments from Jewish Authors*, vol. 1, pp. 130–131.

24 See B. Z. Wacholder, *Eupolemus: A Study of Judaeo-Greek Literature* (Cincinnati, OH: Hebrew Union College Press, 1974), pp. 217–223; D. Mendels, *The Land of Israel as a Political Concept in Hasmonean Literature* (Tübingen: Mohr Siebeck, 1987), pp. 133–143.

25 Providing a gold column to enhance a pagan shrine was a very different matter from financing actual sacrifices to a pagan deity. Even Jews who were sympathetic to Hellenic practices could balk at the latter; see 2 Maccabees 4.18–20.

26 Artapanos, in Eusebius, *Praeparatio Evangelica* 9.27.3–6 (trans. E. H. Gifford), p. 463; Holladay, *Fragments from Jewish Authors*, vol. 1, pp. 208–211.

27 See the discussion of G. Mussies, "The Interpretatio Judaica of Thot-Hermes," in *Studies in Egyptian Religion*, ed. M. Voss et al. (Leiden: Brill, 1982), pp. 87–120.

28 Artapanos, in Eusebius, *Praeparatio Evangelica* 9.27.4–12 (trans. E. H. Gifford), p. 463; Holladay, *Fragments from Jewish Authors*, vol. 1, pp. 208–213.

29 L. H. Feldman, *Jew and Gentile in the Ancient World: Attitudes and Interactions from Alexander to Justinian* (Princeton, NJ: Princeton University Press, 1993), p. 208; E. Koskenniemi, "Greeks, Egyptians, and Jews in the Fragments of Artapanus," *Journal for the Study of the Pseudepigrapha* 13 (2002): 17–31; H. Jacobson, "Artapanus Judaeus," *Journal of Jewish Studies* 57 (2006): 210–221.

30 See Gruen, *Diaspora*, pp. 201–211.

31 Pseudo-Eupolemos, in Eusebius, *Praeparatio Evangelica* 9.17.2–3, 9.17.8–9 (trans. E. H. Gifford), p. 451; Holladay, *Fragments from Jewish Authors*, vol. 1, pp. 170–173.

32 T. Rajak, *The Jewish Dialogue with Greece and Rome: Studies in Cultural and Social Interaction* (Leiden: Brill, 2002), pp. 373–391.

33 *Inscriptiones Judaicae Orientis* II, #168. See the treatment by P. Trebilco, *Jewish Communities in Asia Minor* (Cambridge: Cambridge University Press, 1991), pp. 58–60, and the thorough discussion of Ameling, *Inscriptiones Judaicae Orientis* II, pp. 348–355.

34 Pannonia: *Inscriptiones Judaicae Orientis* I, Pan 4; Cirta: Y. Le Bohec, "Inscriptions juives et judaisantes de l'Afrique romaine," *Antiquités Africaines* 17 (1981): #71.

35 A. Scheiber, *Jewish Inscriptions in Hungary* (Leiden: Brill, 1983), p. 45; R. S. Kraemer, "On the Meaning of the Term 'Jew' in Greco-Roman Inscriptions," *Harvard Theological Review* 82 (1989): 41–43.

36 M. H. Williams, "The Meaning and Function of *Ioudaios* in Graeco-Roman Inscriptions," *Zeitschrift für Papyrologie und Epigraphik* 116 (1997): 250–251.

37 *Inscriptiones Judaicae Orientis* I, Ach44.

38 E. L. Gibson, *The Jewish Manumission Inscriptions of the Bosporus Kingdom* (Tübingen: Mohr Siebeck, 1999).

39 *Inscriptiones Judaicae Orientis* I, BS 20.

40 *Inscriptiones Judaicae Orientis* II, #196.

41 See the discussions of Trebilco, *Jewish Communities*, pp. 178–179; and P. A. Harland, "Acculturation and Identity in the Diaspora: A Jewish Family and 'Pagan' Guilds at Hierapolis," *Journal of Jewish Studies* 57 (2006): 227–232.

42 *Inscriptiones Judaicae Orientis* II, #189.

43 D. Noy and H. Bloedhorn, *Inscriptiones Judaicae Orientis* III (Tübingen: Mohr Siebeck, 2004), Cyp7.

44 *Inscriptiones Judaicae Orientis* II, #218.

45 E. Eshel, H. Eshel, and A. Lange, "'Hear O Israel' in Gold: An Ancient Amulet from Halbturn in Austria," *Journal of Ancient Judaism* 1 (2010): 43–64.

46 See the valuable work of D. D. Binder, *Into the Temple Courts: The Place of the Synagogues in the Second Temple Period* (Atlanta, GA: Society of Biblical Literature, 1999); and the comprehensive survey by L. I. Levine, *The Ancient Synagogue: The First Thousand Years* (New Haven, CT: Yale University Press, 2000).

47 *Inscriptiones Judaicae Orientis* III, Syr44.

48 Hermippos in Josephus, *Contra Apionem* 1.165 (LCL pp. 228–229).

49 Philo, *De Vita Mosis* 1.5 §23 (LCL vol. 6, pp. 286–289).

50 *M. Avodah Zarah* 3:4. Among numerous discussions, see S. Schwartz, "Gamaliel in Aphrodite's Bath: Palestinian Judaism and Urban Culture in the Third and Fourth Centuries," in *The Talmud Yerushalmi and Graeco-Roman Culture*, I, ed. P. Schäfer (Tübingen: Mohr Siebeck, 1998), pp. 203–217; A. Yadin, "Rabban Gamliel, Aphrodite's Bath, and the Question of Pagan Monotheism," *Jewish Quarterly Review* 96 (2006): 149–179.

51 Clement of Alexandria, *Stromata* 1.22.150.4 (see *Ante-Nicene Fathers*, vol. 2, pp. 334–335).

4

Were the Ancient Jews a Nation?

SETH SCHWARTZ

Questions about national, cultural, ethnic, or religious identity are always controversial. For Jews, the controversies are now more than two centuries old, but they remain peculiarly urgent: are the Jews a nation, a people, a race, an ethnic group, or a religious community? What is the content of their group identity and what should it be? Do they/should they share sacred texts and theological ideals, or cultural practices, or genes? Important issues in contemporary politics and culture seem to hinge on the answers to such questions. How legitimate is the Zionist project? Which version of it, if any, deserves to be supported? How should diaspora Jewish communities allocate resources, and how should they decide whom to include and whom to exclude? It may be helpful to start with a very brief survey of the main tendencies in Jewish scholarship on the question of the nationhood or peoplehood of the Jews in general, before tightening our focus on antiquity.[1]

Wissenschaft des Judentums, the earliest version of modern, "scientific" Jewish scholarship, which originated among young Jewish university graduates in the German states around 1820, had as its central project the rediscovery of a Jewish historical and textual legacy that had been neglected or forgotten in traditional Ashkenazic Judaism. Most of these scholars were convinced that they were engaged in "objective" research but concurrently had a political and religious program: they wished to demonstrate that the traditional feudal arrangements that had restricted the Jews politically and economically should be abandoned. The Jews, still subject to corporate disabilities and privileges, deserved emancipation and enfranchisement, or rather they would deserve it if they could be convinced that Judaism in its essential form was a highly refined version of ethical monotheism and not a set of outmoded and unattractive rituals meant to generate an artificial national solidarity, which had no place in a progressive setting: this, for example, was the view of Isaak Markus Jost (1793–1860) in his ten-volume *Geschichte der Israeliten seit der Zeit der Maccabäer bis auf unsre Tage.*[2] Such scholars argued that if the Jews had ever constituted a nation, they emphatically ceased to do so after the Romans destroyed Jerusalem and its temple in 70 CE. This event was a blessing in disguise because it allowed the Jews to fulfill their world-historical mission of spreading monotheism, purified of atavistic elements like animal sacrifice, to the four corners of the world. This perspective presupposes that the scattered Jewish communities might attain a high degree of integration in their host societies. Anyone seeking a success story, of worldly and civilized Jewish philosophers, poets, scholars, and scientists, fully integrated in a tolerant and progressive political regime could find it in Moorish Spain in the eleventh century, the world of Hasdai ibn Shaprut, Solomon ibn Gabirol, Samuel ha-Nagid, and Judah ha-Levi. Inevitably, though, in the harsh conditions of medieval Christendom, Judaism declined, its beautiful essence obscured by the need for self-protection against degradation and torment. Be this as it may, the Jews did not possess a meaningful national culture that could have united them across national borders in Europe, western Asia, and North Africa. In every country they shared more with their neighbors than they did with Jews in distant lands, aside from a set of religious principles. They were thus comparable to Christians, whose occasional feelings of religious solidarity did not necessarily lead to shared political loyalties.

As the quest for emancipation stalled in German lands in the course of the nineteenth century (it barely even got under way in the Russian Empire before it was brought to a halt by the May Laws of 1882) and an anti-Semitic movement began to take shape, the antinational position of early *Wissenschaft* and Reform began to seem less attractive to many Jews, even highly acculturated ones. The most influential and popular German Jewish historian, Heinrich Graetz (1817–1891), shared many *Wissenschaft*-based prejudices, for example, against Polish Jews, Kabbalah, and Hasidism and for philosophical rationalism and Moorish Spain. But he was also an ardent Jewish romantic nationalist, who regarded the Jews' resistance to their rulers and their uninterrupted dedication to their religio-intellectual traditions in conditions of persecution as aspects of heroic nationhood. Later writers, all critical of Graetz's persecutions-and-great-books version of Jewish history, nevertheless shared his nationalism. The Russian Jewish historian Simon Dubnow (1860–1941) aspired to write a properly *national* history of the Jews, which focused not on the literary production of an elite but on the autonomous institutional structures in which all Jews lived. Salo Baron (1895–1989) pursued a similar agenda, underpinned by a similar romantic nationalism, but with greater sophistication and professionalism as befitting the first of the great Jewish historians to occupy a university professorial chair (at Columbia).

Graetz's life and work largely predated the Zionist movement, and the later diaspora nationalist historians tended to be ambivalent about Zionism. But by the early twentieth century, especially after the foundation of the Institute for Jewish Studies at the Hebrew University of Jerusalem in 1925, the first university to offer regular employment to large numbers of Judaic scholars, the academic study of the Jewish past came to be dominated by zealous nationalists of Zionist orientation. There was, to be sure, never really a unitary "Jerusalem school."[3] The naïve Palestinocentrism of Ben-Zion Dinur (1884–1973), which held, to put it rather reductively, that the most significant feature of Jewish life in the diaspora was that the Jews collectively pined away for the Land of Israel, was surely influential in Palestine-Israel in general due to Dinur's role as minister of education in the early state. But it did not appeal to such colleagues as Gershom Scholem (1897–1982), Yitzhak Baer (1888–1980), or Jacob Katz (1904–1998), whose understanding of the Jewish past was more complex and refined. Nevertheless, almost all the Jerusalem scholars shared the conviction that the Jews were and always remained a nation or a people, and all furthermore believed that it was only in the environment of the actualized Zionist project, the pre-state Yishuv and then the state of Israel, that Jewish history could be written without the apologetics and the need to curry favor with gentile authorities that had invalidated so much of the scholarly work of *Wissenschaft des Judentums.*

Meanwhile, both Dubnovian and Baronian diaspora nationalism and Zionism have faced powerful challenges as master narratives. There is, after all, something to the critical view that the Jews have for most of their history been too scattered and out of touch to constitute a national entity in any meaningful way.[4] Local Jewish cultures have been shaped by their varied environments.[5] Premodern rabbinic contacts indubitably crossed cultural boundaries because rabbis shared a professional and intellectual culture based on the mastery of a corpus of texts, expressed in rabbinic Hebrew, which could transcend other types of cultural distinction. They could constitute a "republic of letters" not unlike that of intellectuals and clerics in early modern Christian Europe. But average Jews might find it easier to communicate and get along with their German, Italian, Polish, Moroccan, Syrian, and other neighbors than with one another. One form of this argument might echo the old *Wissenschaft* view and see German Jews as primarily a variety of Germans, and so on. The most extreme version should be seen less as scholarly hypothesis than as political provocation: this is the view of the Israeli scholar Shlomo Sand that the Jews actually have no connection one with another and, more to the point, no connection to ancient Judaeans—at least not genetically. All major diaspora communities, in this view, are the product of local conversion to Judaism (by Khazars in Eastern Europe, Berbers in North Africa, etc.). In other words, the Jews are an aggregation of local religious communities having no integrity as a people/ethnic group. The conviction of modern Jews that they constitute a nation with origins in and so a contemporary claim to Palestine is mere false consciousness, generated to suit its own needs by the Zionist movement.[6]

Sand's book was a *succès de scandale*. It had particular appeal to three groups: Israeli "post-Zionists," diaspora Jews annoyed at local Jewish communities' blind devotion to benighted Israeli policies and weak attempts to generate tribal feelings among their constituents, and non-Jewish opponents of Israel. But the book is intellectually nugatory, effective only if one is willing to accept long-discredited accounts of early medieval Jewish history and if one furthermore takes the racialism—the conviction that all Jews are genetically related and that this fact is significant because it means that they share a set of (positive) characteristics—of some early Zionist discourse at face value.

By the later twentieth and twenty-first centuries, the terms of the argument over what the Jews are changed. Racialism no longer plays a role in respectable Zionist discourse (although it flourishes, alongside plain racism, at the increasingly influential right extreme) and Dinurian Palestinocentrism can no longer be found even among the most avidly nationalist Israeli historians. For their part, diasporists, as they have begun to be called, have long since abandoned the apologetic search for Judaism's high-minded essence. The struggle for emancipation is over and with it the need to gloss over the Jews' distinctiveness. Yet the debate continues between those who see Judaism primarily as a religion and those who see it as a national/"tribal" affiliation. To be sure, things look a bit different outside the world of scholarship: an ever more populous and assertive Orthodox world sees Judaism in strong terms as both religious and national/tribal, rejecting both the denatured and compromised religiosity of diaspora liberals and the tribalism-lite of secular Zionists. And at the other end of the spectrum, growing numbers in the diaspora are—if we read the recent Pew Center report with the requisite degree of cautious skepticism—Jews largely by assertion, without the fact having any impact on their affiliations, practices, beliefs, or modes of socialization.[7] For them, as for many of the Orthodox, the old debate is no longer relevant. Be this as it may, its persistence in other circles (and it is worth remembering that for the time being those circles remain the dominant forces in Jewish life, both in the United States and in Israel) means that the question of what sort of a group if any the Jews were in antiquity can never avoid entanglement in contemporary concerns. Yet we must make every effort to bracket those concerns, to avoid using the past to learn contemporary lessons, if we wish to attain a rich, deep, and nonanachronistic understanding of it.

Ancient Nations

We may start by confronting the fact that words like "nation" and "religion," though they and their cognates and counterparts have been in use since antiquity (whereas "culture" and "ethnicity" are a priori modern terms), have been irrevocably altered by the experience of modernity. "Nation" inescapably means something different to us than *natio* did to Julius Caesar or than its ostensible Hebrew counterpart, *'am*, would have to Caesar's contemporary, Hillel the Elder. Precise ancient Hebrew counterparts to "religion" are harder to come by, but Latin and Greek provide *religio* and *threskeia*, respectively, and these, too, are utterly different from what we mean by the term, which itself should not be assumed to be any one simple thing. To be more specific, in modernity "nation" strongly implies a claim of political sovereignty that *natio* or *'am* most emphatically did not. On the other hand, our "nation" implies at most a weak sense of connection, familial or otherwise, among its constituents, whereas both *natio* and *'am* referred primarily to kinship groups, and though that sense weakened over time, it was never completely lost.

The scholarly debate provides the outline of this chapter. The positions proceed roughly as follows: some scholars, mainly but not exclusively Israelis/Zionists, assume or argue that the ancient Jews were a precocious nation in the modern sense, that is, a self-conscious group who shared the conviction that they should enjoy political sovereignty in their ancestral land, and the various ancient Jewish rebellions were thus comparable to the nationalist revolts of the nineteenth and twentieth centuries. All or nearly all of the ancient Jews, like a faction of the modern Jews, wished to be "a free nation in their own land." Non-Zionist scholars argue that while the Jews, or more precisely, some of the Jews, may have been a nation in the premodern sense—which is to say, a "people," a group united by certain shared goods, especially, perhaps, the conviction of shared descent—they were not nationalists in the modern sense. In any case, by some time in the later Hellenistic or Roman imperial periods, most Jews lived outside Palestine and showed little discernible attachment to their putative homeland. Thus, even if rebellions did feature elements of behavior and ideology similar to modern nationalism, which is debatable, adherence to quasi-modern ideas of nationhood were episodic characteristics of a minority of ancient Jews.

The debate has often been framed as a question about whether Jews were united by ethnicity or by religion. It has been popular to argue that the Jews began as an ethnic group but became a religious group sometime in antiquity—either in the second century BCE, or in the late first century CE, or in the fourth century; this recent scholarship resonates with the view of *Wissenschaft* and post-*Wissenschaft* scholarship that the Jews ceased to be a nation in 70 CE, but is surprisingly little informed by the older historiography. A more radical position holds that Jews were not united by anything in particular, that the ideology, Judaism, which was supposed to have united them, was so diverse and decentered that it served to divide Jews more than unite them. The strong version of this view—advocated in its day by Jacob Neusner and Jonathan Z. Smith—was never actually widespread, but weaker versions persist, especially in American scholarship. Meanwhile, genome studies have introduced a new wrinkle into the debate, though their relevance to the study of ancient Jewish history remains for the time being controversial. A scientific revolution (not only in genomics) is afoot in the study of antiquity generally, and it remains to be seen whether it will have any impact on ancient Jewish history.[8]

The Nation of the *Ioudaioi*

Every empire under whose rule the Jews lived in antiquity until the Roman Emperor Constantine became Christian in 312 CE regarded the Jews, or some of them, in legal or constitutional terms as a nation—that is, an *ethnos* (pl. *ethne*) or a *natio* (pl. *nationes*). In Hellenistic and Roman usage, *ethne* and *nationes* differed from cities (*poleis, civitates*) in that one was born into an *ethnos* and acquired citizenship in a *polis*, though to be sure there were other ways to become attached to *ethne* than through accident of birth.[9] They were also distinguished by the fact that, at least until the Roman period, part of the definition of the *polis* was that it was in some sense—not necessarily literally—free, not under the domination of a king. This was not true of *ethne*. It was assumed that members of *ethne* shared certain features: political institutions, customs, language, religious rites, and so on, all or some of which they might in some cases have the right to preserve. They might inhabit a specific region but might emigrate and form colonies or other types of scattered settlements. The evidence that the Jews conformed to this model for much of the Second Temple period is overwhelmingly abundant. In 200 BCE the Seleucid king, Antiochus III, officially granted to the *ethnos* of the Jews the right to live according to its ancestral laws. Antiochus's son Antiochus IV retracted this gift in 167 BCE (sparking the Maccabean revolt), but in 162 the gift was restored for good. Jews living in Hellenistic and Roman diaspora communities also often claimed the right to follow their ethnic laws—a claim not invariably recognized by local authorities unless the local Jews had enough political clout to get them to yield.[10] When the Romans took over Syria and Palestine in 63 BCE, they appear to have followed Hellenistic precedent in their treatment of the Jews, but the Jewish rebellion that erupted in 66 CE and culminated in the destruction of the city and temple of Jerusalem in 70 swept away all prior arrangements.

I have argued that the Jewish nation was deconstituted in 70 CE, meaning that the Jews lost the recognized corporate right to live according to their ancestral laws.[11] They now became Roman subjects and in some cases Roman citizens and lacked all other legal personality. It would only be fair to point out that this position, first elaborated by Theodor Mommsen, is not universally accepted, but I would nevertheless observe that there is no evidence whatsoever that the Jews retained any corporate legal status after 70.[12] It has furthermore recently been argued that the Jews' denationalization preceded the destruction. The emperor Nero is said to have decided to regard the rebellious Jews of Palestine not as a *natio* subjected to the Roman Empire, but as a foreign tribe—hence the rebellion was in effect a foreign attack on Rome and was treated in response not as an uprising but as a war.[13] If this is correct, then it is unthinkable that the Jewish survivors continued to constitute a recognized *natio*. Nevertheless, a vestige of the Jews' former status persisted in the obligation imposed on all the Jews of the Roman Empire to pay two *denarii* per annum to a fund called the *fiscus iudaicus* (the Jewish chest), intended to replace the two-*sheqel* tax formerly paid to the temple of Jerusalem. This demonstrates that the Roman state did not make any constitutional distinction between the Jews of Palestine and those who resided elsewhere in the empire, though it was naturally easier for the latter to opt out, conceal their Jewishness, and so on.

It is furthermore a matter of legal fact that, whatever one thinks of the status of the Jews after 70, the Christian emperors regarded all the Jews of the Roman Empire not as a *natio* but as a *secta*, a *superstitio*, or a *religio*. As far as the empire was concerned, then, the Jews now had a clergy and parishes and, once again, the right to observe their own religious rites, though not the right to their own civil courts.[14] The Jews thus shifted, in the course of the fourth century, from a deconstituted nation to something like a church. In popular parlance—Jewish, Christian, and pagan—they often remained, though, an *'am*, an *ethnos*, or a *natio*. For its part, for example, Rabbinic literature (200–600 CE) always contrasted Jews either with the (other) nations or with idol worshipers. In other words, the rabbis continued, until the end of antiquity, to regard the Jews as both a national and a religious group.

Were the Jews *Really* a Nation?

It is obvious that constitutional status tells only a very small part of the story. Every scholarly account of the ancient Jews has had to grapple with the fact that group or corporate status is a much richer and more complex issue. Classical Zionist scholarship used its a priori conviction of the full-blown nationhood of the Jews throughout their history as a tool for interpreting the Jewish past in general. The fact that before 70 CE at the earliest the Jews apparently had a recognized territorial center and so something like a normative national history as conventionally understood in an era when national histories were the order of the day made the task relatively easy. A highly simplified nationalist reading of the Jewish history of the Second Temple period, in which the Jews were united in their devotion to their national institutions and also in their opposition to foreign rule, already was well established in late *Wissenschaft* historiography when the Zionists took it up in the 1920s and following. Thus, there was widespread agreement that all Jews except a few ultra-acculturated outliers or collaborationist traitors opposed the decrees of Antiochus IV and supported the Maccabees; that all Jews rejected and hated the not-even-fully-Jewish quisling Herod (reigned 37–4 BCE); and that all Jews supported the *goals* of the Jewish rebellions against the Romans, though there were some pragmatists who counseled patient diplomacy rather than a rush to arms.[15] The novelty of classical Zionist/Israeli historiography, though, was to argue—against the historiography of *Wissenschaft des Judentums* even in its most national-romantic, Graetzian form—that the Jews remained a territory-based nation long after the destruction and even after the Bar Kokhba revolt (132–135 CE) had ended in the near depopulation of Judaea. Ben-Zion Dinur, the chief ideologue of "Jerusalem school" history, argued already in the 1920s that Palestine—mainly northern Palestine after 135—retained a strongly Jewish character long after the failed revolts, down to and even beyond the Arab conquest of the country in 638, and that Palestinian Jewish authorities continued to exercise some control over the Jews of the diaspora. His position was elaborated and given real scholarly heft by Gedalyah Alon (1902–1950), who explicitly described the Jews as having all the attributes of a nation dug into its native soil until deep into late antiquity or beyond.[16] In other words, for Zionist scholarship, although the Jews remained throughout their history a nation yearning to return to its homeland, they had a genuine, not merely an aspirational, national history long after such a history had been previously supposed to have ended.[17]

This hypothesis had a certain explanatory power: if the post-70 rabbis were not merely spiritual but national leaders, then it follows that they had politics with all that that implies (rivalries, factionalism, etc.). Though the Alon school continued to idealize the rabbis, they were more recognizably human than the purely spiritual figures posited by late *Wissenschaft* (early *Wissenschaft* had been stridently antirabbinic). The rabbis' political engagement was surely overstated by Alon and his followers, but their positing a national history for the Jews gave them a highly fertile interest in social and economic history (executed very crudely) and the history of daily life, sometimes thought of as talmudic realia and following the traditions not of the French *annalistes* but of nineteenth-century German antiquarianism.

But the hyper-reification and idealization of the Jewish nation and an exceptionally positivistic reading of rabbinic literature as an authentically Jewish expression of resistance to Rome led to historiographic disaster. In Zionist history, so successful was rabbinic-Jewish cultural-social resistance after 135 that historians of the Jews of Palestine in the rabbinic period felt little need to refer to Rome at all—the Jews of Palestine were thought to have had a nearly entirely self-enclosed history. There were and are Israeli historians of Roman administration in Palestine, but even these have tended to bracket the Jews off from their accounts. The highly competent Roman historian Michael Avi-Yonah, in his popular textbook, wrote an "internal" history of the Jews of Roman Palestine, which is completely detachable from the larger history of the province in which it is embedded.[18] At least in Palestine, Jewish history was "closed": the Jews had a closed economy, a closed culture (the fundamental assumption of all "Alon-school" scholarship), and did not even speak the language of the empire for the most part, or farm their land in the same way as their neighbors.[19] Indeed, with their retreat from the larger historical stage in the wake of the failed rebellions, the Jews attained in Palestine a kind of quintessence of Jewish national authenticity and resistance to outside influence. That this was an illusion created by the peculiar poetics of rabbinic literature, the only source many of Alon's followers bothered to take seriously, does not appear to have occurred to them, though it was noted quite emphatically by their colleagues in the Hebrew University's Hebrew Literature department, following the lead of a New Criticism–oriented scholar of Midrash and talmudic narrative, Jonah Fraenkel (1928–2012).

Furthermore, with some very distinguished exceptions, Zionist-Israeli historians were reluctant to pay much attention to the diaspora, especially after the period of the Revolts. When they did, they tended to imagine it in highly ideological terms: the diaspora Jews yearned for the homeland and tended to yield to the political and religious will of Judaean authorities without real challenge. This position was, I believe, not shared by Victor Tcherikover and others who worked on Hellenistic and early Roman Jewish documents from Egypt, which undeniably told a different story, and needless to say specialists on the Babylonian Talmud and its historical context had to acknowledge some of the complexities of the relationship between the Palestinian and Diasporic rabbinic centers while still in some cases considering the Palestinian center truly central down to the geonic era.[20] In sum, Zionist scholarship had for the most part a strong center-periphery model (not necessarily theorized in these terms) for thinking about the diaspora, which may not do it full justice at every period, though it is arguably valid for some (e.g., the first century CE, predestruction). It also tended, far more problematically, to imagine "the nation" acting as a single organism—the crudest possible intrusion of ideological aspiration on historical analysis.

Scattered amidst the standard scholarly production of the high Zionist tradition, whose landmarks include not only the works of the Dinur tradition (G. Alon, S. Safrai, A. Oppenheimer, M. D. Herr), but also, on an earlier period, and various less easy to classify works like J. Efron on the Hasmoneans, A. Schalit on Herod, the synthetic as opposed to the (excellent) monographic writings of Menahem Stern, are several works that do not merely assert but set out to demonstrate the nationhood, in the strong modern sense, of the ancient Jews.[21]

One of the best known of these is Doron Mendels's *The Rise and Fall of Jewish Nationalism*, which assembles in a positivistic vein all evidence that he can find that the ancient Jews possessed or aspired to possess what Mendels regards as the primary symbols of ancient "nationalism": a territory, a king, a temple, and an army of citizens.[22] It is, of course, not difficult to find Jewish texts that praise such things (though the "army of citizens" is something of a sticking point and, of course, many fundamental Jewish texts were antimonarchic), but it is impossible to show that all Jews always regarded these items as core group values, since the views of the nonelite mass of the Jews cannot be learned from surviving literature. It is also unclear why this complex of items should be labeled "nationalism," a word with a very specific range of modern meanings quite different from what Mendels is writing about. Elsewhere, Mendels declares that when he writes of nationalism he means ethnicity, adding to the confusion. Mendels's use of these terms is untheorized: he has not thought deeply enough about the denotations and connotations of the key words and concepts of his study. His argument thus reads as highly tendentious or unintentionally confused, apart from its other flaws. An incomparably more sophisticated attempt to argue for the episodic presence of something like nationalism among some ancient Jews is David Goodblatt's *Elements of Ancient Jewish Nationalism*.[23] This book, unlike Mendels's, cannot be pigeonholed as naïvely Zionist and will be discussed in more detail below.

Liberal/Diasporic Scholarship

Liberal/diasporic scholarship has tended to be more ruminative than Zionist scholarship about the "groupness" of the Jews.[24] But much of it—especially before the turn of the millennium—has tended, like Zionist scholarship, to be objectivist. It has attempted to discern whether the Jews *really did* constitute a single group, often by evaluating what we know about the ancient Jews against what were in effect checklists of integrative features. The alternative to this method would be to draw on the Weberian tradition, as elaborated in the work of Ernest Gellner and Benedict Anderson, which focused on the ideological or subjective component of national identity: groups constitute groups because their members think they constitute a group, whatever else they share or fail to share (it is helpful but not essential for "outsiders" to agree with the members' intersubjective self-evaluation).[25] Objectivist liberal/diasporic scholarship mobilized as evidence against the hypothesis that the ancient Jews constituted a national-type group, the existence of a diaspora even before the Hellenistic period (332–31 BCE), the importance of sectarianism in Palestine before 70 CE, and much other evidence for the variety of Jewish practice and belief: the Jews did not even share a language, let alone other more subtle indices of national identity. Some scholars have also tried, though as yet without the requisite level of sophistication in historical-demographic method, to determine whether the Jewish communities of the diaspora could really all have been the product of emigration from Palestine; if they were not, then the notion that the Jews shared a meaningful ethnicity becomes harder to sustain.[26]

This approach has been characteristic of American scholarship especially after 1970. It arose from a reaction to the positivism, synthesizing impulse, and absence of methodological rigor that has seemed characteristic of earlier scholarship on ancient Judaism. If older scholarship had been the province of "lumpers," in the second half of the twentieth century "splitters" came to prevail. This was, to be sure, part of a general trend in postwar Anglo-American humanistic and social scientific scholarship: sources were in general treated with more suspicion, and they began to be read as texts and not mined as if they were archives. In general scholars began to think more cautiously about how we know things and were less frequently content simply to assemble a plausible-sounding narrative by stringing together bits and pieces of information extracted from a variety of sources. In an environment where the study of ancient Judaism was closely proximate to New Testament studies, more true now than previously since ancient Judaism now fully entered the academy, the latter had a decisive impact on how (other?) Jewish texts were approached. Biblical and New Testament studies had been developing a methodological orientation since the late nineteenth century, but this had little impact on Jewish scholars until they began to share classroom and departmental space with their colleagues.

The most influential agent of change in Jewish studies was Jacob Neusner (1932–2016), who advocated for, and voluminously performed, form-criticism and synoptic criticism of rabbinic texts in the highly skeptical vein of the German New Testament scholar Rudolf Bultmann (1884–1973). It is important to note that in the course of the 1970s Neusner's epistemological restraint (as he considered it) led him more or less to repudiate history: he regarded it as unrecoverable from the meager evidence at our disposal. Indeed, his first Bultmannesque books, published in the early 1970s, constituted a resounding refutation of the entire structure of talmudic history as produced by Alon and his school: Neusner followed the American historian of religions E. R. Goodenough in regarding the rabbis more as a sect than as a politico-religious leadership and systematically criticized the common practice of reading talmudic stories about rabbis as if they were episodes in Jewish political history.[27] Neusner believed that rabbinic Judaism was a new entity, not the continuation of the predestruction populist Pharisaic mainstream (whose existence he also did not accept), and that rabbinic literature provides plenty of evidence that the rabbis *claimed* authority but next to none that they actually possessed it. Neusner viewed rabbinic claims as propaganda, or as wishful thinking, not as historical description, and fought Israeli hyperpositivism with a withering hermeneutics of suspicion.

But when this critical work was completed by the later 1970s and the field of talmudic history lay in ruins, at least for those who took Neusner's criticisms seriously (which included almost no one in Israel, but many though not all scholars in the United States, the United Kingdom, and Germany).[28] Neusner dedicated much of the rest of his career to describing the history of rabbinic traditions and to the taxonomic project of describing the central ideas he thought were embodied in the different rabbinic texts. Behind this project were the ideas that ancient Judaism was infinitely varied, not uniform, that surviving evidence (for Neusner primarily textual) must be scrutinized carefully for evidence of difference, and that in the case of rabbinic texts it was possible to posit that each one informed us of a different "Judaism." Other scholars had already gotten to work on evidence for Judaism in the Second Temple period, where signs of variety were much easier to detect. The treatises of Philo of Alexandria, the First Book of Maccabees, the Exagoge of Ezekiel the Tragedian, the Wisdom of Ben Sira, and the War Scroll from Qumran really do seem to testify to a surprising degree about linguistic, cultural, and religious variety among an ancient Jewish literate elite. Neusner argued that rabbinic texts, for all that they share with one another, provide evidence for the survival of such variety into late antiquity.

In the late 1980s, the debate about whether the Jews constituted an ethnicity or a religious group received new impetus from the work of Shaye Cohen. In that decade Cohen published a series of papers on ancient Jewish personal status, which in their tough-minded, skeptical minimalism raised a series of new issues.[29] Cohen noted that many markers of Jewish identity whose antiquity and essential quality scholars among others have taken for granted are not attested until surprisingly late dates: prohibition of marriage with foreigners, matrilineal transmission of Jewish identity, ritualized conversion to Judaism—all were either unknown or known but controversial until the late Second Temple period or beyond. Cohen was arguing for a highly dynamic, variegated, and fluid conception of ancient Jewish identity. In 1990 he explored the implications of his argument that formal conversion is unattested before the Hasmonean period, one of which was, in his initial formulation of the issue, that the introduction of the idea that exclusive worship of the God of Israel could in some circumstances turn a gentile into a Jew marked the transformation of Judaism from an ethnicity into a religion. The biblical heroine Ruth left her Moabite gods behind in her father's house but despite this never ceased to be a Moabite from the perspective of the biblical storyteller (who probably lived in the fifth or fourth century BCE). But when, in the apocryphal story of Judith (mid-second century BCE) an Ammonite general recognized the greatness of Israel's God, he actually became a Jew. The conception of what it meant to be a Jew had clearly changed. Subsequently Cohen softened his argument, because it was obvious that so many Jews among others continued to regard Jews as a nation/clan group even after the introduction of conversion: Judaism shifted from ethnicity to ethno-religion.

In the following decades this discussion has shifted focus. Cohen assumed that it was appropriate to refer to an ideological system that emphasized the relations between a specific group and its god/s as a religion, but some scholars, influenced by the heightened theoretical self-consciousness of contemporary anthropology and religious studies, approached the issue in a rather more fussy way. Daniel Boyarin argued (relying in part on an over-reading of a stray comment in my 2001 book, *Imperialism and Jewish Society*) that there was no such thing as religion before the fourth century.[30] I had actually stated that religion was "disembedded" in the fourth century, meaning that it was only then, when the Roman Empire was in the process of Christianization, that large numbers of people began to think of religion as a separate category of human experience. I borrowed the terminology from Moses Finley's work on the ancient economy, who in turn borrowed it from Karl Polanyi's work on the medieval European economy. These premodern economies, like ancient religion, were embedded; that is, premodern historical agents did not aggregate and conceptualize their components abstractly. This does *not* mean that religious phenomena, or economic phenomena, did not exist prior to their disembedding, only that people lacked the language and/or the abstract conceptualizations. What I was trying to explain was the shift in the Jews' status in Roman law and policy, discussed earlier in this chapter, not primarily in the Jews' self-understanding. My argument was actually that the Jews remained what they had always been, primarily an ethnic group, bound by a myth of shared ancestry, the content of whose "groupness" had an especially prominent religious component because it was overwhelmingly focused on God's covenant with Israel in a way that made much other cultural stuff secondary or trivial. Almost all other ancient groups with ethnic self-conceptions also had shared gods, but their relations with their gods did not monopolize their self-understanding to the same extent. In my view, this was probably true in the fourth century BCE, certainly true in the second century BCE, the first century CE, the fourth century CE, and indeed the sixteenth century CE. There were, of course, shifts along the way: the introduction of the ritual of conversion did matter, if not quite as much as Cohen argued, as did the Christianization of the Roman Empire (if not quite in the way Boyarin thought). But the Jews' failure to fit comfortably in either purely ethnic or purely religious categories seems a stable fixture of their corporate identity, challenged only in modernity.

The value of methodology-conscious skepticism was that it required the dismantling of so many simplifying narratives. The variety that it claimed to have discovered in ancient Judaism also problematized and complicated any idea that "the Jews" constituted a nation or any type of group in any simple way. It pushed to the forefront the problem of how we know anything about the past at all and thematized the perils of the leap from texts to history. Liberal/diasporic scholarship did not demonstrate that the Jews were not a nation. If anything, in its latest manifestation it seemed excessively committed to the notion that they were an ethnicity, which may just be the modern translation of the ancient *'am/ ethnos/natio*. It was rarely interested in the implications of this, since it was more often a subfield of religious studies than of history. But it did drive home the point that the question is very difficult to answer on the basis of the information we have at our disposal.

But liberal/diasporic scholarship paid a price for its neglect of history. Neusner's Judaisms were mainly ideational structures or intellectual systems. Sometimes they corresponded to social groups in relatively straightforward ways, sometimes not. For example, "apocalyptic Judaism" or "Enochic Judaism" (this is not a specifically Neusnerian concept) was thought to have been practiced by specific groups or "conventicles." Though this hypothesis is no more than weakly plausible, it remains almost certain—notwithstanding some recent criticism of the idea—that some of the Dead Sea Scrolls reflected the ideas and interests of a small sectarian organization. On the other hand, "the rabbis" are responsible for all of Neusner's slightly varied versions of rabbinic Judaism, and Neusner himself never tried to tie the different "Judaisms" to specific rabbinic subgroups. Be this as it may, the splitting of Judaism into an infinity of loosely related subgroups eventually backfired: its critical work of dismantling old master narratives was brilliantly successful, but its constructive work ended up raising serious problems in that it was hard to reconcile with those few things we actually do know about ancient Jewish history.

Back to History

No ancient source acknowledges the existence of Judaisms. The most ardent sectarians, like those who appear to have lived near the site of Qumran, regarded themselves as the true remnant of Israel and the rest of the Jews as sinners (though salvageable if they repented and joined the sect), but other Jews as far as we can tell all regarded themselves as members of a single group, Israel (in more theologically loaded language) or the Jews (in the language of international politics).[31] By the middle of the Second Temple period, "the Jews" actually possessed a norm-creating, politically authorized, institutional center, consisting of the Jerusalem temple, its staff, and its laws—some version of the Torah (Pentateuch). It was, to be sure, possible to opt out on ideological grounds, but this entailed at least partial withdrawal from society, as in the case of the Dead Sea sect. Presumably there was still more give in the system in diasporic environments, but even there many Jews strove to attain the right to follow their ancestral laws, again, presumably some version of the Torah.[32]

In practical terms, the institutional center tended to grow and strengthen over time, though there were complicating factors. The Hasmonean conquests of Idumaea, Samaria, and Galilee (c. 112–100 BCE) brought many newly converted Jews under the authority of the Temple and the Torah, but in reality their integration was gradual and partial; they retained some autonomous political structures and cultural norms, and the Samaritans soon parted company with the rest altogether. The century before the Roman conquest of Syria was an anarchic one in the eastern Mediterranean basin, and this meant that there was little regular contact between diaspora communities (whatever their origins may have been) and Palestine. To be sure, there is evidence for epistolary contact and for the remission of donations to the Jerusalem temple, but no evidence for large-scale pilgrimage. But this changed dramatically starting in the later first century BCE. The Roman Peace, which began after the Battle of Actium in 31 BCE, made travel relatively safe, and Herodian building projects—especially the construction of a massively enlarged temple in Jerusalem and the establishment of a great new seaport at Caesarea Maritima—enabled and encouraged diaspora pilgrimage on the large scale. Jews and money flowed into Jerusalem and its Temple on an unprecedented scale, and religious ideas among other things flowed back into the diaspora. The first century was a period when for all their diversity Jews were joined in an unprecedented way by their contact with and, in many cases, their enhanced loyalty to the institutional center of the Jews. It would be fair to say that the Jews were a version of an imagined community, but that the actual ties were real and in the century between Herod and the outbreak of the first rebellion unusually dense and substantial. It would not be absurd to draw a causal link between the historical contingencies of the post-Herodian period and the disasters that ensued.

This is another way of saying that the ideological background of the Jewish rebellions needs to be historicized: it was not the product—as Jewish nationalist scholarship used to believe—of the Jewish nation's unquenchable desire to be free of foreign rule. Something very specific went wrong under Roman rule. We should first note that the Jews as a nation and the institutions that eventually came to form the core content of their group identity—the temple and the Torah—all coalesced under the rule of empires, which were more or less supportive because they normally worked through local intermediaries and native institutions.[33]

This was true both of the Achaemenids and most Hellenistic rulers. For reasons still unknown, Antiochus IV abrogated this principle, but what ensued hardly constituted an eruption of national outrage. Rather, a small minority took up arms, not to make Judaea independent but to force the king to restore the Jews' autonomy. The king's successors very quickly realized his error and did just that, and the Maccabean revolt was soon over and the *status quo ante* restored. But its conclusion coincided with the outbreak of civil war at Antioch, which initiated the unraveling of the kingdom, at which point the survivors of the Hasmonean family, who still controlled some manpower, stepped in and offered their services to one of the pretenders, who accepted. It was only decades later that Simon the Hasmonean declared Judaea free, but his dynasty did not last a century and had never enjoyed general popularity among the Jews.

Was There a *Freiheitsbewegung* in Roman Palestine?

Most Persian and Hellenistic rulers recognized the Jews' right to use their own laws. The Jews in turn did not question the rulers' right to govern them, with all that that entailed (collecting taxes, installing garrisons, etc.). Initially, the Romans seemed to follow the Hellenistic model, but their intrusions were from the start more blatant and soon the Romans abandoned the Hellenistic model in the east altogether. From the Romans' perspective the cataclysmic disasters endured by the Jews during the first century and a half of Roman rule were simply pangs of adaptation, as the Roman state moved from a model of rule through native intermediaries to one of annexation and provincialization. As it was objectively, Roman rule was more threatening to Jews who wished to retain a separate corporate existence than any prior regime and than many later regimes. There have always been scholars who believe that antipathy to Rome was simply a "default" position for all Jews, especially though not exclusively those living in Palestine. While this view is indubitably exaggerated, we possess snippets of information about groups of Jews who were dedicated to opposing Roman rule over the Jews.[34] The first of these groups appeared in the reign of Herod and the last disappeared with the reduction of the fortress of Masada by Roman forces in 73 or 74 CE. The outbreak of a massively destructive Judaean revolt again in 132 CE demonstrates that opposition to Rome survived or was revived. There is very little information about the Bar Kokhba revolt, but unlike the Great Revolt there is no indication that it was dominated by small rebel organizations. This time the hostility was more general and so the results of the rebellion more dire for the Jews: the district of Judaea was nearly depopulated. Meanwhile, the Jewish communities in Libya, Egypt, Crete, and Cyprus had endured a similar fate: their rebellion, in 115–117 CE, appears to have been similarly widespread but resists evaluation. It may have been less an expression of hostility to Rome than a civil war between the Jews and their Greek neighbors. There is no evidence that it was ideologically Palestine-centered, but we have too little information about it to be sure.[35]

Were these anti-Roman movements and rebellions motivated by nationalism? If so, the conviction that Jews should be free of foreign rule (an essential component of modern nationalisms; according to Josephus, one rebel group believed that the Jews should have no ruler but God) was a relatively novel one in Jewish history.[36] Even the Hasmoneans had not been fully committed to it and did not hesitate to submit to Seleucid rulers if they considered it strategically wise. We know little about the pre-66 rebel groups. It was once customary to ignore or minimize their differences and assemble them into a unified *Freiheitsbewegung*. The issue is complicated also by the fact that Josephus, our main source, often calls them brigands, and there may indeed have been more overlap and slippage between brigandage and anti-Roman or anti-Jewish-collaborationist activity than romantically celebratory modern scholarship has wished to acknowledge. Sometimes, furthermore, the groups may have originally consisted of religious extremists or rigorists; Josephus describes some Jerusalemite teachers who took so hard a line on the biblical prohibition of figurative representation that their disciples martyred themselves to remove the image of an eagle that Herod had placed over one of the Temple gates. Herod was a collaborationist and the eagle may have symbolized Rome, but can we be sure Josephus was wrong about the young men's motivations?

After the failure of the Bar Kokhba revolt (132–135 CE), we hear nothing more about armed Jewish opposition to Roman rule for centuries to come: there may have been a small uprising in Galilee in 352 CE, though this is controversial. It is also possible that, as Byzantine chroniclers claim, when the Sasanians conquered Palestine in 614 CE, the

Jews enthusiastically supported them and took the opportunity to massacre their Christian Roman oppressors in many places. Just as likely, this notice is false or highly exaggerated. If in its initial stages Roman rule, because of both its intrusiveness and its support for the national-institution-building strategies of Herod, lent what had previously been the diffuse subjectivity of Jewish corporate solidarity explosive political urgency, what became of the Jews in the High and Later Empire?

For Zionist scholarship, as we have seen, it was precisely in this period when a Jewish society of untrammeled authenticity took shape in northern Palestine, but an alternative account notes the archaeological evidence that Palestine was on the whole successfully "provincialized" in the wake of the Bar Kokhba revolt. Many Jews (in many cases having undoubtedly learned their lesson the hardest way possible) simply submitted to the process, which entailed significant political and cultural change while maintaining at most a residual or vestigial sense of their separateness as Jews. Judaism had advocates, too, and while they also had to submit in deep and subtle ways to the realities of life under Rome, the rabbis, necessarily largely depoliticized (contra Alon), did preserve a form of cultural opposition.[37] Rabbinic Judaism was indubitably a novel and creative development, but it was based entirely on traditional sources, was expressed in nonclassical languages, and had little about it that was meaningfully Greco-Roman. We can at least speculate that the "crisis of the third century," which eventually depressed the economies of Roman cities and impoverished the pillars of Roman rule in the provinces, the city councilors, worked to the advantage of anti-establishment quasi-elites generally, like rabbis and Christian bishops. And we can also infer that the centuries of Christianization that followed not only redefined the status of the Jews in constitutional terms, but also fatefully changed Jewish politics. In the High Empire, the Jews eventually had to acknowledge the need for their integration into the Roman system. The Christian Roman state had a vested theological interest in combing the Jews out of the fabric of imperial society and politics: the era of the diasporic bargain (the state recognizes the right of the Jews, now organized in local communities, to follow their laws; the Jews recognize the state's right to govern them and to alienate their property)—a slight revision of the Jews' collective bargain with the Hellenistic kingdoms—which remained firmly in place until the nineteenth century was now under way.[38]

Conclusion

The Jews were not a nation in the modern sense but most likely were a nation in an older sense, at least in some periods in Antiquity. There is some evidence that many Jews shared the subjective sense of affiliation with other Jews. Were they "diverse" from the observers' perspective? All groups are by definition diverse, since they consist of more than one individual. But the lesson of this chapter has been that these questions cannot be answered in theoretical terms alone, nor can a phenomeno-logical approach—one that aims at static description—yield satisfactory results. We are obliged instead to approach the topic through theoreti-cally informed historical investigation.

NOTES

1 This introductory survey is indebted to an excellent study by Michael Brenner, *Prophets of the Past: Interpreters of Jewish History* (Princeton, NJ: Princeton University Press, 2010), to which readers who wish to learn more are directed.

2 Isaak Markus Jost, *Geschichte der Israeliten seit der Zeit der Macabäer bis auf unsre Tage* (Berlin: Schlesinger, 1820–1847).

3 See D. Myers, *Re-Inventing the Jewish Past: European Jewish Intellectuals and the Zionist Return to History* (New York: Oxford University Press, 1995).

4 See B. Evron, *Jewish State or Israeli Nation* (Bloomington: Indiana University Press, 1995).

5 This was the main thrust of the influential volume edited by David Biale, *Cultures of the Jews: A New History* (New York: Schocken, 2002).

6 See S. Sand, *The Invention of the Jewish People* (London: Verso, 2010). Sand's work has also fallen afoul of recent genome studies, notwithstanding the efforts of the geneticist Eran Elhaik to defend it: see D. Behar et al., "No Evidence from Genome-Wide Data of a Khazar Origin for the Ashkenazi Jews," *Human Biology* 85 (December 2013): 859–900.

7 See Pew Research Center, "A Portrait of Jewish Americans" (October 1, 2013), www.pewforum.org.

8 For example, R. Fleming, *Britain after Rome: The Fall and Rise, 400–1070* (London: Allen Lane, 2010).

9 This model has been criticized and greatly complicated by B. Eckhardt, "Vom Volk zur Stadt? Ethnos und Polis im hellenistischen Orient," *Journal for the Study of Judaism in the Persian, Hellenistic, and Roman Periods* 45 (2014): 199–228, but retains some limited validity.

10 The exception here may have been Hellenistic Egypt, where Jewish immigrants, along with all immigrants, automatically enjoyed the privilege of following their *politikoi nomoi*, the laws of their communities of origin (at least in the opinion of

J. Mélèze-Modrzejewski, *The Jews of Egypt: From Rameses II to Emperor Hadrian* [Princeton, NJ: Princeton University Press, 1997]). Though the mass of Hellenistic documentary papyri involving Jews shows that Jews tended not to follow Jewish *civil* law in Egypt, there is a fascinating exception: a collection of papyri from the small village/army camp of Herakleopolis, which contains the records of a Jewish *politeuma* that functioned there for a few decades in the second century B C E. This organization—probably consisting of a group of local Jewish military settlers— based its legal life in part on the Greek version of the Torah. On some of the complexities of the Jews' status in Hellenistic and Roman Egypt, see S. Honigman, "*Politeumata* and Ethnicity in Hellenistic and Roman Egypt," *Ancient Society* 33 (2003): 61–102.

11 S. Schwartz, *The Ancient Jews, from Alexander to Muhammad* (Cambridge: Cambridge University Press, 2014).

12 *Provinces of the Roman Empire,* trans. W. Dickson (New York: Scribner's, 1887), vol. 2, pp. 235–240.

13 See G. Gambash, *Rome and Provincial Resistance* (New York: Routledge, 2015). My view is elaborated in *The Ancient Jews.*

14 See Schwartz, *Ancient Jews.*

15 These views can be found repeatedly expressed by the mainstream of mid- to late twentieth-century Israeli ancient Judaic scholars in such publications as H. H. Ben-Sasson, ed., *A History of the Jewish People* (Cambridge, MA: Harvard University Press, 1976); *The World History of the Jewish People,* 11 vols. (Tel Aviv: Jewish History Publications, 1964–1979); S. Safrai et al., eds., *Compendia Rerum Iudaicarum ad Novum Testamentum* (Assen: Van Gorcum, 1974–); and in various contributions to the *Encyclopedia Judaica.*

16 See G. Alon, *The Jews in Their Land in the Talmudic Age, 70–640 CE,* trans. G. Levi (Cambridge, MA: Harvard University Press, 1989; originally published 1952–1955, based on lectures given in the '30s and '40s).

17 For a full discussion of this view, see S. Schwartz, "Historiography on the Jews in the 'Talmudic Period'" in *The Oxford Handbook of Jewish Studies,* ed. M. Goodman (Oxford: Oxford University Press, 2002), pp. 79–114.

18 See M. Avi-Yonah, *The Jews under Roman and Byzantine Rule: A Political History of Palestine from the Bar Kokhba War to the Arab Conquest* (New York: Schocken, 1984; originally published Jerusalem: Mosad Bialik, 1952).

19 See Z. Safrai, *The Economy of Roman Palestine* (London: Routledge, 1994). Y. Feliks, *Agriculture in Eretz Israel in the Period of the Bible and the Talmud,* 2nd ed. (Jerusalem: Magnes Press, 1990; Hebrew); a summary of Feliks's views in English may be found in the articles on agriculture in the *Encyclopedia Judaica.*

20 Nevertheless Tcherikover's work on Egyptian Jewry (see the lengthy introduction to *Corpus Papyrorum Iudaicarum,* ed. V. Tcherikover et al., vol. 1 [Cambridge, MA: Harvard University Press, 1958]) was strongly influenced by nationalist assumptions, as noted by S. Honigman, above, note 10; Aryeh Kasher, *The Jews in Hellenistic and Roman Egypt: The Struggle for Equal Rights* (Tübingen: J. C. B.

Mohr, 1985), is more explicitly Zionist. For a concise statement, see I. Gafni, *Land, Center and Diaspora: Jewish Constructs in Late Antiquity* (Sheffield: Sheffield Academic Press, 1997).

21 The publications of S. Safrai and Herr are almost exclusively in Hebrew and consist mainly of papers and chapters. For Oppenheimer, see, e.g., *'Am Ha-aretz: A Study in the Social History of the Jewish People in the Hellenistic-Roman Period* (Leiden: E. J. Brill, 1977). See V. Tcherikover, *Hellenistic Civilization and the Jews* (Philadelphia: Jewish Publication Society of America, 1959), on the Maccabean revolt and its aftermath, not Hellenistic Egypt. For examples of Stern's work, see his contributions to *A History of the Jewish People*, ed. H. Ben Sasson, and similar collaborative efforts, as opposed to his many fundamental papers on specific aspects of Jewish history under Hellenistic and Roman rule and the irreplaceable *Greek and Latin Authors on Jews and Judaism* (Jerusalem: Israel Academy of Sciences and Humanities, 1976–1984). J. Efron, *Studies on the Hasmonean Period* (Leiden: E. J. Brill, 1987); A. Schalit, *König Herodes: der Mann und sein Werk* (Berlin: DeGruyter, 1969).

22 Doron Mendels, *The Rise and Fall of Jewish Nationalism* (New York: Doubleday, 1992).

23 David Goodblatt, *Elements of Ancient Jewish Nationalism* (Cambridge: Cambridge University Press, 2006).

24 This section adapts and abbreviates S. Schwartz, "How Many Judaisms Were There? A Critique of Neusner and Smith on Definition and Mason and Boyarin on Categorization," *Journal of Ancient Judaism* 2 (2011): 208–238.

25 E. Gellner, *Nations and Nationalism* (Ithaca, NY: Cornell University Press, 1983); B. Anderson, *Imagined Communities: Reflections on the Origins and Spread of Nationalism* (New York: Verso, 1991).

26 L. Feldman, *Jew and Gentile in the Ancient World: Attitudes and Interactions from Alexander to Justinian* (Princeton, NJ: Princeton University Press, 1993), makes the observation, but in the service of a very different kind of argument.

27 Neusner's pre-1970 work was more or less conventional talmudic history; for our purposes the crucial publications are *Development of a Legend: Studies on the Traditions Concerning Yohanan ben Zakkai* (Leiden: Brill, 1970); *Rabbinic Traditions about the Pharisees before 70*, 3 vols. (Leiden: Brill, 1971). His form-critical work on the Mishnah was summed up in *Judaism: The Evidence of the Mishnah* (Chicago: University of Chicago Press, 1981).

28 Neusner's student David Goodblatt argued for its rehabilitation as early as 1980 ("Towards the Rehabilitation of Talmudic History," in *History of Judaism: The Next Ten Years*, ed. B. Bokser [Chico, CA: Scholars Press, 1980], pp. 31–44). A small group of post-Neusnerian scholars kept historical study of the period alive outside Israel—including Goodblatt himself (who began his career in Haifa), Martin Goodman, Shaye Cohen, Seth Schwartz, Catherine Hezser, and Hayim Lapin.

29 The papers are collected and updated in S. Cohen, *The Beginnings of Jewishness* (Berkeley: University of California Press, 1999).

30 D. Boyarin, "Rethinking Jewish Christianity: An Argument for Dismantling a
    Dubious Category (to Which Is Appended a Correction of My *Border Lines*)," *Jew-
    ish Quarterly Review* 99 (2009): 7–36; this has been merged with an argument that
    "Jews" and "Judaism" did not exist in antiquity, that in translating ancient texts
    one should use only the term "Judaeans"—an ethnic designation—because "Jews"
    refers to a religious group and "Judaism" to a religion, things which as everyone
    knows did not exist until the fourth century or even later. Furthermore, early
    Christian texts often use the term "Judaism" as an insulting way to refer to the
    degraded scraps of corrupt practice left to the "Judaeans" after their rejection of
    Christ and the consequent destruction of Jerusalem. This is a nugatory argument
    with the unintentionally problematic implication of positing an absolute discon-
    tinuity between ancient Jews and medieval or modern Jews. It is easily refuted:
    the English word "Jews" does not refer to a religious group. "Judaism" was indeed
    used insultingly by early Christian writers, but the word appears in earlier Jewish
    sources written in Greek in a way that inescapably denotes, well, Judaism. It may
    be worth noting that Church Fathers also used the term Christianity (*christianis-
    mos*): are all –isms then meant as insults? The issue was actually raised long ago,
    as part of a program of defending the Gospel of John, which harps on the hostility
    of "the *Ioudaioi*" to Jesus, against charges of anti-Semitism or anti-Judaism: see M.
    Lowe, "Who Were the *Ioudaioi*?" *Novum Testamentum* 18 (1976): 101–130. Much
    later, Steve Mason was compelled, by his rash policy decision as editor of the Brill
    Josephus to use the term "Judean" (in his preferred spelling) rather than "Jewish,"
    to produce a vigorous though strained and incoherent defense of the practice:
    "Jews, Judaeans, Judaizing, Judaism: Problems of Categorization in Ancient
    History," *Journal for the Study of Judaism in the Persian, Hellenistic, and Roman
    Periods* 38 (2007): 457–512. For fuller discussions, see Schwartz, "How Many Juda-
    isms Were There?"; and Adele Reinhartz, "The Vanishing Jews of Antiquity," *Los
    Angeles Review of Books* (June 24, 2014), www.marginalia.lareviewofbooks.org.

31 The most recent discussion of these terms is in N. Thiel, "'Israel' and 'Jew' as
    Markers of Jewish Identity in Antiquity: The Problems of Insider/Outsider Clas-
    sification," *Journal for the Study of Judaism in the Persian, Hellenistic, and Roman
    Periods* 45 (2014): 80–99.

32 This and what follows summarizes the main argument of S. Schwartz, *Imperialism
    and Jewish Society, 200 BCE to 640 CE* (Princeton, NJ: Princeton University Press,
    2001), and *The Ancient Jews*, and is indebted, too, to D. Goodblatt, *Elements of
    Ancient Jewish Nationalism* (New York: Cambridge University Press, 2006).

33 I acknowledge the existence of the two Israelite kingdoms in the Iron Age and
    assume that some of the biblical stories about the shared ancestry of the Israelites
    were known then, although the biblical account itself greatly complicates the
    issue especially in the opening chapters of Judges. Thus, Israelites might have
    considered themselves descendants of the biblical patriarchs, but might also have
    admitted that some of their ancestors included the peoples that the Israelites had
    failed to displace when they conquered or, in Judges, infiltrated, Canaan. The

Judahites, who emerged as a distinctive group sometime after Cyrus's conquest of Babylon, were still Israelites and so likewise had a conviction of shared descent, though this was again complicated by the knowledge/claim, evinced in the lists in Ezra-Nehemiah, that not all the returning exiles (let alone the 'am ha'aretz) were truly Judahites. So imperial policy probably did not create the Jews from scratch. But it did make them very different from their putative Israelite ancestors.

34 That the various rebel and brigand groups constituted a broad "liberation movement," or *Freiheitsbewegung*, was the argument of M. Hengel, *The Zealots: Investigations into the Jewish Freedom Movement in the Period from Herod I until 70 A.D.* (Edinburgh: T & T Clark, 1989).

35 On this revolt, see M. Pucci Ben Zeev, *Diaspora Judaism in Turmoil, 116/117 CE: Ancient Sources and Modern Insights* (Leuven: Peeters, 2005).

36 D. Goodblatt, mentioned above, provides the most detailed account of the ideological components of the rebellions.

37 See now H. Lapin, *Rabbis as Romans: The Rabbinic Movement in Palestine, 100–400 CE* (New York: Oxford University Press, 2012).

38 On the afterlife of this arrangement in the medieval Christian and Muslim worlds, see Mark Cohen, *Under Crescent and Cross: The Jews in the Middle Ages* (Princeton, NJ: Princeton University Press, 1994).

5

How Christianity Parted from Judaism

ADELE REINHARTZ

Christianity as Judaism

Christmas time in America. Stores and street corners are decorated with pastoral scenes of a manger, in which a tiny bed is surrounded by adoring wise men, angels, shepherds, and livestock, set against the backdrop of a starry night sky. In popular imagination, Christmas Day marks not only the birth of a savior but also the origins of Christianity, the movement to which he is central.[1] History, however, tells a different story.

Jesus, an itinerant Jewish teacher born and active in the first three decades of the first century CE, had no intention of beginning a new movement, let alone a new religion.[2] Rather, Jesus operated within an exclusively Jewish milieu, as did his earliest followers. Although they were different in some ways from other Jewish groups among whom they lived, their ideas and practices fall well within the Jewish spectrum known from numerous written and archaeological sources from this period. And yet, within two or three decades, the movement had spread beyond the Jewish communities of Palestine to both gentile and Jewish communities in the broader Roman Empire; by the early fourth century, Christianity—the name given to that movement devoted to the belief that Jesus was the messiah and son of God—was the dominant religion in the Roman Empire. Why, how, and when did this small Jewish group differentiate itself so thoroughly from other Jewish groups that it could chart an independent course in world history?

In retrospect, it may seem that the differentiation between Judaism and Christianity began with Jesus's birth and the fundamental belief that he was the messiah and son of God. The four gospels of the New Testament, ascribed to Matthew, Mark, Luke, and John, claim as much. For John, Jesus was God's son, the Divine Word who existed before the creation of the world and was sent to dwell among humankind to offer salvation (John 1:1–14). In Matthew and Luke, Jesus's divine identity was announced prior to his conception and birth (Matthew 1:20; Luke 1:35), and in all four canonical gospels it was announced to John the Baptist by God prior to the commencement of Jesus's ministry. The gospels, however, reflect back on Jesus's life from a chronological distance of four or five decades, and a time when a church focused on faith in Jesus's messianic and divine identity had already begun to establish itself. Whether Jesus saw himself as a savior figure is not possible to determine, but from a historical point of view it is clear that he had no intention of beginning a movement that in time would not consider itself or be considered by others to be Jewish. In the beginning, Christianity was Judaism.

Jesus the Jew

Notwithstanding the four canonical versions of Jesus's biography—the Gospels of Matthew, Mark, Luke, and John—there is little certainty about his life. Even his birth and death dates are contested. Nevertheless, historians agree on one point: Jesus was Jewish and lived and worked primarily within the Jewish communities of Galilee and Judea.[3] To be sure, the gospels do not often call Jesus a *ioudaios* (the Greek term for Jew).[4] Nevertheless, they provide ample evidence of Jesus's Jewish identity, or, to be more precise, it is evident that the gospel writers were convinced of Jesus's Jewish identity. In its infancy narrative, the Gospel of Luke describes how the family observed the standard Jewish rites that attend the birth of a male child:

> After eight days had passed, it was time to circumcise the child; and he was called Jesus, the name given by the angel before he was conceived in the womb. When the time came for their purification according to the law of Moses, they brought him up to Jerusalem to present him to the Lord (as it is written in the law of the Lord, "Every firstborn male shall be designated as holy to the Lord"), and they offered a sacrifice according to what is stated in the law of the Lord, "a pair of turtledoves or two young pigeons." (Luke 2:21–24)[5]

Luke also recounts that Jesus's parents went up to Jerusalem for Passover, and at the age of twelve Jesus joined them for this pilgrimage. He may well have gone with them in earlier years, but Luke makes special mention of this occasion (2:41–42).

As an adult, the Gospel of Mark tells us, Jesus taught in the synagogue (1:21–22); he would not have been permitted to do so were he not a Jew. According to John, Jesus attended a wedding at which there stood six stone water jars for the Jewish rites of purification, each holding twenty or thirty gallons (2:6). The reference is likely to the Jewish ritual handwashing that preceded each meal.

Not only Jesus but also his earliest followers were Jewish, not surprising given that he functioned within a generally Jewish milieu. As in their portrayal of Jesus, the gospel writers do not emphasis this point, but it underlies their depiction of Jesus's disciples. An example is the following exchange in which the Galilean follower Philip recruits a new disciple, Nathanael:

> Philip found Nathanael and said to him, "We have found him about whom Moses in the law and also the prophets wrote, Jesus son of Joseph from Nazareth." Nathanael said to him, "Can anything good come out of Nazareth?" Philip said to him, "Come and see." When Jesus saw Nathanael coming toward him, he said of him, "Here is truly an Israelite in whom there is no deceit!" (John 1:45–47)

The First Christians

The term "Christian" occurs for the first time in Acts 11:26, in which the narrator comments that "it was in Antioch that the disciples were first called 'Christians.'" The term also appears in Acts 26:28, in which King Agrippa asks Paul, "Are you so quickly persuading me to become a Christian?" and 1 Peter 4:16, in which the author exhorts his audience: "Yet if any of you suffers as a Christian, do not consider it a disgrace, but glorify God because you bear this name." These verses suggest that "Christian" may already have been a well-established designation for the believers in Jesus as the messiah either by the late first century, when Acts was written, or perhaps even in the mid-first century, when the Acts account is set. The grammatical form does not make it clear whether this term originated with insiders or outsiders, but at the very least its existence demonstrates that even in the first century, when Christianity had not yet separated, it was necessary to find a way of distinguishing these Jews from other Jews. This does not mean that Christianity already constituted an autonomous identity. It does indicate, however, that those who followed Jesus were seen as distinctive, just as Pharisees, Sadducees, and Essenes were distinctive, while still remaining under the Jewish umbrella. While such distinctiveness may have already contained the seeds of separation, it is possible to imagine that, under a different set of historical and social circumstances, Christianity might have remained within Judaism or else disappeared, as did the Essenes.

Metaphors of Identity Formation

It is difficult to talk about the process by which Christianity developed an identity that was fully autonomous from Judaism without resorting to metaphors.[6] Scholars have been inventive in creating metaphors that express their views both about the process and also about the state of the relationship between Christ-believers and non-Christ-believing Jews both before and after the differentiation occurred.

Venn Diagram

Philip Alexander suggested that the process of differentiation can be visualized as a Venn diagram. Judaism and Christianity begin as circles that overlap completely and then gradually separate until they are completely independent. This is not to suggest that both were initially the same or that Christianity occupied the same amount of "space" as Judaism, simply that Christianity did not constitute a circle separate from Judaism but was part of it.[7] The metaphor implies that the circles remained separate, with no contact whatsoever, after they separated. This schema conveys the notion that the separation took place as part of a process, but it is too schematic to convey an appropriately complex understanding of the ongoing relationships between Judaism and Christianity after their separation.

Textile

James Dunn has proposed several metaphors, including a textile metaphor.[8] Dunn pictures first-century Judaism as a richly woven garment in which nascent Christianity was but one strand. Over time, this strand worked its way out of the garment and eventually pulled all the way loose. This metaphor, too, has its limitations, for it does not have a way of weaving yet another rich garment from the strand that came loose from Second Temple Judaism.

Fluvial

Both James Dunn and Daniel Boyarin have suggested river or lake metaphors. Dunn views rabbinic Judaism and Christianity as two strong currents from within the broad stream of ancient Judaism that over time carved out two separate channels (Dunn).[9] Boyarin describes the first-century Jewish movements, including Christianity, as waves that flow out from a single source, like the concentric ripples that flow out when a pebble is tossed into a still pond.[10]

Kinship

In the nineteenth and most of the twentieth centuries, kinship metaphors dominated scholarly discussion of the relationship between Judaism and Christianity.

MOTHER-DAUGHTER

A dominant metaphor in nineteenth-century scholarship on the origins of Christianity was the mother-daughter relationship.[11] At first glance, this metaphor seems apt, for it acknowledges that Christianity was born into and nurtured within a Jewish environment, as well as the theological and other similarities between them that persist from the ancient period to the present. Furthermore, it makes sense of the separation as an inevitable part of the maturation process. Nevertheless, it is problematic, for it implies the eventual demise of the "mother" and the rise of the "daughter" as a replacement.[12] Furthermore, it implies unity of the "mother" over and against the historical reality of the tremendous diversity within first-century Judaism, of which Christianity was one but by no means the only part. In this sense there was no single "Judaism" that could have given birth to a child at all, but rather an ever-shifting set of groups that shared some ideas and practices while disagreeing on others.[13]

SIBLINGS

The notion of kinship seemed to get at something important and organic about the relationship between Judaism and Christianity, even as the problems with the mother-child metaphor became clear to more and more scholars. A modification introduced by Alan Segal still has a following. Segal proposed that Judaism—specifically, rabbinic Judaism—and Christianity were actually more like siblings than they were like mother and daughter. He referred to them as "Rebecca's children"—the twins Jacob and Esau. This metaphor draws on the rabbinic designation of Rome, and consequently post-Constantine Christianity, as Edom. The metaphor acknowledges that rabbinic Judaism and Christianity are both products of one "mother"—Second Temple Judaism—that came to maturity in the first five centuries of the Common Era. While they have much in common, they are also rivals and quite different from one another if, perhaps, not quite able to separate fully.[14] For Segal, their conception occurred in the first century, but their development was spurred by the two revolts against Rome and the process of separation largely completed by the early second century.[15] This metaphor, like most, also has its limitations. Both Judaism and Christianity claim to be the true descendants of the younger twin Jacob, who outsmarted his brother Esau to gain the birthright and his father's blessing and who wrestled with the angel to gain divine favor.[16]

The Parting of the Ways

While kinship metaphors are still used, the current scholarly conversation on this question most often refers to the "parting of the ways." This metaphor can refer to kinship matters, such as divorce, or to human relationships more generally, when business partners or friends simply decide to go their separate ways or no longer see eye to eye. But at its core it is a roadway metaphor, suggesting that two people or groups have simply decided to go different ways, take different routes whether to the same or to different destinations. The roadway metaphor may be used to express the idea that Judaism was the main highway from which Christianity branched off to go in a different direction.[17] There may also be those who see this main highway ending as the secondary route adds more lanes. This reproduces the "late Judaism" position that we have already discussed.[18] But for the most part, it is seen as two equally important roadways that split off from a larger thoroughfare, replicating to some extent Segal's "sibling" image.[19]

Another Roadway Image

Like the metaphors already mentioned, the "parting of the ways" has its limitations. In postulating two major roadways, it implies that these two—rabbinic Judaism and early Christianity—were the only two options. In order to signal the complexity of early Judaism and Christianity, the presence of multiple groups within each one and the messiness of their ongoing relationships both within and between Judaism and Christianity, Judith Lieu has proposed that we speak not of a parting of the ways so much as a "criss-crossing of muddy tracks which only the expert tracker, or poacher, can decipher."[20] Boyarin goes even further, denying the existence of any partitions or criss-crossing but rather a continuous roadway along which an individual could travel along a continuum rather than a sharp divide between rabbinic Judaism and Christianity. This would challenge the very idea that the ways ever parted at all or that it would have been possible in the ancient world (or now, or at many points in between) to differentiate clearly if at all among these various groups.[21]

Why Part Ways?

Even the muddiest of these metaphors cannot express the full complexity or the various theories concerning the "parting of the ways." For this reason they provide only a starting point for the diverse views on how, when, and why the ways parted. To some degree, these diverse perspectives reflect different assessments of the reasons that the ways parted.

Theology

It is safe to assume that most people would see theology as a major factor in the eventual separation of Christianity from Judaism, and they would also agree that the essential theological difference between Judaism and Christianity pertains to Jesus. Christians believe that Jesus is the Messiah

(Christ, in Greek) and Son of God, a figure both human and divine, who was crucified and then resurrected on the third day. Jews do not believe that Jesus was anything more than a man, charismatic, maybe even prophetic, but merely a man. Yet in the ancient world, such beliefs did not constitute the absolute divide that many would argue today.[22]

According to Josephus, numerous individuals claimed to be saviors in the decades leading up to the first revolt against Rome in 70, including Theudas, who "persuaded the majority of the masses to take up their possessions and to follow him to the Jordan River"; an Egyptian "who declared that he was a prophet and advised the masses of the common people to go out with him to the mountain called the Mount of Olives"; a "certain imposter who had promised them salvation and rest from troubles, if they chose to follow him into the wilderness"; and a "false prophet, who had on that day proclaimed to the people in the city that God commanded them to go up to the temple court, to receive there the tokens of their deliverance."[23] These "false messiahs" may have been misguided and even destructive, but they occasioned no theological distress.

This basic theological difference, however, had implications for issues that went well beyond the question of messianism to touch on points that were fundamental to Jewish identity. According to James Dunn, pressure on certain key elements—monotheism, election, Torah, and Temple—eventually built to the point where rupture was the only option.[24] Monotheism was threatened by the belief that Jesus was divine and by the development of binitarian (two divine beings) and trinitarian (three divine beings) theologies.[25] The concept of election was challenged by the claim that the covenantal relationship between God and Israel was now being mediated by Christ and not by Torah, as Jews believe.[26] Finally, critique of the Temple (see Acts 7 and John 4:21–23) and its displacement from its central place in communal ritual would have been a challenge even in the period after its destruction, as the Temple and sacrificial cult remained important symbolically and ritually.[27]

Social Factors

In contrast to Dunn, some scholars do not see even these theological differences as decisive in the eventual rift between Judaism and Christianity. They point out that social contact continued to take place long after these theological positions developed. Judith Lieu points to "evidence of Jews and Christians not only living in the same areas but even being buried in the same cemeteries."[28] Yet ongoing social contact does not preclude separation. Well into the modern period, Christians and Jews continued to engage with each other personally, liturgically, and theologically.[29] Indeed, some have argued that not only was Judaism formative for Christianity but Christianity was formative for Judaism, especially in the development of what most see as distinctive Jewish practices such as the Passover Seder.[30]

The Gentile Mission

A major sociological factor in the process of differentiation was the Christ-believers' mission to the gentiles. The letters of Paul, the earliest documents of the New Testament dating from the mid-first century, show that this mission began in the years immediately following Jesus's death. Scholars differ in their evaluations of the importance of the gentile mission. Craig Evans, for example, sees the gentile mission as important but not as a "root cause."[31] My own view is that the gentile mission and, specifically, the position that gentile converts to Christianity did not have to undergo circumcision or observe Jewish laws such as *kashrut* was a major though not the sole factor in the complex process of Christian differentiation.

The genuine letters of Paul testify amply to his self-understanding as an apostle to the gentiles and his conviction that through faith in Jesus as the Christ, gentiles become part of God's covenant community. Paul's mission to the gentiles was based on the belief that Israel maintained a primary covenantal relationship with God. As Paul declares in Romans 9:4–5, "To Israelites (Jews) belong: the glory, the covenants, the giving of the law, the worship, and the promises; to them belong the patriarchs, and from them, according to the flesh, comes the Messiah, who is over all, God blessed for ever. Amen." The new covenant (as he called it in 2 Corinthians 3:6) or "Christians" as, according to Acts, they were called in Antioch, did not create a new covenant, but provided a path that gentiles could take into that covenantal relationship without converting to Judaism. "But when the fullness of time had come, God sent his Son, born of a woman, born under the law, in order to redeem those who were under the law, so that we might receive adoption as children. And because you are children, God has sent the Spirit of his Son into our hearts, crying, 'Abba! Father!' So you are no longer a slave but a child, and if a child then also an heir, through God" (Gal 4:4–7).

But Paul also insisted that gentile believers did not need to—indeed, they should not—take on primary Jewish identity markers. According to his letters, this position put him at odds with the Jerusalem church led by Peter (also known as Cephas) and James, who had sent representatives to Galatia in Paul's absence to persuade the gentile believers that they had to undergo circumcision in order to belong fully to the church. In Galatians 1:13–17, Paul responds by proclaiming his apostolic credentials as well as his independence from the Jerusalem church:

> You have heard, no doubt, of my earlier life in Judaism. I was violently persecuting the church of God and was trying to destroy it. I advanced in Judaism beyond many among my people of the same age, for I was far more zealous for the traditions of my ancestors. But when God, who had set me apart before I was born and called me through his grace, was pleased to reveal his Son to me, so that I might proclaim him among the Gentiles, I did not confer with any human being, nor did I go up to Jerusalem to those who were already apostles before me, but I went away at once into Arabia, and afterwards I returned to Damascus.

Later, Paul says, he did go up to Jerusalem, where he received the seal of approval for his mission from the pillars of the Jerusalem church:

> And from those who were supposed to be acknowledged leaders (what they actually were makes no difference to me; God shows no partiality)— those leaders contributed nothing to me. On the contrary, when they saw that I had been entrusted with the gospel for the uncircumcised, just as Peter had been entrusted with the gospel for the circumcised (for he who worked through Peter making him an apostle to the circumcised also worked through me in sending me to the Gentiles), and when James and Cephas and John, who were acknowledged pillars, recognized the grace that had been given to me, they gave to Barnabas and me the right hand of fellowship, agreeing that we should go to the Gentiles and they to the circumcised. (Gal 2:6–9)

Acts of the Apostles, written some decades after Paul's letters, also approves of the gentile mission but smooths over the conflict between Paul and the Jerusalem church:

> Then Peter began to speak to them: "I truly understand that God shows no partiality, but in every nation anyone who fears him and does what is right is acceptable to him. You know the message he sent to the people of Israel, preaching peace by Jesus Christ—he is Lord of all. That message spread throughout Judea, beginning in Galilee after the baptism that John announced: how God anointed Jesus of Nazareth with the Holy Spirit and with power; how he went about doing good and healing all who were oppressed by the devil, for God was with him. We are witnesses to all that he did both in Judea and in Jerusalem. They put him to death by hanging him on a tree; but God raised him on the third day and allowed him to appear, not to all the people but to us who were chosen by God as witnesses, and who ate and drank with him after he rose from the dead. He commanded us to preach to the people and to testify that he is the one ordained by God as judge of the living and the dead. All the prophets testify about him that everyone who believes in him receives forgiveness of sins through his name." (Acts 10:34–42)

Admitting gentiles to the covenant community meant eliminating at least two important boundary markers: the observance of the dietary laws (*kashrut*) and circumcision. In his letter to the Galatians, Paul is particularly adamant about the latter. Indeed, he warns the Galatians:

> Listen! I, Paul, am telling you that if you let yourselves be circumcised, Christ will be of no benefit to you. Once again I testify to every man who lets himself be circumcised that he is obliged to obey the entire law. You who want to be justified by the law have cut yourselves off from Christ; you have fallen away from grace. For through the Spirit, by faith, we eagerly wait for the hope of righteousness. For in Christ Jesus neither circumcision nor uncircumcision counts for anything; the only thing that counts is faith working through love. (Gal 5:2–6)

He also, however, notes that observance of the dietary laws is not essential. He criticizes Peter (Cephas) for hypocrisy on this score and recounts that when Cephas came to Antioch, I opposed him to his face, because he stood self-condemned; for until certain people came from James, he used to eat with the Gentiles. But after they came, he drew back and kept himself separate for fear of the circumcision faction. And the other Jews joined him in this hypocrisy, so that even Barnabas was led astray by their hypocrisy. But when I saw that they were not acting consistently with the truth of the gospel, I said to Cephas before them all, "If you, though a Jew, live like a Gentile and not like a Jew, how can you compel the Gentiles to live like Jews?" (Gal 2:11–14)

As this latter quotation makes clear, Paul is not arguing against Judaism as such, but against the Jerusalem church, which continued to insist that gentile converts observe Jewish ritual law.

The admission of gentiles to the church without requiring observance of dietary laws, circumcision, or other laws would have had a deleterious effect on social contact, as marriage as well as table fellowship would not have been possible. The inability to share in such fundamental social practices helped to set the stage for eventual separation, once the size of the gentile Christian communities had grown.[32]

When Did the Parting Happen?

Scenario 1: 70–135 CE

Scholars agree that the ways did not part suddenly, but there are diverse opinions as to when the process was complete. Many argue that the process of separation began in earnest with the first Jewish revolt against Rome (66–74 CE) and was largely complete by the end of the Bar Kokhba revolt (132–135 CE).[33] Within this period, several events stand out as significant.

THE FLIGHT TO PELLA

The first point pertains to the Christians' participation—or, rather, lack of participation—in the first revolt. Eusebius recounts that the Jerusalem Christians fled before the revolt to a town called Pella:

The people of the church in Jerusalem had been commanded by a revelation . . . before the war, to leave the city and to dwell in a certain town of

Perea called Pella. And when those that believed in Christ had come there from Jerusalem, then, as if the royal city of the Jews and the whole land of Judea were entirely destitute of holy men, the judgment of God at length overtook those who had committed such outrages against Christ and his apostles, and totally destroyed that generation of impious men.[34]

Whether the flight to Pella occurred in fact or only in imagination is uncertain. Gerd Lüdemann argues that the tradition originated with Jewish-Christians who wished to establish an ancient pedigree in Jerusalem in the decades before the revolt.[35] Jonathan Bourgel, on the other hand, sees this as a credible story and argues that these members of the Jerusalem church did indeed flee in 68 just ahead of the revolt, and then encountered Vespasian's garrisons in the vicinity of Jericho, just east of Jerusalem.[36] The Roman forces, viewing these Christians as Jews, allowed them to negotiate the terms of their surrender and sent them to Peraea.[37]

BIRKAT HA-MINIM

Some scholars argue that this period saw a second milestone: the insertion of a "curse" on the heretics into the daily Jewish liturgy that was formulated in the years immediately after the first revolt. This curse is euphemistically referred to as a "blessing" on the heretics (*Birkat Ha-Minim*). The earliest texts of this curse were found in the Cairo Geniza.[38] The almost 280,000 Jewish manuscript fragments included more than a hundred copies of this blessing, in several variations. What was striking about many of them was the inclusion of a formula *hanotzrim ve-haminim* (lit. "the Christians and the heretics"). Here is one version:

> For those doomed to destruction may there be no hope
> and may the dominion of arrogance be quickly uprooted in our days
> and may the Nazarenes and the heretics be destroyed in a moment
> and may they be blotted out of the book of life
> and may they not be inscribed with the righteous.
> Blessed are you, O Lord, who subdues the arrogant.[39]

Birkat Ha-Minim was drawn into the question of the parting of the ways by the work of J. Louis Martyn, who, in his book *History and Theology in the Fourth Gospel,* argued that *Birkat Ha-Minim,* or something very much like it, underlies the Gospel's references to expulsion from the synagogue.[40] His argument is based on three passages in the Gospel of John that refer to *aposynagogoi:* people who are excluded from the synagogue.

The most substantial is John 9. After Jesus heals a blind man on the Sabbath, the Jewish authorities call in his parents and ask them, "Is this your son, who you say was born blind? How then does he now see?" (v. 19). The parents acknowledge that this is indeed their son and that he was born blind, but "we do not know how it is that now he sees, nor do we know who opened his eyes. Ask him; he is of age. He will speak for himself" (v. 21). The narrator comments that "His parents said this because they were afraid of the Jews; for the Jews had already agreed that anyone who confessed Jesus to be the Messiah would be put out of the synagogue. Therefore his parents said, 'He is of age; ask him'" (vv. 22–23).

In John 12:42–43, near the end of Jesus's public ministry, the narrator states that "many, even of the authorities, believed in him. But because of the Pharisees they did not confess it, for fear that they would be put out of the synagogue; for they loved human glory more than the glory that comes from God." Finally, in his farewell discourses to the disciples on the eve of his arrest, Jesus warns the disciples that "[t]hey will put you out of the synagogues. Indeed, an hour is coming when those who kill you will think that by doing so they are offering worship to God" (John 16:2).

Martyn argued that the three expulsion passages refer to a real experience of the gospel's first audience, and that the mechanism for such exclusion can only have been liturgical. Only *Birkat Ha-Minim* can fit the bill of a liturgical element that could have been used to exclude Jewish-Christians. The argument is that a person would be exposed as a Jewish-Christian—a heretic—if he was asked to be a prayer leader and refused to recite the blessing against the heretics. He supported this argument by referring to rabbinic literature, in which the institution of *Birkat Ha-Minim* is dated to the late first century, precisely the same time as the Gospel of John. The principal text is found in the Babylonian Talmud:

> Our rabbis taught: Simeon ha-Paquli organized the Eighteen Benedictions in order before Rabban Gamaliel in Yavneh. Rabban Gamaliel said to the sages: "Isn't there anyone who knows how to fix the Benediction of

the Heretics?" Samuel the Small stood up and fixed it, but another year he forgot it. And he thought about it for two or three hours, [and he did not recall it], but they did not remove him. Why then did they not remove him? Did not R. Judah say that Rav said: "If someone makes a mistake in any of the benedictions, they don't remove him, but if [he makes a mistake] in the Benediction of the Heretics, they do remove him, since they suspect that perhaps he is a heretic"? Samuel the Small is different, because he formulated it.[41]

Many, though by no means all, New Testament scholars agree with Martyn's hypothesis concerning the use of *Birkat Ha-Minim* to expel Jewish-Christians from the synagogue and for that reason consider it to be relevant to the parting of the ways.[42] Specialists in rabbinic literature and the history of Jewish liturgy, however, are less certain. In the first place, the rabbinic passages are unlikely to be historically accurate, particularly concerning the late first century dating of the curse. The rabbis had a vested interest in backdating their practices, including liturgy, to the first two decades of the postdestruction period as support for their authenticity and authority. As Ruth Langer has pointed out, the earliest sources for *Birkat Ha-Minim* date to the third or early fourth century, casting doubt on the existence of the curse in the period between the two revolts.[43] Second, even if there were such a curse, it is difficult to understand how it would have functioned to exclude Jewish-Christians from the synagogue. Steven Katz notes that the use of *Birkat Ha-Minim* as an exclusion mechanism would have required that Christians consider themselves heretics, an unlikely supposition. Furthermore, Jewish-Christians would likely already have been known to other synagogue goers. If so, more direct measures would have been more useful if indeed the intention was to exclude them.[44] Once this curse is no longer seen as a factor in the first century, the Johannine expulsion passages are often no longer seen as a reference to the exclusion of Christianity writ large, but rather as a local phenomenon, if indeed historical at all.[45]

FISCUS IUDAICUS

Another event often mentioned as a marker of the process of Jewish-Christian differentiation is the Roman head tax—the *fiscus iudaicus*—imposed in the aftermath of the first revolt. Whereas Jews throughout the empire had previously paid a tax for upkeep of the Jerusalem temple, the Romans collected a tax for the building and maintenance of Jupiter Capitolinus, the temple to Jupiter in Rome.[46] In contrast to the temple tax, which was required only of men between the ages of twenty and fifty, the *fiscus* was imposed on all, including women, children, and slaves. Domitian expanded the tax's purview to include not only those who were Jews but also those who lived like Jews, perhaps aiming at "godfearers" (gentiles who attended synagogue but did not undergo conversion to Judaism). The tax, therefore, in principle provided an opportunity for those who did not consider themselves Jewish to formalize their separation from the Jewish community. Marius Heemstra argues that many Jewish-Christians took advantage of this opportunity. For this reason, in his view, the *fiscus*, coupled with the exclusion of Jewish-Christians from the synagogue, provided the circumstances for a definitive break between Jews and Jewish-Christians.[47]

BAR KOKHBA REVOLT IN 132–135 CE

The first revolt was followed by a second diaspora-based revolt in 117–119 and a third revolt based in the land of Israel under the leadership of Simon Bar Kosiba, nicknamed Bar Kokhba. Some rabbinic sources suggest that he was perceived in messianic terms by the prominent Rabbi Akiva. The earliest reference is in the Palestinian Talmud, in which Rabbi Akiva is reported to have referred to the military leader as King Messiah and the fulfilment of the messianic prophecy in Numbers 24:17: "A star [*kokhav*] shall step forth from Jacob."[48] Patristic sources imply the leader's uneasiness with regard to Jewish-Christians. Justin Martyr claims that "in the Jewish war which now occurred, Bar Kochba, the leader of the revolt of the Jews, ordered that Christians alone should be led to terrible punishments unless they would deny Jesus, the Christ, and blaspheme."[49] The historicity of this claim is difficult to demonstrate, but further evidence of uneasiness may be found in one of the letters apparently penned by Bar Kokhba himself, in which he refers to Galileans being held in custody by one of his followers.[50]

The hypothesis that the process of separation between Judaism and Christianity occurred between the first revolt and the Bar Kokhba revolt is supported by the tensions that are apparent in the New Testament literature, which, aside from the letters of Paul, were also written in this period. These tensions are reflected in the deicide charge, in which the Jews are seen as bearing the moral if not the legal responsibility for Jesus's death. This is expressed most stridently in Matthew 27:24–26, in which Pilate, who had been sympathetic to Jesus, "saw that he could do nothing, but rather that a riot was beginning. He took some water and washed his hands before the crowd, saying, 'I am innocent of this man's blood; see to it yourselves.' Then the people as a whole answered, 'His blood be on us and on our children!' So he released Barabbas for them; and after flogging Jesus, he handed him over to be crucified."

Another very problematic passage is John 8:44, in which Jesus tells the Jews, "You are from your father the devil, and you choose to do your father's desires. He was a murderer from the beginning and does not stand in the truth, because there is no truth in him. When he lies, he speaks according to his own nature, for he is a liar and the father of lies." Like the deicide charge, the association of Jews and the devil became a staple of anti-Semitism, both Christian and secular, to the present day.

Scenario 2: Early Fourth Century CE

The consensus that Christian differentiation and separation from Judaism were more or less complete by the time of the Bar Kokhba revolt has been challenged by scholars who argue that the boundaries between Judaism and Christianity took much longer to form than the earlier view had acknowledged. Some scholars suggest that separation was hastened by Roman measures limiting Jewish access to Jerusalem and proscribing circumcision in the aftermath of the Bar Kokhba revolt.[51]

Others point to the diversity and theological flexibility of first-century Judaism, within which fledgling Christianity was only one strand and by no means the most extreme. They also emphasize the strong evidence of ongoing contact between those who believed Jesus to be the messiah and those who did not. On this basis, they argue that it is not appropriate to speak about separation until the Christianization of the Roman Empire in the early fourth century.[52] This recent argument reflects at least in part the postmodern tendency to break down the neat binary oppositions that characterized earlier scholarship, for example, the absolute opposition between Judaism and Christianity. It also builds on the growing understanding of the tremendous variety of Second Temple

Judaism as well as of ongoing social contacts and the fluidity of ethnic and religious identity that may have characterized the period before Constantine's conversion.

According to Scenario 2, the process of differentiation took place over the course of three centuries, with firm markers of separation occurring in a cluster of events that took place in the early fourth century, between 311 and 325 CE. The first was the Edict of Toleration in 311, issued by the Roman tetrarchs Galerius, Constantine, and Licinius, which brought an official end to the persecution of Christianity. The edict comments on the persecution to which the empire had subjected Christians on account of their refusal to "conform to the institutes of antiquity" and announced the decision to cease such persecution:

> since most of them persevered in their determination, and we saw that they neither paid the reverence and awe due to the gods nor worshipped the God of the Christians, in view of our most mild clemency and the constant habit by which we are accustomed to grant indulgence to all, we thought that we ought to grant our most prompt indulgence also to these, so that they may again be Christians and may hold their conventicles, provided they do nothing contrary to good order. But we shall tell the magistrates in another letter what they ought to do. Wherefore, for this our indulgence, they ought to pray to their God for our safety, for that of the republic, and for their own, that the republic may continue uninjured on every side, and that they may be able to live securely in their homes.[53]

The next milestone was Constantine's conversion in 312, followed by the Edict of Milan in 313. The edict exists in different versions in Lactantius's *De Mortibus Persecutorum* and in Eusebius's *History of the Church*.[54] The edict is the outcome of a meeting between Constantine and Licinius in Milan at which they agreed to change their policies toward Christians and to treat them benevolently. Constantine and Licinius decided to "grant to the Christians and others full authority to observe that religion which each preferred . . . [and] to arrange that no one whatsoever should be denied the opportunity to give his heart to the observance of the Christian religion, of that religion which he should think best for himself, so that the Supreme Deity, to whose worship we freely yield our hearts, may show in all things His usual favor and benevolence."[55]

While these three events paved the way for rapid growth in size, strength, and power, it was the Council of Nicaea in 325 that sealed the separation of Christianity from Judaism. One of the main achievements of this council was to impose a single date for the celebration of Easter, which to this point had been celebrated at different times by different groups, and to separate it definitively from the Jewish feast of Passover.

> At this meeting the question concerning the most holy day of Easter was discussed, and it was resolved by the united judgment of all present, that this feast ought to be kept by all and in every place on one and the same day. . . . And first of all, it appeared an unworthy thing that in the celebration of this most holy feast we should follow the practice of the Jews, who have impiously defiled their hands with enormous sin, and are, therefore, deservedly afflicted with blindness of soul. . . . Let us then have nothing in common with the detestable Jewish crowd; for we have received from our Saviour a different way.[56]

Whether the events of the early fourth century merely put the final seal on a process that was already very far advanced if not complete by this point or whether it was instrumental in moving Christianity out of the Jewish fold—arguments can be made in both directions—it is nevertheless clear that by the year 325 Christianity had not only fully separated and differentiated itself from Judaism but also become a major social, economic, and political institution in the Roman Empire.

Conclusion

Christianity began as one of many Jewish groups in the first century of the Common Era. On either scenario outlined above, the development of an autonomous identity on the part of Christianity—the parting of the ways, the eddying of waters, separating the siblings, dismantling of textiles—was not a neat linear or onetime occurrence but the result of a lengthy, messy, difficult-to-describe process that took place over the course of one to three centuries, at different times in different locales.[57] However we view the process of separation, it is clear that by the early fourth century, Christianity was no longer Judaism. Indeed it positioned itself firmly over and against Judaism, a position that most mainstream branches of Christianity rejected only in the twentieth century. Christianity developed its own ways of understanding monotheism; its own practices, rites, and rituals; and its own life-cycle events and identity markers. In many ways, however, Christianity remains Judaism, or, to be more precise, Christianity and Judaism continue to agree on some fundamental points: belief in or, at least, some form of orientation toward a divine being who is concerned about humankind, and a commitment to social justice that requires human beings to strive for the well-being of others. It behooves all of us to strive to understand the other and the other's history in order to live together productively and peacefully in the modern world.

NOTES

1 Jesus's actual birth date is unknown. For a brief discussion, see Everett Ferguson et al., *Encyclopedia of Early Christianity* (New York: Garland, 1990), p. 251.

2 A number of scholars now question whether the category "religion" existed in the first century. See, for example, Steve Mason, "Jews, Judaeans, Judaizing, Judaism: Problems of Categorization in Ancient History," *Journal for the Study of Judaism in the Persian, Hellenistic and Roman Periods* 38 (2007): 480–488; Daniel Boyarin, "Rethinking Jewish Christianity: An Argument for Dismantling a Dubious Category (To Which Is Appended a Correction of My *Border Lines*)," *Jewish Quarterly Review* 99 (2009): 228–230. For a thoughtful counterargument, see Seth Schwartz, "How Many Judaisms Were There?" *Journal of Ancient Judaism* 2 (2011): 228–230.

3 Jesus's Jewishness was vigorously denied in the Nazi era by scholars associated with the Institute for the Study and Eradication of Jewish Influence on German Religious Life; see Susannah Heschel, *The Aryan Jesus: Christian Theologians and the Bible in Nazi Germany* (Princeton, NJ: Princeton University Press, 2008), p. 62. Others do not deny Jesus's Jewishness so much as the existence of "Judaism" in the first century. See, for example, John Elliott, "Jesus the Israelite Was Neither a 'Jew' Nor a 'Christian': On Correcting Misleading Nomenclature," *Journal for the Study of the Historical Jesus* 5 (2007): 119–154. For a thorough discussion of the history of scholarship on the "Jewish Jesus," see William E. Arnal, *The Symbolic Jesus: Historical Scholarship, Judaism and the Construction of Contemporary Identity* (Hoboken, NJ: Taylor and Francis, 2015).

4 The exception is John 4, in which Jesus stops by a well in Samaria to rest and refresh himself en route from Judea to Galilee. There he meets a Samaritan woman, whom he asks for a drink of water. She is surprised: "'How is it that you, a Jew, ask a drink of me, a woman of Samaria?' (Jews do not share things in common with Samaritans)" (v. 9). Otherwise, however, Jesus is not referred to explicitly as an *ioudaios*. This silence is understandable, for generally, as John 4:9 shows, there is

no need to employ an ethnic label to describe an individual except when there is a need to differentiate that person from some other person or group.

5 All quotations from the New Testament are taken from the New Revised Standard Version unless otherwise noted.

6 For more detailed discussion, see Adele Reinhartz, "A Fork in the Road or a Multi-Lane Highway? New Perspectives on the 'Parting of the Ways' between Judaism and Christianity," in *Changing Face of Judaism, Christianity, and Other Greco-Roman Religions in Antiquity*, ed. Ian H. Henderson and Gerbern S. Oegema (Gütersloh: Gütersloher, 2006), pp. 280–295.

7 Philip S. Alexander, " 'The Parting of the Ways' from the Perspective of Rabbinic Judaism," in *Jews and Christians: The Parting of the Ways A.D. 70–135*, ed. James D. G. Dunn (Tübingen: J. C. B. Mohr [Paul Siebeck], 1992), pp. 1–25.

8 James D. G. Dunn, *The Partings of the Ways: Between Christianity and Judaism and Their Significance for the Character of Christianity* (London; Philadelphia: SCM; Trinity Press International, 1991), p. 230.

9 Ibid.

10 Daniel Boyarin, *Dying for God: Martyrdom and the Making of Christianity and Judaism* (Stanford, CA: Stanford University Press, 1999), p. 9; Daniel Boyarin, "Justin Martyr Invents Judaism," *Church History* 70 (2001): 460.

11 For discussion, see Wayne A. Meeks, "Breaking Away: Three New Testament Pictures of Christianity's Separation from the Jewish Communities," in *"To See Ourselves as Others See Us": Christians, Jews, "Others" in Late Antiquity*, ed. Jacob Neusner and Ernest S. Frerichs (Chico, CA: Scholars Press, 1985), pp. 104–108; Daniel Stokl Ben Ezra, "On Trees, Waves, and Cytokinesis: Shifting Paradigms in Early (and Modern) Jewish-Christian Relations," in *Interaction between Judaism and Christianity in History, Religion, Art and Literature*, ed. Marcel Poorthuis, Joshua Schwartz, and Joseph Turner (Leiden: Brill, 2009), pp. 128–129.

12 As E. P. Sanders has shown so convincingly, this tendency came along with a subtle or often overt anti-Judaism or even anti-Semitism, including surprise that Judaism—an empty and stagnant religion—has nevertheless managed to endure for so many years after it was eviscerated by Christianity (*Paul and Palestinian Judaism: A Comparison of Patterns of Religion* [Philadelphia: Fortress Press, 1977], pp. 33–59).

13 Jacob Neusner popularized the notion that there were many "Judaisms" in the first century. Cf. Jacob Neusner, Ernest S. Frerichs, and William Scott Green, *Judaisms and Their Messiahs at the Turn of the Christian Era* (Cambridge: Cambridge University Press, 1987); Alan F. Segal, *The Other Judaisms of Late Antiquity* (Brown Judaic Studies 127; Atlanta, GA: Scholars Press, 1987). For the view that there was a "common Judaism" that overrode differences among various groups, see E. P. Sanders, *Judaism: Practice and Belief, 63 BCE–66 CE* (London; Philadelphia: SCM; Trinity Press International, 1992); and Schwartz, "How Many Judaisms Were There?" In recent scholarship, usage has reverted to the singular, at least in part as a result of Sanders's cogent critique.

14 Boyarin, *Dying for God*, p. 3.

15 Alan F. Segal, *Rebecca's Children: Judaism and Christianity in the Roman World* (Cambridge, MA: Harvard University Press, 1986), p. 173.

16 Boyarin, *Dying for God*, p. 5.

17 Hyam Maccoby, *The Mythmaker: Paul and the Invention of Christianity* (London: Weidenfeld & Nicolson, 1986); Lawrence H. Schiffman, *Who Was a Jew? Rabbinic and Halakhic Perspectives on the Jewish Christian Schism* (Hoboken, NJ: Ktav, 1985).

18 See E. P. Sanders's discussion of Weber and Bousset in his *Paul and Palestinian Judaism*, pp. 33–59.

19 Judith Lieu, "The Parting of the Ways: Theological Construct or Historical Reality?" *Journal for the Study of the New Testament* 56 (1994): 101–119. See also F. J. Foakes-Jackson, William Ralph Inge, and Jesus College (University of Cambridge), *The Parting of the Roads; Studies in the Development of Judaism and Early Christianity* (London: E. Arnold, 1912).

20 Lieu, "Parting of the Ways," p. 119.

21 Boyarin, *Dying for God*, p. 9. See Adam H. Becker and Annette Yoshiko Reed, *The Ways That Never Parted: Jews and Christians in Late Antiquity and the Early Middle Ages* (Tübingen: Mohr Siebeck, 2003).

22 Many adherents of the modern Jewish Hasidic group known as Lubavitch or Chabad believe that their rebbe, Rabbi Menachem Mendel Schneerson, who died in 1994, still lives and is the messiah. For discussion, see Samuel C. Heilman and Menachem Friedman, *The Rebbe: The Life and Afterlife of Menachem Mendel Schneerson* (Princeton, NJ: Princeton University Press, 2010).

23 Josephus, *Jewish Antiquities* 20.5.1 §§97–99, 20.8.6 §§169–172, 20.8.10 §188 (Loeb Classical Library [LCL] vol. 13, pp. 52–54, 92–93, and 102–103); *Jewish War* 6.5.1 §285 (LCL vol. 3, pp. 458–459).

24 Dunn, *Partings of the Ways*, p. 35.

25 Segal, *Rebecca's Children*, p. 156; Dunn, *Partings of the Ways*, pp. 240–245 and 148. But see Boyarin, who argues that such elements are present within Judaism as well ("The Gospel of the *Memra*: Jewish Binitarianism and the Prologue to John," *Harvard Theological Review* 94 [2001]: 244).

26 For discussion, see Meeks, "Breaking Away," p. 107.

27 Richard Bauckham, "The Parting of the Ways: What Happened and Why?" *Studia Theologica* 47 (1993): 142–146.

28 Ibid., p. 117. See also Paula Fredriksen, "What 'Parting of the Ways'? Jews, Gentiles, and the Ancient Mediterranean City," in Becker and Reed, *Ways That Never Parted*, p. 38.

29 G. N. Stanton, "Aspects of Early Christian-Jewish Polemic and Apologetic," *New Testament Studies* 31 (1985): 377.

30 See Israel Jacob Yuval, *Two Nations in Your Womb: Perceptions of Jews and Christians in Late Antiquity and the Middle Ages* (Berkeley: University of California Press, 2006).

31 Craig A. Evans, *From Jesus to the Church: The First Christian Generation* (Louisville, KY: Westminster/John Knox Press, 2014), p. 145.

32 On other social factors that contributed to the growth of the church, including the Gentile church, see Rodney Stark, *The Rise of Christianity: A Sociologist Reconsiders History* (Princeton, NJ: Princeton University Press, 1996).

33 Adolf von Harnack, *The Expansion of Christianity in the First Three Centuries*, trans. James Moffatt (London; New York: Williams & Norgate; G. P. Putnam's Sons, 1904); S. G. F. Brandon, *The Fall of Jerusalem and the Christian Church; A Study of the Effects of the Jewish Overthrow of* A.D. *70 on Christianity* (London: SPCK, 1951); Marcel Simon, *Verus Israel: A Study of the Relations between Christians and Jews in the Roman Empire, 135–425* (Oxford: Published for the Littman Library by Oxford University Press, 1986); Dunn, *Partings of the Ways*, pp. 230–253; S. G. Wilson, *Related Strangers: Jews and Christians, 70–170 C.E.* (Minneapolis, MN: Fortress Press, 1995).

34 Eusebius, *Ecclesiastical History* 3.5.3 (cf. LCL vol. 1, pp. 198–201).

35 Gerd Lüdemann, "The Successors of Pre-70 Christianity: A Critical Evaluation of the Pella Tradition," in *Jewish and Christian Self-Definition*, ed. E. P. Sanders (Philadelphia: Fortress Press, 1980), vol. 1, p. 172.

36 Josephus, *Jewish War* 2,18.6 §486 (LCL vol. 2, pp. 510–511).

37 Jonathan Bourgel, "The Jewish-Christians' Move from Jerusalem as a Pragmatic Choice," in *Studies in Rabbinic Judaism and Early Christianity*, ed. Dan Jaffe (Boston: Brill, 2010), p. 129. For Bourgel, however, the revolt and the flight to Pella were not a significant point in the relationship between Jews and Jewish-Christians (ibid., p. 135).

38 On the Cairo Geniza, see Adina Hoffman and Peter Cole, *Sacred Trash: The Lost and Found World of the Cairo Geniza* (New York: Schocken, 2011). The most detailed study of *Birkat Ha-Minim* is Ruth Langer, *Cursing the Christians? A History of the Birkat Haminim* (New York: Oxford University Press, 2011).

39 As quoted in Joel Marcus, "Birkat Ha-Minim Revisited," *New Testament Studies* 55 (2009): 524.

40 J. Louis Martyn, *History and Theology in the Fourth Gospel*, 3rd ed. (Louisville, KY: Westminster John Knox Press, 2003).

41 B. *Berakhot* 28b–29a.

42 See, for example, Marcus, "Birkat Ha-Minim Revisited," pp. 523–551.

43 Langer, *Cursing the Christians?*, p. 39. For an earlier study, see R. Kimelman, "Birkat Ha-Minim and the Lack of Evidence for an Anti-Christian Jewish Prayer in Late Antiquity," *in Sanders, Jewish and Christian Self-Definition*, vol. 2, pp. 226–244 and 291–403.

44 Steven T. Katz, "Issues in the Separation of Judaism and Christianity after 70 CE: A Reconsideration," *Journal of Biblical Literature* 103 (1984): 74.

45 For a critique of this theory, see Adele Reinhartz, "The Johannine Community and Its Jewish Neighbors: A Reappraisal," in *"What Is John?"* ed. Fernando F. Segovia (Atlanta, GA: Scholars Press, 1998), vol. 2, pp. 111–138.

46 Josephus, *Jewish War* 7.6.6 §218 (LCL vol. 3, pp. 566–567).

47 Marius Heemstra, *The Fiscus Judaicus and the Parting of the Ways* (Tübingen: Mohr Siebeck, 2010).

48 *Y. Ta'anit* 68b; Adele Reinhartz, "Rabbinic Perceptions of Simeon Bar Kosiba," *Journal for the Study of Judaism in the Persian, Hellenistic, and Roman Periods* 20 (1989): 172.

49 Justin Martyr, First *Apology* 31.6; cf. *The Ante-Nicene Fathers*, ed. Alexander Roberts and James Donaldson (Grand Rapids, MI: Wm. B. Eerdmans, 1951), vol. 1, p. 173.

50 Reinhartz, "Rabbinic Perceptions of Simeon Bar Kosiba," p. 175.

51 Lawrence H. Schiffman, "At the Crossroads: Tannaitic Perspectives on the Jewish-Christian Schism," in Sanders, *Jewish and Christian Self-Definition* (Philadelphia: Fortress Press, 1981), vol. 2, p. 155.

52 Boyarin, *Dying for God*, p. 17.

53 Lactantius, *Of the Manner in Which the Persecutors Died* §34, *Medieval Sourcebook* www.fordham.edu/halsall/source/edict-milan.asp; cf. *The Ante-Nicene Fathers*, vol. 7, p. 315.

54 Eusebius, *Ecclesiastical History* 10.5 §§1–14 (LCL vol. 2, pp. 444–453) and Lactantius, *Of the Manner in Which the Persecutors Died* §48 (*The Ante-Nicene Fathers*, vol. 7, p. 320). A translation of the text is available at www.fordham.edu/halsall/source/edict-milan.asp. On Constantine's conversion, see Michael Grant, *Constantine the Great: The Man and His Times* (New York: Scribner's; Maxwell Macmillan International, 1994).

55 A translation of the decree is available at www.fordham.edu/halsall/source/edict-milan.asp.

56 Eusebius, *Church History*, "Life of Constantine" 3.18; translation taken from *Nicene and Post-Nicene Fathers: A Select Library of the Christian Church*, 2nd ser., ed. Philip Schaff and Henry Wace (Peabody, MA: Hendrickson, 1999), vol. 1, p. 524.

57 See especially the essays in Becker and Reed, *Ways That Never Parted*.

PART II

Emerging Normativity

6

The Emergence of the Synagogue

STEVEN FINE

While in prison awaiting execution by the Gestapo in 1944, the great French-Jewish historian Marc Bloch penned his important *Apologie pour l'histoire, ou, métier d'historien,* published by his students after the war.[1] This central volume of modern historical reflection was translated in 1952 as *The Historian's Craft.* Of Bloch's many insights and approaches, one that has stayed with me throughout my career is his disdain for what he calls the "idol of origins."[2] By this he means that ideas and institutions are best understood not by the search for where they originated, but rather by their function within any given social setting. Nowhere is this more the case than with the synagogue, an institution that did not develop in a revolutionary manner, but slowly over centuries. Nevertheless, generations of scholars, beginning already during the eighteenth century, have focused on the "origins" of this institution. Some have placed them in the Babylonian captivity of 586 BCE, others in the biblical city gate, some in Ptolemaic Egypt, and others more generally in "the diaspora."[3] Truth said, none of these scholarly guesses is more valuable than any other or closer to the origins than the others. Each is a guess. They often tell us much more about the predilections of interpreters than the origins of the synagogue. These represent just the kinds of questions that Bloch warned against.

Yet the quest for origins, "idolatrous" or not, is one that has enticed Westerners for generations. The question is no less than "where do we come from and where are we going?" These are the kinds of existential questions that often stand behind the question of origins. With this awareness, this chapter aims to explore some of what we know about the emergence of the synagogue, focusing on two archaeological discoveries from Roman antiquity and broadly contextualizing these sites in terms of what we know about the synagogue sometime after it "originated."

We will focus on the synagogue of Theodotus in first-century Jerusalem and the Dura Europos synagogue in third-century Syria. Each of these early buildings raises questions regarding the "origins" of the synagogue, expressing broader trends in the history of the synagogue, of Judaism in the Roman world, and of Judaism's modern interpreters.

The Synagogue of Theodotus

In 1913–1914 a French-Jewish archaeologist, Raymond Weill, excavated a tract on the biblical City of David in Jerusalem, a plot that had been recently purchased with the help of Baron Édouard de Rothschild. In what were the first excavations of the Holy Land under Jewish auspices, Weill uncovered what he believed were the tombs of the kings of Judah. Alas, Weill was wrong, and he did not find the Davidic tombs. Digging deep into a cistern on the Jerusalem hillside, however, he found neatly stacked a large limestone block, carved with a fine Greek inscription. It read: "Theodotus, son of Vettenos the priest and synagogue leader [*archisynagogos*], son of a synagogue leader and grandson of a synagogue leader, built the synagogue for the reading of the Torah and studying of the commandments, and as a hostel with chambers and water installations to provide for the needs of itinerants from abroad, which his fathers, the elders, and Simonides founded."[4] Weill had uncovered the first and, to date, the most important evidence for the synagogue during the first century CE. Since that time, the Theodotus inscription has been the linchpin for all studies of the first-century synagogue—indisputable literary evidence that has not gone through the filters of later authors and copyists. When placed beside these sources—in the writings of Philo of Alexandria, Flavius Josephus, the New Testament, and the rabbis, not to mention considerable archaeological discoveries since—the Theodotus synagogue springs to life and may serve as a focal point for understanding the early history of this institution.[5]

The inscription, which is truly massive (41 by 75 centimeters), was likely colored in antiquity and not the stark tan limestone slab it is now. The donors present themselves in our inscription publicly before God and man as the benefactors of the synagogue (lit. "the [place of] assembly") as was customary for public gifts in the Roman world. Theodotus and his father were priests, at the very top of the religious hierarchy, who undoubtedly served in the Temple. Their names are typical of the array used by Greek-speaking Jews in this period. Theodotus, "he who is pious toward God," is parallel to the modern name Theodore ("gift of God") and the modern Hebrew name Doron, Greek for "gift." Many Jews used Greek and sometimes Latin names that did not include reference to pagan divinities—thus, for example, Stefanos (Steven, "garland"), Philo ("beloved"), Vettenos (a Greek-Latin name), and Alexandra (after Alexander the Great). Simonides, by contrast, is a Greek version of the Hebrew Shimon/Simon, like Judas for Judah the Maccabee (or Jesus for Yeshua, for that matter).

It was clearly important to Theodotus to distinguish himself as a "priest and a synagogue leader" in that order, beginning with his priestly lineage—which must have had especial significance in Jerusalem, where Theodotus could officiate in the Temple sacrifices. The term "synagogue leader"—whether the Greek *archisynagogos* of our inscription, the Hebrew *rosh ha-knesset*, or the Aramaic version of the Greek, *archon*—is well known from antiquity, but all evidence is later than our inscription. Theodotus's family had this role as synagogue patron for three generations, apparently beginning with Vettenos's father. Imagine, then, that the inscription was set in stone around 60 CE (more or less the last possible date before the start of the Jewish revolt in 66 CE). In that case, the family of Theodotus would have been synagogue leaders as early as the first century BCE. If the stone is fifty or more years earlier, certainly a possibility, their position would date deep into the first pre-Christian century. This suggests that the synagogue was a well-established "institution" with its own hierarchies by then. No wonder that the Jewish historian Flavius Josephus, the New Testament's Acts of the Apostles, and the rabbis could claim haughty antiquity for this relatively recent religious innovation, claiming that it originated with Moses himself.[6]

The synagogue of Theodotus must have been set within a rather large building, though little of that structure has survived. Remnants of ancient wall paintings decorated with flowers were discovered together with this artifact, as well as a carved stone decorated with rosettes and geometric patterns.[7] The Theodotus synagogue was apparently quite a colorful place.

Spaces for public assembly have been discovered across Jewish Palestine of the later Second Temple period, from the monumental buildings at Gamla in the Golan Heights and the recently discovered synagogue of Magdala on the Sea of Galilee to modern Qiryat Sefer and Modi'in in the Judean hill country, as well as a space transformed into a synagogue by the Zealots on Masada and perhaps Herodian in the midst of the Jewish War (66–74 CE).[8] What these buildings have in common is both a sense of internal intimacy and benches surrounding a central hall.

The Masada synagogue building provides the most information regarding the ways in which religious life was carried out prior to the destruction of the Temple in Palestinian synagogues. It was built on the western wall of Masada by the Zealots around 66 CE. The architecture of the rebels' meeting house reflects the centrality of the Holy Scripture and its public reading.[9] Benches with four tiers on three sides of the room direct attention toward the center of the hall, where scripture was most likely read. The interior measurements of the hall are 12.5 by 10.5 meters. On the fourth side, at the northwestern end of the building, a large protruding room (measuring 3.6 by 5.5 meters) was constructed within which biblical scrolls were buried while the synagogue was still in use. Fragments of Deuteronomy and Ezekiel were discovered in two pits excavated there.[10] Significantly, most ancient documents that were discovered on Masada—a veritable library that includes liturgical texts—were found covered with Roman projectiles, within meters of the synagogue.

At Magdala, a large rectangular stone with four small legs, which some have identified as a reading table (I am unconvinced), was found at the center of the synagogue hall. It is decorated with various figures, most prominent among them a seven-branched menorah, which connects the synagogue to the Temple and its iconography even before 70.[11] This, too, is relevant to the Theodotus inscription. Our synagogue is part of a group known from ancient sources that were organized around groups of Jews from abroad. The Tosefta, a third-century rabbinic collection, refers to a "synagogue of the Alexandrians," and the New Testament Acts of the Apostles to synagogues of "the Freedmen (as it was called) and of the Cyrenians and of the Alexandrians, and of those from Cilicia and Asia" (6:9). These undoubtedly served diaspora communities in Jerusalem, particularly visiting pilgrims. The "water installations," likely ritual baths (miqvaot), and lodging all point in this direction, as the purity of body and soul achieved through ritual immersion was a requirement for ascent to the Temple. The discovery of a *miqveh* next to the synagogue of Gamla points to broader concerns for ritual purity. The close proximity between Jerusalem synagogues and the Temple is imagined in a later rabbinic source, which describes the chock-filled day of a pilgrim during the fall festival of Sukkot, Tabernacles:

> Said Rabbi Joshua son of Hananiah:
>
> All the days of the celebration of the Water Drawing [a carnivalesque evening celebration in the Temple during the week of Sukkot] we never saw a moment of sleep. We would arise in time for the morning daily whole-offering [in the Temple].
>
> From there we would go to the synagogue,
>
> From there to the additional (*musaf*) offering [in the Temple],
>
> From there to eating and drinking,
>
> From there to the study house (*beit ha-midrash*),
>
> From there to the Temple for the whole sacrifice at dusk,
>
> From there to the celebration of the Water Drawing. (*Tosefta Sukkah* 4:4)

The Theodotus inscription provides a sense of the overriding significance of the public reading and interpretation of scripture within places of assembly. Paradoxically, the most complete description of the public reading and interpretation of scripture from antiquity appears in the Gospels, likely to explain Jewish ritual to an increasingly non-Jewish audience. Thus we read in Luke 4:14–26:

> And Jesus returned in the power of the Spirit into Galilee, and a report concerning him went out through all the surrounding country. And he taught in their synagogues, being glorified by all. And he came to Nazareth, where he had been brought up; and he went to the synagogue, as his custom was, on the Sabbath day. And he stood up to read; and there was given to him the book of the prophet Isaiah. He opened the book and found the place where it was written, "The Spirit of the Lord is upon me, because He has anointed me to preach good news to the poor. He has sent me to proclaim release to the captives and recovering of sight to the blind, to set at liberty those who are oppressed, to proclaim the acceptable year of the Lord." And he closed the book and gave it back to the attendant and sat down; and the eyes of all in the synagogue were fixed on him. And

he began to say to them, "Today this scripture has been fulfilled in your hearing." And all spoke well of him and wondered at the gracious words which proceeded out of his mouth.

It is noteworthy that our inscription does not mention any form of prayer. This seeming "lack," at least from the perspective of hindsight, has been the subject of considerable scholarship, which reflects as much about modern Jewish identity as about antiquity. Up until the 1980s it was generally assumed that this is just an omission and that some sort of prayer, probably loosely associated with that of the rabbis of the post-Temple period, took place in synagogues. This changed with the application of a basic principle to ancient Judaism associated previously with Protestant New Testament scholarship. According to this approach, later sources cannot be used to explain earlier situations. As a general rule, this is a good one—until we reach the case where later sources actually preserve nuggets of earlier knowledge or approach issues that are nascent earlier but can only be seen once they develop a bit. Thus, in 1987, during the heyday of this approach, Lee I. Levine, followed somewhat less starkly in 1989–1990 by Ezra Fleischer, argued, based upon this inscription together with a range of literary parallels, that prayer—meaning for Fleischer formal obligatory prayer the likes of the rabbinic *amidah*—was not an essential element of Second Temple synagogues.[12] If it is not mentioned, the logic goes, it was not there.[13] However, origins are generally nonrevolutionary and "quiet"; new phenomena do not often leave their mark on the historical record for some time. In 2005, Levine rightly moderated his position, noting the considerable evidence of Jewish prayer during this period—from the Dead Sea Scrolls, from Josephus, and even from the Gospels, arguing that prayer, while perhaps not central to the synagogue, might have existed in some form.

In Egypt, Jews assembled in meeting halls called *proseuchei* (prayer places), beginning during the third century BCE; this term is known mostly from Western diaspora contexts from the Roman period. During the first century, Philo of Alexandria brings together both the term *proseuche* and the study function of the synagogue. He writes, for example, that

the Jews every seventh day occupy themselves with their ancestral philosophy, dedicating that time to acquiring knowledge and the study of the truths of nature. For what are our prayer places throughout the cities but schools of prudence and bravery and control and justice, as well as of piety and holiness and virtue as a whole, by which one comes to recognize and perform what is due to men and God.[14]

My own sense is that prayer (though not that of the later rabbis) must certainly have been an element of synagogue life in the land of Israel—most everyone in the Roman world engaged in some sort of "cult" sometimes. Synagogues were the Jewish parallel of Greco-Roman "associations," societies of like-minded individuals, often based on place of origin, where various groups assembled in smaller groups for cultural, social, and, yes, religious reasons. Thus, Egyptians came together in Isis temples, Mithraites (followers of a Persian religion reformulated into a Roman one) in Mithra temples, and Jesus followers, who first assembled in private homes, soon established Christian assemblies. For Jews, the unique element of their associations was, as we have seen, scriptural reading and study.[15] The fact that prayer is not mentioned in the Theodotus inscription (or ancient sources referring to Palestinian synagogues) does not necessarily mean that it did not happen. It may just mean that since prayer—of any sort—was not uniquely Jewish, it was not, therefore, worthy of special mention. This might especially be the case for authors whose audience was generally not specifically Jewish, like Philo (to some degree), Josephus, and the New Testament, who needed to explain the unique element of synagogue life, not the obvious one.

The Theodotus inscription has served us as a window into the world of the earliest known synagogues in the land of Israel. In a text like this each word matters, and we have discussed most of the pertinent issues. While we cannot reach back to the "origins" of the synagogue through this artifact, we can clearly see the first flowering of the synagogue as a full-blown institution through it and the various other sources—literary and archaeological—that survive from this formative period.

The Dura Europos Synagogue

Few discoveries relating to the history of Judaism in late antiquity rival the synagogue of Dura Europos. Reflecting on his discovery of the Dura synagogue, the archaeologist Clark Hopkins reports,

We stood together in mute silence and complete astonishment. A casual passerby witnessing the paintings suddenly emerging from the earth would have been astonished. If he had been a Classical archaeologist, with the knowledge of how few paintings survived from Classical times, he would have been that much more amazed. But if he were a biblical scholar or a student of ancient art and were told that the building was a synagogue and the paintings were scenes from the Old Testament, he simply would not have believed it. It could not be; there was absolutely no precedent, nor could there be any. The stern injunction in the Ten Commandments against the making of graven images would be sufficient to prove him right. If, finally, this passerby had been in my shoes, the director of the excavations, responsible for the success of the expedition, and the one who would be credited most with its achievements, then the discovery of the Synagogue that day would be like a page from the Arabian Nights. Aladdin's lamp had been rubbed, and suddenly from the dry, bare desert had appeared paintings, not just one nor a panel nor a wall, but a whole building of scene after scene, all drawn from the Old Testament in a way never dreamed of before.[16]

Jewish communal associations thrived during the late Roman period, taking on ever more significance and even holiness. The early history of the synagogue in the late Roman period, sometimes called "late antiquity" or, in Israeli scholarship, "the period of the Mishnah and the Talmud," is nowhere better expressed than in Dura Europos.[17] Called Europos in Greek and Dura in Persian, it was a small city on the trade route between Rome and Persia, a border city set on the bluffs on the western shore of the Euphrates River. There, distant from the civic center and located near the western city walls, no fewer than three associations procured housing units and converted them into meeting houses: the Mithraites, the Christians, and the Jews.[18] The synagogue, discovered in 1932, was the largest and the most grand of these. In fact, the Dura synagogue is the most beautiful ancient synagogue yet discovered anywhere. Sometime during the later second century, the Jewish community of this border city acquired a house and refurbished it as their synagogue, beginning a process of decoration and embellishment that reached its peak in 244/245 CE, when all of the walls were covered with paintings representing episodes from biblical history. The Dura Europos synagogue together with the entire city was destroyed and thus preserved around 256 CE during one of the periodic border wars between Rome and Persia. Because it was near the city wall, the Roman defenders filled the prayer hall with dirt to buttress the walls. Any part of the building that was filled was preserved, to be discovered by a team of French and American archaeologists; any part that was not is lost. About 60 percent of the walls were preserved. It is now safely—we hope—at the National Museum in Damascus, though there is a half-scale model at the Museum of the Jewish People in Tel Aviv and smaller models at Yeshiva University Museum and the Jewish Museum in New York.

The discovery of the paintings of the Dura Europos synagogue was a landmark in the history of both art and Jewish studies—something that the site archaeologist intuited would be the case and expressed in the quote above. In fact, the discovery of this small sacred space changed the way that scholars looked at the art of Judaism forever. In a single stroke the Dura frescos upended the long-standing prejudice whereby Jews are a "nation without art," blinded by a rigorous interpretation of biblical law and thus having little visual capacity and perhaps even genetic color-blindness. For a broad swath of Europeans and Americans, Jews were racially lacking of visual acumen, a charge that Jews as individuals and as a community labored to overcome through much of the nineteenth and twentieth centuries. Though Jews denied the racial elements of this characterization, many Westernizing Jews (liberalizers and traditionalists, "Reformers" and "Orthodox"), eager to stress their well-known literary acumen over perceived artistic deficiencies, embraced this characterization of Judaism as a religion that is not skilled in "art." The implications for Jewish nationalism were enormous. In order to be a "nation" in the sense of nineteenth-century European nationalism, whether a diaspora nation or the landed nation of Zionism, Jews needed to show a well-developed national art like all other "nations." Jewish culturalists, particularly in the Austro-Hungarian Empire and then under the Zionist flag, embraced the notion of "Jewish art" and went on the offensive against notions of Jewish artlessness, expressed in a proliferation of monumental synagogue construction and Jewish museums, and especially the Bezalel National Academy of Art in Jerusalem (now part of the Israel Museum).[19] These prejudices, which tell us far more about the mainly Protestant originators of the myth and modernist Jewish and

Christian identities than about premodern Jews, were only finally tackled and disproved by historical scholarship in the last fifteen or so years by Kalman Bland, Margaret Olin, and myself.[20]

The first scholars to focus on the content of the Dura Europos synagogue paintings, most prominently E. L. Sukenik in his exhaustive study of the synagogue and its paintings, and Carl H. Kraeling in his preliminary and final reports of the synagogue, asserted a close relationship between the iconography of the Dura synagogue and Jewish lore as preserved in rabbinic literature, showing numerous parallels between them.[21] The American Joseph Gutmann went so far as to write an article in 1983 titled "The Illustrated Midrash in the Dura Europos Synagogue Paintings: A New Dimension for the Study of Judaism," and rightly so.[22] Yet some scholars, particularly during the second half of the twentieth century, built on the Protestant conception of the "artless Jew"; the presence of images at Dura was thus proof of the "nonrabbinic nature" of this community.[23] Good rabbis, they argued, did not tolerate such art—a supposed violation of biblical law—so it must be the product of "nonrabbinic Jews." In other words, the myth of the "nation without art" was now seen to be untrue. Not to abandon a perfectly good (if incorrect) paradigm without a fight, though, this modern misnomer was limited to rabbis exclusively. Thus, the presence of art was taken as a marker of a form of Judaism that was different from that of the rabbis. For the small number of Jewish culturalists who knew the history of Jewish manuscript illumination, ceremonial art, beautifully painted synagogues in Eastern Europe, and the nimbleness of Jewish law, however, the assumption that the presence of art is a marker of nonrabbinic attitudes was at best a skewed image of Judaism. While in western Europe and in much of Lithuanian rabbinic culture, not to mention Islamicate Jewry, such painting was anathema, in a broad swath ranging from Bavaria through Ukraine and Poland it was rather common. They, and for that matter I, read the imagery of the Dura synagogue within this tradition, which talmudic rabbis grappled with and some, like later rabbis, disliked vehemently (and all rejected when clear idolatry was suspected), but most made their peace with.[24] The Dura Europos synagogue opened a new chapter, then, in the interpretation of the synagogue, of Jewish art, and of the rabbis, serving as a kind of touchstone for twentieth-century constructions of the late antique Jewish past.

According to my understanding of the sources, Dura does indeed reflect Judaism beyond the rabbis, but my nuance is somewhat different and less stark. The rabbis were, after all, a relatively small group, though they seem to have had many acolytes beyond their immediate circles, people who considered them to be "holy men."[25] They were the literate scholars within Jewish culture, the only Jewish scholastics that we know of from late antiquity. Parallels between rabbinic conceptions and those expressed in the remains of a local synagogue suggest that rabbis and the general population shared a broad Judaism that the rabbis, being intellectuals, discussed, argued about, and eventually wrote up. Parallels do not mean that rabbis were politically influential within any particular setting, only that the Jews of that place, in this case Dura Europos, were part of a larger culture that the rabbis also inhabited. If a rabbi were to pass through Dura (which may well have happened, because Dura was on the route between Palestine and the Jewish centers of Babylonia), I would imagine that this synagogue would be thoroughly familiar, though, being a member of an elite, he would likely hold his own pretensions in relation to the local community.

The Dura Europos synagogue was equally important for the history of Christian art, as art historians, particularly Princeton University's Kurt Weitzmann and his students, interpreted the synagogue paintings as evidence of a tradition of Jewish manuscript illumination that was the source of early Christian art.[26] For this reason, the Dura synagogue appears in every survey of Christian art and has achieved iconic status. Weitzmann went further, interpreting Dura during the third century as a kind of happy, multicultural city, where religious communities met and somehow got along. Weitzmann projected postwar America into antiquity in response to his own wartime experiences. He traced his interest in relationships between Jewish and Christian art to a seminar on Dura taught by the venerable Berlin art historian Hans Lietzmann in 1933–1934, soon after Hitler came to power. This theme was apparently chosen by Lietzmann as an act of resistance against Nazism. As a student of the Jewish art historian Adolph Goldschmidt, Weitzmann found himself unemployable in Germany without a course of Nazification. He therefore left for Princeton, where he developed his prewar interests and continued to imagine—and project—a Weimar-like multicultural Dura Europos. This message fit well with the work of Salo W. Baron of Columbia University and his cadre of students, who sought to discover a similarly happy history of the Jews, one different from the "lachrymose" and rabbi-centered history imagined by his predecessors. This was to be a new "usable history," one that Americanizing Jews could embrace. The Dura Europos synagogue as interpreted by Weitzmann fit well with the needs of this group. Thus, it has carried quite a heavy burden for a small provincial synagogue building, even as the interpretations of this structure have tended to stress meta-theories and to play down the more mundane "religious" significance of the synagogue and its decoration.

My interest, unlike many other recent interpreters, is not related to power relationships. My concern is more anthropological and less global, focusing on the ways in which the synagogue expresses the liturgical life of the community that built and lived out its communal life there. The study of buildings as "sets" for liturgical performance is relatively new. Historically, buildings have been studied for their iconography, their style, and what they can tell us about temporal power, but seldom as religious spaces. This approach changed largely in response to the Second Vatican Council of the early 1960s and its call to reform Catholic liturgy and thus liturgical spaces. As Catholic scholars reassessed their own church architecture, historians looked back on historic spaces to understand how they "worked" in the liturgical lives of their communities. Most prominent among these was the art historian Thomas Matthews.[27] This approach was first imported to Jewish studies by Lawrence Hoffman of Hebrew Union College, though it was beginning to appear as early as the first generation of Dura interpreters.[28] As my teacher Stephen S. Kayser wrote as early as 1953, "The pictures were an integral part of the house of worship, related to the order of prayer or readings and perhaps used as 'illustrative' material for sermons," an approach given sinews in terms of Dura by Annabel Wharton.[29] How was the interior of the Dura synagogue formed as a site for religion, as a "set" upon which Judaism was performed? In what follows, I will suggest just a few examples of how this "set" operated.

The First Phase, before 244/245 CE

Sometime during the second century the Jews of Dura renovated their "house synagogue," created a large meeting hall (13.65 by 7.68 meters) on its western side, and decorated its interior. To reach this room, one needed to traverse a series of small rooms and a large courtyard. We have no idea what went on in these rooms. A large meeting hall was constructed, its walls lined with benches as in Second Temple–period Palestinian synagogues. They also built a large Torah shrine on the western wall of the synagogue. We cannot know if this wall was used as a matter of convenience, since it is opposite the entrance, or whether this is the first sure attempt to align the synagogue with Jerusalem, a notion that appears in the literature of the rabbis dating to around the same time. The façade of this large shrine includes the earliest known biblical imagery in synagogue art—all reflecting connection to the Temple. This panel is decorated with images of the Jerusalem Temple that is much like the image of a building whose façade is supported by four columns (a tetrapylon) that appears on the coins of Bar Kokhba (132–135 CE). The Temple is flanked by a menorah and lulav to its left and the binding of Isaac (Genesis 22), which 2 Chronicles 3:1 associated with the Temple Mount, to the right. In this latter image Abraham holds a large knife, a *ma'akhelet* (which the rabbis describe as "a knife that eats much flesh"). The hand of the God of Israel is shown reaching down to stop the killing. This portrayal of God is no metaphor. Jews in antiquity, before the rationalist impulse set in in the Islamic world, believed that God had a body. God's hand is a well-known theme in the second phase of the synagogue, but that is getting ahead of ourselves. Nonetheless, the presence of even this much figurative art is surprising and new, since we see no such imagery in Second Temple–period Jewish contexts. It is completely "normal" for Dura, however, where all of the religious spaces are lavishly painted with murals. Clearly, by this time, Jews had gotten used to this kind of flat image and adopted it rather than rejecting it as a form of religious expression, communication, and propaganda. Similar use of images is seen in Israel a century later, but only on floors—likely because no walls survive![30]

The Torah shrine of the synagogue bears two Aramaic inscriptions in a typical "Jewish" script, the language and script used by Jews both in Babylonia to the east across the Euphrates and in the land of Israel to the west. The most important of these reads, "I, Uzi, made the house of the ark" (*beit arona*). The designation of the Torah shrine as "the house of the ark" is significant. By calling it an "ark," the donor is associating this shrine with the biblical ark of the covenant, which stood in Solomon's Temple. Further, the conch-shaped tympanum of the shrine is mimicked in a similar conch in the image of the Temple, creating a visual association between the synagogue "ark" and the façade of the Temple. All of this Temple imagery strengthens the notion that the alignment of the synagogue with Jerusalem is intentional, connecting the local assembly with the lost, yet eternally significant shrine, which had been destroyed in 70 CE.

At about the same time that the Jews of Dura made this association, the connection between the synagogue shrine and the biblical ark was made explicit by another group of Jews, the rabbis in Palestine and Babylonia, whom we refer to as Amoraim. These rabbis made this association based upon ideas that were nascent in earlier rabbinic (Tannaitic) sources, reflecting rabbinic thought mostly during the second century. Thus, far from the rabbinic centers in Eretz Israel and in Sasanian Babylonia, though on the trade route between Persia and Palestine, a small Jewish community imagined its local Torah shrine as a *beit arona*, a "house of the ark" and by implication associated their local synagogue with the now-lost Temple of Jerusalem. We have come a long way from the Theodotus synagogue, as the unique furnishings suitable to house the Torah were now developed and given meaning derived from the Temple, a phenomenon occurring simultaneously in rabbinic literature, where the synagogue was increasingly conceived as a "small temple" (*miqdash me'at*), a dwelling place for the divine presence.[31]

The Second Phase of the Synagogue, 244/245–Ca. 256 CE

During the second phase of the Dura Europos synagogue, all of the walls were covered with paintings showing the sacred history of biblical Israel, the Torah shrine serving as a kind of keystone to the entire environment. The frescoes, in brilliant colors, depict biblical stories as read through the lenses of Jewish folk tradition. Imagery includes the discovery of Moses by the daughter of Pharaoh, the crossing of the Red Sea, the tribes of Israel encamped around the tabernacle, Elijah on Mt. Carmel, the ark of the covenant in the land of the Philistines, Ezekiel's vision of the dry bones, and Esther before King Ahasuerus. They are arranged in three registers on all four walls, the various sizes of each panel creating a sense

Figure 6.1. Tabernacle panel, Dura Europos synagogue, Syria, 244/245 CE. Photograph by Fred Anderegg, after E. R. Goodenough, *Jewish Symbols in the Greco-Roman Period* (New York: Pantheon, 1964), vol. 11, p. 11, pl. XIV.

of movement that to a modern eye looks like a comic strip. The presence of Greek and Aramaic inscriptions as well as Persian graffiti directly on the panels makes it hard to know whether to "read" the walls from left to right or right to left, and some of the images can be read either way. This, too, creates a sense of centering, as the entire composition portrays both stability and movement, but no particular directionality. The palette of colors is consistent across the images and the other decorative panels of the synagogue, further imposing unity. The ceiling itself was brightly colored with mostly store-bought standard tiles, with images ranging from human faces to the evil eye, with some inscribed dedicatory tiles in Aramaic and Greek that give voice to Jews with biblical, Greek, and even Persian names, a priest named Samuel who was the *archon* ("leader," the same term we saw in Jerusalem), a Persian convert known in an Aramaic inscription as Arshakh and in a Greek inscription as Arcases, and many other men (no women) who were fundamental to the synagogue project. In the floor are notches, probably for large lamp stands that supported oil lamps—thus, the entire room, much darker than we would tolerate in a world after Edison, would have been both brightly colored but more dark than we see now, with uneven flickering lights giving a sense of movement to each composition and to the entire menagerie of biblical characters, Torah shrines, and even broken idols on the walls and animals and mythological creatures decorating the walls and ceilings.

The prominence of the Torah shrine carried over into the synagogue renovation. The ark of the covenant, formed as a Torah shrine, appears three times in the middle register. Thus, in an image to the left of the shrine, we see the tabernacle, with Aaron the priest standing to the right of the shrine. Above Aaron's head is a Greek inscription (a second language within this synagogue), identifying this biblical priest. The Torah shrine is prominent, and within its rounded gable, just as on the synagogue ark, is an image of a menorah. The ark is also shown vanquishing the Temple of Dagon in Ashdod on the north wall and the defeat of the Israelites at Eben-Ezer. The image of the ark of the covenant before the Temple of Dagon in Ashdod is especially evocative.[32] In 1 Samuel 2–4, we read,

> the Philistines took the ark of God and brought it into the house of Dagon and set it up beside Dagon. And when the people of Ashdod rose early the next day, behold, Dagon had fallen face downward on the ground before the ark of the Lord. So they took Dagon and put him back in his place. But when they rose early on the next morning, behold, Dagon had fallen face downward on the ground before the ark of the LORD, and the head of Dagon and both his hands were lying cut off upon the threshold; only the trunk of Dagon was left to him.

In illustrating this scene, the artists included numerous images of Dagon's broken body parts and cult utensils. Dagon is portrayed as none other than a Palmyrene god—a divinity of the sort worshipped in nearby temples. The artists went out of their way to illustrate the triumph of the ark over the very gods that were worshiped by their neighbors. This and other images of God's power are thus set within a very local context. Here the ark and, by implication, the Torah ark as well is in the end triumphant.

The paintings at the center of the western wall were arrayed to highlight the centrality of the Torah shrine. They show just how much thought went into the process, as they were redone so many times that we cannot be sure what was originally painted there. Two rectangular panels containing portraits of standing men, one above the other, were placed on either side of a central panel above the ark, a symmetry that is unknown elsewhere in the synagogue. Each faces frontally, "looking" outward from his panel. Above and to the right of the Torah shrine is the image of a man holding a biblical scroll, emphasizing the significance of scripture within the synagogue. It is my sense that the man holding the scroll is Moses himself, though scholars have posited every possible identification—any biblical character who at any time carried a scroll. Moses is the most prominent character in the synagogue images. In the lower tier to the right of the ark is his discovery by the daughter of Pharaoh in the river. Incidentally, the frontal nudity of the daughter of Pharaoh has struck some as deeply unrabbinic (whatever that means), though I hasten to note that nudity, whether the daughter of Pharaoh in Spanish Passover haggadahs or the "fountain of youth" in an Ashkenazi one, is not uncommon in medieval Hebrew manuscripts produced within "rabbinic" cultures and reproducing rabbinic texts. In one delightful image, a beautiful blond woman dips in the *miqveh* as her husband awaits in bed. I have collected nearly a hundred nude women in Jewish art from antiquity through the eighteenth century and am not really surprised by the presence of Pharaoh's daughter in all her glory at Dura, though I point out that, although nude males appear in later synagogue mosaics, never does such blatant female nudity appear in synagogue contexts. Nudity, including nude slaves wandering about, was a constant on the Roman street. For comparison, I remind you that the presence of nude figures in public spaces was "normal" in the 1920s world of art deco: witness the friezes of Rockefeller Center (something that would never be considered today) or the zodiac floor with Virgo in all her glory on the historic 1928 Yeshiva University campus.

In the upper tier, also to the right of the Torah shrine, is a large panel showing Moses and the children of Israel crossing the Red Sea, chased by the Egyptian army, which, in the sequence of this panel, is shown drowning. Moses appears three times, as in a modern comic strip, first leading the "armies of Israel," then crossing the sea, and finally closing the sea on the defeated pursuers. In case the identity of Moses is unclear (as it is in the scroll panel), the artisans added inscriptions in Aramaic to identify the main protagonist three times. One of these reads, "Moses when he went out of Egypt and split the sea."[33] This language is very close to the known Aramaic paraphrases of the Torah.[34] Hovering above the entire scene are the arms of the Divine, referencing such verses as Exodus 15:6 ("Your right hand, O LORD, is glorious in power") and 5:12 ("You did stretch Your right hand, the earth swallowed them").

There is no overarching global theme to the paintings. One might imagine a preacher within the synagogue turning to the images and using them to homiletic effect according to the content of his homily and the assembled community, focusing upon different images according to their interests, concerns, and visual facility. The use of synagogue decorations as "props" by homilists is known from rabbinic sources, as is a similar process within somewhat later church contexts.[35] There was no one exclusive meaning for each image, but rather a range of interconnected interpretations as possibilities.[36] The preacher likely interpreted the images differently depending on the lesson he was teaching, the audience, the liturgical calendar, and the particular text that he was explicating. The vast quantity of images at Dura certainly facilitated a wide variety of possibilities. Depending upon the context, a homilist could choose one or another. This approach fits well with the rabbinic midrashic approach to scripture itself.

Astonishingly, we have some idea what the Jews of Dura, and perhaps others, were "thinking" when they looked upon these paintings. Graffiti was scrawled on many of the images in the lowest registers. Thus, an illustration of a prophet reviving a dead child, likely Elijah reviving the son of the widow of Zarephath as described in 1 Kings 17, is accompanied by the Aramaic label "Elijah." A Persian inscription was painted over Elijah's foot: "When Hormezd the scribe came and he looked at this [picture]: 'Living the child (who has been) dead.'"[37] Another inscription reads: "The month [Ardwahist?], day Hormezd [the name of the day], When Ardaw the scribe came and he looked at this picture and he looked at the child (?): 'Living the dead (be)come.'"[38] Similarly, on images of Ezekiel's vision of the valley of dry bones (Ezekiel 37), a prophecy that took place in Babylonia and appears on the northern wall of the synagogue, someone wrote: "This make known: Be joyous and hear the gods' voice. Then well-being [or, peace] will be upon us."[39]

The Dura synagogue served as a setting not only for study and exegesis, but also for liturgical prayer in the more specific sense of the word.

Some characters are shown in prayer positions, either with hands raised or, in the Babylonian mode, folded at the waist, and a prayer text in Hebrew was discovered in the street next to the synagogue. This is the earliest Jewish prayer text known from the post-Temple period.[40] The fragments read as follows:

Fragment "A":

Blessed is X king of the world/eternity	ברוך X מלך העלם	1.
apportioned food, provided sustenance	חלק מזון התקין מ[חיה]	2.
sons of flesh cattle to...	בני בשר בהמה ל...	3.
created man to eat of...	יצר אדם לאכול מ...	4.
many bodies of...	גויות רבאות ממ...	5.
to bless all cattle	לברך כלם בהמות	6.
	...מ..ה.ה...	7.
...provides...	ל... תקן	8.
	ל...ק	9.

Fragment "B":

for	כי	1.
pure (animals) to (eat?)	[ט]הרות לא[כל]	2.
provides sustenance	מכלכל	3.
small and large	קטנות עם גדו[לות]	4.
all the animals of the field...	כל חית השדה	5.
...feed their young	...ל מאכל טפם...	6.
and sing and bless	ושיר וברך	7.

Even in its fragmentary state, this document provides ample evidence for the liturgical life of Jews at Dura. It is written in Hebrew and is the only evidence for the use of this language at Dura Europos. Hebrew is thus the fourth language to appear in this small community, reflecting the multilingual nature of this synagogue on the cusp of the Persian and Roman empires. The parchment is rich in phraseology that closely parallels that in classical rabbinic literature and among the many variant prayer forms discovered in the Cairo Geniza. The text with which the prayer opens, "Blessed is X king of the world/eternity . . . ," directly parallels the rabbinic introductory blessing formula, "Blessed are You, LORD our God, king of the world/eternity." This formula first appears in rabbinic literature during the mid-third century, but not in biblical or Second Temple–period sources.[41] The text has been associated with versions of the grace after meals (*Birkat Ha-Mazon*) that are preserved in the Geniza. The Jews of Dura not only maintained traditions that closely parallel those of the rabbis, but also some prayed using texts that parallel rabbinic sources.

Conclusion

We have explored two important discoveries in the history of the early synagogue that exemplify the ways that this institution developed from the later Second Temple period until the third century. The focus on scripture that was essential to Second Temple–period synagogues was concretized at Dura in the construction of a Torah shrine, called an "ark" after the ark of the covenant. Scripture, as read through the prism of Jewish tradition, was so significant to this community that they projected it on the walls of their synagogue, interacting with the imagery through comments written on it in Aramaic, Greek, and Persian. Were it not for the small scraps of parchment found near the synagogue, we would not know that at least some Jews in Dura prayed in Hebrew.

The very small amount of evidence that exists for the Roman world requires real circumspection in its interpretation, especially in any search for "origins." We just know so little. Still, there is much that can be said. The Dura synagogue "looks" like a synagogue, the sort that would continue to develop through antiquity and into later periods, each age adding its own wrinkles and ways of creating communal space. Here at Dura, however, we have the first synagogue we are aware of that a member of a "modern" congregation might clearly recognize without the intervention of academic interpretation. It is a synagogue that the ancient rabbis would have "recognized" as such as well, thus expressing the broad culture of Judaism that this group of intellectuals and more common folks shared—at least sometimes.

This discussion has dipped into the waters of modern scholarship, where academics of varying perspectives bring their own experiences to bear in filling the spaces between the scraps of knowledge that survive and our own desire to understand. From the destruction of the Theodotus synagogue, likely in 70 CE with the rest of Jerusalem, to the destruction of Dura around 256 CE, something like 186 years had passed. During this time, the "origins" of the synagogue had matured into the beginnings of the institution we know today, a place of assembly, a synagogue, a *beit knesset*.

NOTES

1 Marc Bloch, *Apologie pour l'histoire, ou, métier d'historien* (Paris: Armand Colin, 1949).

2 Marc Bloch, *The Historian's Craft*, trans. P. Putnam (New York: Knopf, 1953), p. 29.

3 See Lee I. Levine, *The Ancient Synagogue: The First Thousand Years* (New Haven, CT: Yale University Press, 2000), pp. 19–40. I made this point more tentatively in "From Meeting House to Sacred Realm: Holiness and the Ancient Synagogue," in *Sacred Realm: The Emergence of the Synagogue in the Ancient World*, ed. S. Fine (New York: Oxford University Press and Yeshiva University Museum, 1996), p. 21.

4 My translation generally follows Jonathan J. Price, "Synagogue Building Inscription of Theodotus in Greek, 1 c. BCE–1 c. CE," in *Corpus Inscriptionum Judaea/Palaestinae*, ed. H. M. Cotton et al., volume 1: Jerusalem, part 1, 1–107 (Berlin: De Gruyter, 2010), no. 9, pp. 53–56. The original publication of this artifact is still of considerable significance. See Raymond Weill, *La cité de David* (Paris: P. Geuthner, 1920), vol. 1, pp. 184–190, translated as *The City of David: Revisiting Early Excavations; English Translations of Reports by Raymond Weill and L.-H. Vincent*, ed. R. Reich and H. Shanks (Washington, DC: Biblical Archaeology Society, 2004), pp. 84–89.

5 The evidence for first-century synagogues is surveyed conveniently in Levine, *Ancient Synagogue*, pp. 42–159, where the relevant bibliography is cited.

6 *C. Apion*, 2.175; Acts 15.21; *y. Megillah* 4.1, 75a.

7 Weill, *La cité de David*, 184 (English translation, p. 84).

8 Detailed in Levine, *Ancient Synagogue*. On Migdal, see R. Steven Notley, "Genesis Rabbah 98, 17: 'and Why Is It Called Gennosar?' Recent Discoveries at Magdala and Jewish Life on the Plain of Gennosar in the Early Roman Period," in *Talmuda de-Eretz Israel: Archaeology and the Rabbis in Late Antique Palestine*, ed. S. Fine and A. Koller (Berlin: De Gruyters, 2014), pp. 141–158.

9 See the final report of this excavation: E. Netzer, *Masada III, The Yigael Yadin Excavations 1963–1965, Final Reports, the Buildings: Stratigraphy and Architecture* (Jerusalem: Israel Exploration Society, 1991), pp. 402–413.

10 Ibid., p. 410.

11 See my "From Synagogue Furnishing to Media Event: The Magdala Ashlar," *Ars Judaica* 13 (2017): 27–38.

12 L. Levine, "The Second Temple Synagogue: The Formative Years," in *The Synagogue in Late Antiquity*, ed. L. I. Levine (Philadelphia: American Schools for Oriental Research, 1987), pp. 7–31. Levine's position is nuanced in his *Ancient Synagogue*, pp. 151–159; Ezra Fleischer, "On the Beginnings of Obligatory Jewish Prayer," *Tarbiz* 59 (1989–1990): 397–441 (Hebrew). See Ruth Langer, "Revisiting Early Rabbinic Liturgy: The Recent Contributions of Ezra Fleischer," *Prooftexts* 19 (1999): 179–194; Ezra Fleischer, "On the Origins of the 'Amidah: Response to Ruth Langer," *Prooftexts* 20 (2000): 381–384; Ruth Langer, "Considerations of Method: A Response to Ezra Fleischer," *Prooftexts* 20 (2000): 384–387.

13 Steven Fine, *Art, History, and the Historiography of Judaism in Roman Antiquity* (Leiden: Brill, 2013), pp. 7–16.

14 *The Life of Moses* 2, line 216; my translation follows E. R. Goodenough, *Jewish Symbols in the Greco-Roman Period* (New York: Pantheon, 1954), vol. 2, p. 88. See also Philo's *Embassy to Gaius*, line 132.

15 See L. Michael White, *Building God's House in the Roman World* (Baltimore, MD: Johns Hopkins University Press, 1990); Philip A. Harland, *Associations, Synagogues and Congregations: Claiming a Place in Ancient Mediterranean Society* (Minneapolis, MN: Fortress Press, 2003).

16 Clark Hopkins, *The Discovery of Dura Europos*, ed. B. Goldman (New Haven, CT: Yale University Press, 1979), p. 131.

17 The final report on the Dura synagogue was prepared by C. H. Kraeling, *The Synagogue*, with contributions by C. C. Torrey, C. B. Welles, and B. Geiger (New Haven, CT: Yale University Press, 1956). See my discussions of this synagogue in *Art and Judaism in the Greco-Roman World: Toward a New Jewish Archaeology*, rev. ed. (Cambridge: Cambridge University Press, 2010), pp. 101–122, 106, 131–132, and 174–185.

18 On the relationships between the various religious buildings at Dura, see M. H. Gates, "Dura-Europos: A Fortress of Syro-Mesopotamian Art," *Biblical Archaeologist* 47 (1984): 166–181.

19 Fine, *Art, History*, pp. 12–34 and the bibliography there.

20 Kalman Bland, *The Artless Jew: Medieval and Modern Affirmations and Denials of the Visual* (Princeton, NJ: Princeton University Press, 2000); Margaret Olin, *The Nation without Art: Examining Modern Discourses on Jewish Art* (Omaha: University of Nebraska Press, 2002), pp. 127–156; and Fine, *Art, History*, pp. 5–59, 131–132, and 174–185.

21 E. L. Sukenik, *The Synagogue of Dura-Europos and Its Frescoes* (Jerusalem: Mosad Bialik, 1947), in Hebrew.

22 *Proceedings of the American Academy for Jewish Research* 50 (1983): 91–104.

23 E. R. Goodenough, *Jewish Symbols in the Greco Roman Period*, 13 vols. (New York: Pantheon, 1953–1967). The review literature on Goodenough's work is vast and representative of the various approaches to ancient Judaism from midcentury through the 1980s. Perhaps the most insightful of these is Morton Smith, "Goodenough's *Jewish Symbols* in Retrospect," *Journal of Biblical Literature* 86 (1967): 53–68. For Smith's own approach to Dura and related material, see most conveniently "Morton Smith on the Dura Europos Synagogue," in "*Symposium on the Dura-Europos Synagogue Paintings, in Tribute to Dr. Rachel Wischnitzer*, November 6, 1968: The Contributions of Morton Smith and Meyer Schapiro," ed. Steven Fine in *Images: A Journal of Jewish Art and Visual Culture* 3 (2010): 129–134. On both of these scholars, see Fine, *Art, History*, pp. 35–46.

24 See, for example, E. L. Sukenik, *Ancient Synagogues in Palestine and Greece* (London: Oxford University Press, 1934), pp. 63–64n1, and the responsa translated by Vivian B. Mann, *Jewish Texts on the Visual Arts* (Cambridge: Cambridge

University Press, 2000). A focus on rabbinic literature referring to issues of idolatry skews the question of art toward this issue; see Fine, *Art, History, pp.* 97–121. Similarly, use of responsa literature to determine Jewish attitudes provides a skewed image of actual practice, not general practice, because it represents only those troubled enough—usually by issues of idolatry—both to ask questions and to answer them.

25 On the rabbis in late antique Palestine, see Lee I. Levine, *The Rabbinic Class of Roman Palestine in Late Antiquity* (Jerusalem: Yad Izhak Ben-Zvi; New York: Jewish Theological Seminary of America, 1989); Catherine Hezser, *The Social Structure of the Rabbinic Movement in Roman Palestine* (Tübingen: Mohr Siebeck, 1997); Alexei Sivertsev, *Private Households and Public Politics in 3rd–5th Century Jewish Palestine* (Tübingen: Mohr Siebeck, 2002). For Sasanian Babylonia, Isaiah Gafni, *The Jews of Babylonia in the Talmudic Era* (Jerusalem: Shazar Institute, 1990), pp. 137–148 (Hebrew); Isaiah Gafni, "Babylonian Rabbinic Culture," in *Cultures of the Jews: A New History,* ed. D. Biale (New York: Schocken, 2002), pp. 225–265; Yaakov Elman, "Middle Persian Culture and Babylonian Sages: Accommodation and Resistance in the Shaping of Rabbinic Legal Tradition," in *The Cambridge Companion to the Talmud and Rabbinic Literature,* ed. C. E. Fonrobert and M. S. Jaffee (Cambridge: Cambridge University Press, 2007), pp. 165–197. On the "holy man" in late antiquity, see Peter L. Brown, *The Cult of the Saints* (Chicago: University of Chicago Press, 1981); Peter L. Brown, *Society and the Holy in Late Antiquity* (Berkeley: University of California Press, 1982), pp. 103–152.

26 K. Weitzmann, *Sailing with Byzantium from Europe to America: The Memoirs of an Art Historian* (Munich: Editio Maris, 1994), pp. 345, 397, 437, 442, and 474; K. Weitzmann, "The Illustration of the Septuagint" and "The Question of the Influence of Jewish Pictorial Sources on Old Testament Illustration," both of which appear in *No Graven Images: Studies in Art and the Hebrew Bible,* ed. J. Gutmann (New York: Ktav, 1971), pp. 201–231 and 309–328. See also Olin, *The Nation without Art,* pp. 127–154; Fine, *Art, History,* pp. 201–206.

27 T. F. Mathews, *The Early Churches of Constantinople: Architecture and Liturgy* (University Park: Pennsylvania State University Press, 1971); P. Brown, "Art and Society in Late Antiquity," in *The Age of Spirituality: A Symposium,* ed. K. Weitzmann (New York: Metropolitan Museum of Art, 1980). For a survey of scholarly approaches to this issue, see S. De Blaauw, "Architecture and Liturgy in Late Antiquity and the Middle Ages: Traditions and Trends in Modern Scholarship," *Archiv für Liturgie-Wissenschaft* 33 (1991): 1–34.

28 Lawrence A. Hoffman moved in this direction in his *Beyond the Text: A Holistic Approach to Liturgy* (Bloomington: University of Indiana Press, 1989), pp. 16–17.

29 S. S. Kayser, "Defining Jewish Art," in *Mordecai M. Kaplan Jubilee Volume* (New York: Jewish Theological Seminary of America, 1953), pp. 457–467; Annabel Wharton, *Refiguring the Post Classical City: Dura Europos, Jerash, Jerusalem, and Ravenna* (Cambridge: Cambridge University Press, 1995), pp. 15–23.

30 Fine, *Art, History,* pp. 121–124.

31 E.g., *b. Megillah* 29a. On this development, see S. Fine, *This Holy Place: On the Sanctity of the Synagogue during the Greco-Roman Period* (Notre Dame, IN: Notre Dame University Press, 1997).

32 Kraeling, *Synagogue*, pp. 99–105.

33 C. Torrey, "The Aramaic Texts," in Kraeling, *Synagogue*, p. 269.

34 A. Díez Macho, *Neophyti 1: Targum Palestinense Ms de la Biblioteca Vaticana* (Madrid and Barcelona: Consejo Superior de Investigaciones Científicas, 1968); E. G. Clarke, *Targum Pseudo-Jonathan of the Pentateuch: Text and Concordance* (Hoboken, NJ: Ktav, 1984).

35 Marc Bregman, "The Darshan: Preacher and Teacher of Talmudic Times," *Melton Journal* 14 (1982): 3, 19, 26.

36 Fine, *Art, History*, pp. 107–173.

37 David Noy and Hanswulf Bloedhorn, *Inscriptiones Judaicae Orientis*, vol. 3, *Syria and Cyprus* (Tübingen: Mohr Siebeck, 2004), pp. 196–198.

38 Ibid., pp. 200–202.

39 Ibid., pp. 204–207.

40 Fine, *Art, History*, pp. 176–178.

41 *Y. Berakhot* 9:1, 12d; *b. Berakhot* 40b; R. Kimelman, "Blessing Formulae and Divine Sovereignty in Rabbinic Literature," in *Liturgy in the Life of the Synagogue*, ed. S. Fine and R. Langer (Winona Lake, IN: Eisenbrauns, 2005), pp. 1–39.

7

New Directions in Understanding Jewish Liturgy

RUTH LANGER

When Jews hold in their hands a Jewish prayer book today, no matter of what movement, they are participating in a form of worship about which the Bible tells us nothing, but one which derives from the earliest layers of rabbinic teachings.[1] The origins of what Jews do in their formal scripted prayer intersect deeply with the origins of rabbinic Judaism itself; consequently, our understanding of how Jewish liturgy took its form has shifted with debates and emerging understandings of larger questions about rabbinic Judaism in general. Jewish liturgists ask not only how and when rabbinic liturgy emerged and how it took shape, but also how and when this nonsacrificial, highly scripted verbal and communal worship of God come to be the universal Jewish mode of worship.[2] That it did so is an undeniable marker of the success of rabbinic influence; it is also one that can, to a degree, be traced through evidence that goes beyond the authoritative books of the rabbis' own library.

In 2001, I enumerated some emerging questions and methods in the discipline.[3] In the interim, the study of early rabbinic liturgy itself has been fairly quiescent, but there have been some exciting changes on its borders that have the potential to affect it deeply. This chapter explores some ways in which these scholarly developments put us on the verge, potentially, of a radical rethinking of method that might lead us to revolutionary new understandings of Jewish liturgical history. This rethinking not only builds on specifically liturgical work of the past few decades, but also requires us to think about liturgy with the tools and methods that scholars apply today to the rabbinic sources on which liturgical studies relies. "From where and how did Jews get the liturgy that became the prayers familiar today?" has been the central question of Jewish liturgical studies. I do not seek to decenter this question so much as to ground our answers to it more securely.

In my 2001 survey, I highlighted the ways in which the study of Jewish liturgy was beginning to incorporate much more than just the search for the origins of the words of the liturgy. Instead, it was also considering non-textual elements like its setting, the *halakhah* governing it, and the ways that it was performed. I also mentioned that our new knowledge about Qumran liturgy was made possible both as the publication of the Dead Sea Scrolls neared its completion, and as increased attention to the prayer texts found in the Cairo Geniza were reshaping our understandings of the earlier history of prayer texts.[4] Ultimately, though, our tools for recovering the Jewish liturgical life of the past remain limited. We learn from synagogue archaeology and from the texts that happen to be preserved, some describing the liturgical experience and some containing liturgical texts. However, while synagogues are important, each ancient building's remains can raise the perpetual question of to what extent the rituals within it followed the norms of rabbinic prayer. We cannot recover the sounds, the music, the smells, or the sight and feel of the gathered community. What language or languages were they using for prayer, learning, and conversation among themselves? Were women present, and where? For these questions and more, we have only spotty textual evidence that needs careful integration as it spans about a millennium: prayer texts from the Second Temple period, rabbinic literature about liturgy with occasional prayer texts embedded, and liturgical texts of the distinctive rites of the Land of Israel and Babylonia, including liturgical poetry, preserved in medieval manuscripts, especially from the Cairo Geniza.[5]

Before looking forward, though, it is helpful to offer a brief survey of where we have been. Questions about the origins of rabbinic liturgy intrigued some of the earliest leaders of the academic study of Judaism in the nineteenth century, most notably Leopold Zunz (1794–1886), whose 1832 volume tracing the history of Jewish preaching included a discussion of liturgical poetry. This led him to write a brief overview of the origins of the liturgy in which it is embedded.[6] His question of origins focused mostly on individual blessings and even phrases within them, that is, on the trees and not on the forest. This focus on small textual details remained the dominant concern for Jewish liturgical scholarship for over a century. What clues could be found by which to date the original composition and/or reediting of individual prayer texts? This approach presupposed that liturgy consisted from the beginning of words that some individual presumably composed and wrote down for others to use. It could thus be analyzed like other texts, using the tools of historical-critical scholarship.[7] This presupposition, of course, is coherent with how we know the prayers: we open up a text that someone else has composed and read it. This enables communal prayer to function. There seemed no reason to imagine a different scenario. However, challenges to this presumption began to emerge with the discovery of the Cairo Geniza in the mid-1890s and the first publication of radically different liturgical texts from it in 1898.[8] Initially, these findings led only to modifications of these presuppositions and no radical reworking. The classic text of Jewish liturgical scholarship, Ismar Elbogen's (1874–1943) tome *Jewish Liturgy: A Comprehensive History*, translated into English in 1993, belongs to this world.[9] At the extreme, this method supposed that we can also recover original compositions, a task to which Louis Finkelstein (1895–1991) brought enormous erudition in a series of long articles; however, he generated very questionable results.[10]

New methods began to emerge in the mid-twentieth century, but they became influential with the 1963 dissertation of Joseph Heinemann (1915–1978).[11] Heinemann demonstrated the implausibility of presuming such authored prayers and instead posited that different modes of prayer language had emerged in different social contexts during the Second Temple period. These contexts, which he enumerated as the synagogue, Temple, house of study, law court, and private, each created prayers with identifiable linguistic characteristics, like the way that they addressed God. When the rabbis adopted individual prayers, they preserved these characteristics. In addition, Heinemann claimed that within these norms of language there was great freedom in the actual composition of any particular prayer. The numerous versions we have received of prayers for rebuilding Jerusalem, all "synagogue style," point to a lack of preformulated, composed prayers. Thus, according to Heinemann, Jews in the early rabbinic period knew how to generate prayers appropriately, and they gradually evolved more and more fixed texts out of the wealth of available possibilities.

Until 1990, Heinemann represented the latest and the best academic thinking. However, beginning then and continuing for most of a decade, Ezra Fleischer (1928–2006) published a series of articles raising serious challenges to the fundamental presuppositions undergirding Heinemann's theories. Fleischer's fundamental claim was that the destruction of the Jerusalem Temple in 70 CE and the end of animal sacrifices created a covenantal void. Relatively quickly the rabbis constructed a system of mandatory verbal worship to replace the lost sacrificial worship. Because such verbal worship was not previously necessary, it did not exist. In order for this system to function, the rabbis could only have composed and disseminated verbatim prayer texts. Otherwise, it would have been impossible for most people to meet their new responsibilities. It can be demonstrated that prayer was not previously a function of synagogues, and now the rabbis inserted it.[12]

Fleischer was too important a scholar to be ignored, and his challenge has thrown the study of Jewish liturgical origins into significant disarray ever since.[13] Fleischer's point about there being no demonstrable use of Second Temple–era synagogues for prayer relied on evidence now widely accepted by those studying the synagogue itself. Numerous texts describe gatherings for reading and studying scripture, but none mentions regular communal prayer. This does, correctly, remove a key social setting from Heinemann's list, as he assigned the central rabbinic prayers to the synagogue. Fleischer's insistence on new fixed written compositions also contradicts Heinemann at a fundamental level but is more questionable. Fleischer rejected as irrelevant the evidence for organized verbal prayer from the Dead Sea Scrolls. In his understanding, the nature of rabbinic prayer as fulfilling Jews' covenantal obligations to worship God was determinative, and sacrifice had fulfilled this role previously. That Qumran sectarians who rejected the legitimacy of their contemporary Temple's prayers also might have need of substitute worship seemed immaterial to him, and that meant that the nature of their prayer texts was also unimportant. The study of Second Temple prayer language that emerged in the English-speaking world beginning in the late 1990s also seems not to have shaped Fleischer's deliberations.

Jewish liturgical studies today thus is in need of a more coherent explanation of origins.[14] So what stops me from writing my own book right now, from offering the Langer theory that would cut through this situation of confusion? In what follows, I will explain why this is a particularly ambitious and challenging project, one that is still a task for the future because it requires establishing first some new directions for the field. We will look first at the new scholarship on prayer in the Second

Temple period, then at the impact of new methods in study of the rabbinic period itself, and then at the impact of deeper knowledge about the liturgical findings of the Geniza on our possible understandings of earlier Jewish liturgy. All of these are areas in which there have been significant developments since Fleischer's publications that might or might not have influenced him but that definitely influence me.

Second Temple Prayer Texts

In the late 1990s, three revised doctoral dissertations appeared almost simultaneously, looking at prayer in the Second Temple period.[15] These studies opened the door to a new set of possibilities in understanding the precursors to rabbinic (and Christian) liturgy. They teach us that even though it cannot be demonstrated, based on current evidence, that *any* of the elaborate prayers that the rabbis would require, those that came to constitute Jewish liturgy, existed in recognizable form in the Second Temple period, it can be demonstrated that people then had developed a strong sense of what constituted appropriate kinds of language to use for their prayers. In other words, they demonstrate in detail what Heinemann intuited about Second Temple–era prayer, though without his discussion of specific social settings, for which there is insufficient evidence. This prayer language paraphrases or reuses that of the Bible (what Judith Newman terms "scripturalization").[16] They demonstrate continuities from the prayers found in later biblical books to biblical-style books not admitted to the Jewish canon (Apocrypha and pseudepigrapha), to Qumran prayer texts, to early Christian prayers, and to later Jewish liturgy.

One accessible example, with implications for later Jewish liturgy, is the reuse of Deuteronomy 10:17, where Moses refers to God as *"ha'el hagadol hagibbor vehanora"* (the great, mighty, and awesome God). This language appears in later biblical prayer texts: in full in Nehemiah 9:32a, in Jeremiah 32:18 without the third adjective (*hanora*), and without the second adjective (*hagibbor*) in Nehemiah 1:5 and Daniel 9:4.[17] Of course, this language, also in full, became part of the familiar opening blessing of what is arguably the most important prayer of rabbinic liturgy, the *amidah*. Indeed, the rabbis invoke this biblical precedent explicitly to justify this prayer's listing of such a select list of divine attributes:

Someone went down [before the ark to lead the *amidah*] in the presence of Rabbi Ḥanina. He recited: "The great, might, awesome, majestic, powerful, terrible, strong, fearless, sure, and honored God." [Rabbi Ḥanina] waited until he had finished, and when he had finished, said to him, "Have you fully completed praising your Master? What is all this? If Moses our Teacher had not said in the Torah these three words [great, mighty, and awesome] that we normally recite and had the Men of the Great Assembly not established them in the prayer, we could not recite even them—yet you recited all of them and added even more! This could be compared to a human king who had thousands upon thousands of dinars of gold and they praised him for his silver. Would that not be an insult to him?"[18]

What Newman and her colleagues demonstrate is that this pattern of constructing new prayers from language given an imprimatur from scripture, in this case a description of God that carries with it the authority of a Torah text, emerges in the period of the Babylonian exile and becomes increasingly characteristic of Jewish prayer in the Second Temple period.

The confluence of interests underlying these three books led to a decision to convene a three-year consultation on their common concern, the emergence of penitential prayer, at the Society for Biblical Literature. Deeply involved were also leading scholars of Qumran liturgy and scholars studying other Second Temple–era texts. The first year focused on penitential prayer in the Bible, the second on Second Temple literature, and the third on the influence of these forms in subsequent periods. The papers, with some additions, were published in a three-volume set titled *Seeking the Favor of God.*[19] Although these volumes look only at a single genre of prayer, they collectively make a strong claim about the functioning of prayer language in the Jewish world and its early history.

Newman's concept of scripturalizing not only applies to penitential prayer, but also provides a starting point for understanding emerging prayer language in other sorts of liturgical language like petition or praise. In all these modes, psalms especially, but any biblical poetic text, also form rich models of prayer language, whether cited directly or alluded to more or less obliquely in subsequent compositions. This scholarship has also demonstrated that this scripturalizing does not occur in only Hebrew prayers. Those composing prayer texts in Greek, whether Jews or Christians, cited and alluded to the Septuagint in completely analogous ways.[20]

Rabbinic prayer originated in a world that knew this linguistic and literary model for constructing prayers. All we know about rabbinic prayer texts—which is not much, but more about that later—suggests that the rabbis fully accepted this inherited model as well. Initially, this seems to have extended to allowing prayer in languages other than Hebrew, at least for those who could not manage the sacred tongue.[21] However, as we know, rabbinic prayer texts emerged almost entirely in Hebrew, and this is reflected in the hints of actual texts preserved in the literature.

The material available for these discussions has been vastly expanded by the complete publication of the Dead Sea Scrolls. Of course, these scrolls present their own challenges of interpretation. They include a not-insignificant number of liturgical texts, but it is less obvious which texts represent sectarian texts and which reflect a more normative Judaism of the period, if such a thing existed.[22] In addition, the texts are mostly fragmentary to various degrees, meaning that reading them and deciphering their meaning often requires significant interpretation. This, of course, opens the door to reading into a text what one seeks to find in it, a serious methodological issue. However, the insights of the new work on the nature of prayer in the Second Temple period, work that does incorporate the Qumran literature, is very helpful in this regard and needs to be heeded in turn by the scrolls-focused scholars. Some make dubious claims to find direct precursors to later rabbinic prayers in particular Qumran texts. It is much more valid to understand these texts as participating in—and as important witnesses to—the emerging vocabulary and grammar of appropriate Hebrew prayer, a grammar and vocabulary that would also inform later rabbinic liturgy.

An example is the Dead Sea Scroll 4Q521, known also as 4Q Messianic Apocalypse, which clearly contains both language of resurrection of the dead and language drawn from Psalm 146:7–8 that lists God's attributes as one who frees captives, gives sight to the blind, and makes straight those who are bent.[23] A few scholars have pointed to the similarity between this cluster of themes and language and the second blessing of the *amidah* in its familiar versions, suggesting that it is witness to an early form of the prayer.[24] But there are significant problems with this observation. First of all, 4Q521 is not obviously a liturgical text, although perhaps it echoes one. More importantly, the recent work on our earliest evidence for rabbinic prayer texts demonstrates that while resurrection is an early and central theme of the second benediction of the *amidah* universally, Geniza texts show that this allusion to Psalm 146 appears only in the Babylonian rite and not in that of the Land of Israel.[25] Were the Qumran text a precursor of the rabbinic prayer, it would be surprising to find its language in Babylonia only. The introduction of language from Psalm 146 into the *amidah* seems to be a later elaboration of the rabbinic prayer text, one that does accord, though, with the principles of Jewish prayer language that emerged from the Second Temple period.

This suggests that the search for the origins of specific rabbinic prayers in the Second Temple period is an extremely dicey venture. This, of course, is precisely what characterized much of the early academic scholarship on Jewish liturgy, which generally presupposed that prayers were authored and promulgated by someone, presumably someone with authority, and that the task of the historian was to try to retrieve as much as possible about that initial stage. According to this method, a prayer that names resurrection of the dead multiple times must have been composed in response to those objecting to it. Thus, the prayer must have been a Pharisee response to known Sadducee opposition. Maybe. But this emphasis on resurrection could also have arisen from a world in which it was important in its own right, as demonstrated by 4Q521 and Christianity. Similarly, those who place the origins of the *amidah*'s curse of sectarians (the *Birkat Ha-Minim*) in specific Second Temple curse texts ignore the ubiquity of cursing as a mode of discourse then.[26] I could give many more examples of such overreading.[27]

What we can say is that rabbinic liturgy continues a number of features found in the prayer texts from Qumran. These include the preference for biblical-style language, in both vocabulary and rhetorical structuring. The Qumran community also definitely preferred Hebrew prayer, although other literature proves that this was not a universal norm among Jews at the time.[28] Their texts also demonstrate that the idea of regular daily scripted verbal prayer existed during the Second Temple period and was apparently fully independent of Jerusalem's sacrifices. Moreover, these texts demonstrate the emerging use of a blessing formula to structure prayer. Thus, while it is problematic to look for precursors of specific rabbinic prayer texts, it is equally problematic to understand rabbinic prayer as completely without precedent in the way that Fleischer did.

Rereading Rabbinic Literature about Prayer

How then, do we understand the various *rabbinic* reports about Second Temple liturgy? Are these bases for historical conclusions, or are they, alternatively, rabbinic retrojections about what they wish had been happening while the Temple still stood? In general, how do we derive history from any of the rabbinic reports about liturgy?

The traditions of Jewish liturgical scholarship have, for the most part, taken rabbinic texts at their face value, reconstructing history from them unless they are obviously mythological. This has meant, at a minimum, dating a particular concern by the rabbi(s) to whom it is attributed and tracing the emergence of the details of the liturgy accordingly. In addition, if words of the liturgical text appear in rabbinic texts, they are presumed to be accurately attributed and transmitted. However, these presumptions do not integrate a whole slew of methodological issues currently being discussed in the larger study of rabbinic literature or in the study of the greater Jewish world of late antiquity and beyond. In order to move our question of the origins of rabbinic liturgy onto a firmer basis, we absolutely must engage with these issues, which have the potential to rewrite our historical understandings dramatically.

Much ink has been spilled over the question of when the received liturgy began and under whose auspices. Is it purely rabbinic, or did it have a pre-rabbinic existence? As should be clear from the previous section, precursors to rabbinic liturgical language seem not to have taken the form of specific prayers. However, this is not always the presumption of the rabbinic texts themselves. For instance, rabbinic tradition teaches that the biblical patriarchs instituted the three daily times of prayer, that Jacob began the nonbiblical response customarily recited after the first verse of *Shema*, and that the *amidah* originated with the Men of the Great Assembly who gathered early in the Second Temple period.[29] Such narratives, even when obviously mythological, contribute significantly to the sense that at least some elements of rabbinic prayer did have a prehistory. However, there are other liturgical elements for which the rabbis seem not to remember any such prehistory. What then, was the rabbinic self-understanding, or by asking this question are we imposing a modern sense of history on the ancient words?

The rabbinic texts suggest that even if the *amidah* originated with the Men of the Great Assembly, it had been forgotten and needed to be reinstituted at the formative gathering of rabbis at Yavneh after the Romans destroyed the Jerusalem Temple in 70 CE.[30] Thus, the rabbis recognize that it was not really recited in the late Second Temple period. All other prayers they present as having existed prior to the destruction of the Temple, either explicitly or implicitly. They understand the Grace after Meals to have acquired a fourth blessing after the fall of Beitar (135 CE), but they present only mythological origins for the rest of the prayer.[31] Similarly, the rabbis state that the Sabbath Torah reading began with Moses, and Ezra expanded it to weekdays and Sabbath afternoons.[32] In this case, external evidence from a whole slew of Second Temple period sources establishes that Jews did indeed read Torah at least on the Sabbath during that period.[33]

For the *Shema*, the evidence is more equivocal. Its core is, of course, passages from Deuteronomy and Numbers received at Sinai. Rabbinic texts presume its liturgical preexistence and present a fanciful *aggadah* about its pre-Sinai origins, constructing a deathbed dialogue where Jacob's sons assure him of their loyalty to God, addressing him as Israel, "Listen Israel, the LORD *is our* God, and we know that the LORD is one."[34] Concrete nonrabbinic evidence for ritual use of the *Shema* text from Deuteronomy in the Second Temple period does exist in the second-century BCE Nash papyrus, which may have been an amulet of some sort, and in *tefillin* found at Qumran. However, the liturgical texts from Qumran do not hint at a recitation of the *Shema* itself. Jesus also seems to have cited the first two verses as the most important of commandments.[35] But none of this external evidence reflects a liturgical unit where Jews recite this biblical text regularly or within a larger ritual context. Did Second Temple–era Jews recite this biblical text, as it commands, upon lying down (at night) and rising up (in the morning)? Perhaps, but there is no evidence *from that time* one way or another.

The Mishnah's report stands in contrast to the silence of the nonrabbinic sources. It records that before completing the morning sacrificial offering, the priests would abandon it and go to one of the Temple's chambers, where an appointed leader would call upon them to recite one unspecified blessing, the Ten Commandments, the paragraphs of the *Shema*, and then three more blessings (*m. Tamid* 4:3–5:1). The Mishnah goes on to name these three blessings as the familiar one immediately following the *Shema* and two from the *amidah*. The difference between this text and actual rabbinic practice, even at the time of the redaction of the Mishnah, suggests that this memory indeed might be authentic. Mishnah *Berakhot* explicitly calls for *two* blessings before *Shema* (though it still does not specify their content) and *one* after it in the morning.[36] Mishnah *Berakhot* also knows another liturgical element, called *tefillah* (lit. "prayer," what we have been calling *amidah*), consisting of eighteen benedictions (on weekdays), but it does not explicitly specify whether or how these two elements should be combined. The last two blessings named in the Temple liturgy of Mishnah *Tamid* are familiar to us from the conclusion of this prayer.[37]

However, how do we understand the Mishnah's traditions about the Temple? Are they early layers preserving authentic memories and hence good historical sources, or are they constructs of the Mishnah's redactors, a century and more after its destruction? Naftali S. Cohn argues that the Mishnah includes narratives about Temple practice that the rabbis constructed in order to claim authority over this central but lost institution and thus help to consolidate their own ritual power.[38] If Cohn is correct, then we need to question the historical value of any report of nonrabbis performing rabbilike rituals. That would include this priestly ritual as well as the High Priest's Torah readings with blessings on Yom Kippur and kings' readings on Sukkot.[39] Here, too, the Mishnah's details differ from later rabbinic practice, but neither does the Mishnah describe Second Temple–style liturgies of the sorts witnessed by other sources. More significantly, what late Second Temple kings might have performed such a reading? Certainly not the Roman puppets of the first century CE! Is this then more an ideal construction than historical memory?

I see little reason to doubt that the *halakhic* discussions in the Mishnah and other tannaitic texts record the fundamental outlines of the rabbis' own system of worship of God in the post-Temple era. However, one critical question, discussed by some historians of this period but little by liturgical scholars, is how much influence the rabbis had and how their system of worship intersected with the reality of other Jews of their world.[40] The tendency has been very much to presume that the rabbis were the religious leaders of their time, successfully determining the parameters of actual Jewish practice. This may be a naïve reading, taking what the rabbis wished were the case as reality.

We return now to the debate over the nature of early rabbinic prayer. Did it involve fixed texts, decreed by a central rabbinic authority, or did the rabbis only outline the structure of the prayers, all that the Mishnah itself specifies, more or less leaving individuals or communities free to develop their own wording? This, too, involves questions of rabbinic authority as it affects the mechanisms by which we reconstruct the spread of the rabbinic system.

The Mishnah records Rabban Gamliel (late first century) as teaching about the daily recitation of eighteen benedictions (i.e., the *amidah*).[41] Ezra Fleischer interprets the Mishnah's ambiguous language not as a minimalist description, "Every day a person recites eighteen," but rather as a universal prescription, "Every day *each* person *must* recite eighteen." This is a plausible reading, one that Fleischer argues suits the promulgation of a new ritual. The continuation of the Mishnah records objections from Rabban Gamliel's colleagues, not about his call for people to pray, but rather about precisely how complex a prayer should be expected of them. Should most people just recite an abbreviated version, or should this depend on the individual's ability to pray fluently? In other words, they debate the realism of his decree: will people go along with it?[42]

Fleischer's presumption, and, indeed, the presumption of essentially all liturgists before him, was that Rabban Gamliel and his colleagues could issue such a decree successfully. This Mishnah would thus reflect an (almost) immediately accomplished revolutionary shift from the priestly daily worship of the Temple, in which most Jews participated only vicariously at best, to a universally accepted obligation for prayer placed upon every individual in every location. In order for this to happen, Fleischer claimed, Rabban Gamliel's court must have scripted the full text of these eighteen benedictions.[43] Heinemann, in contrast, had claimed that only the order of themes had been roughly scripted. When Rabbi Akiva spoke about requiring the full prayer only from one whose prayer is fluent, he was not speaking about memorization but rather the person's ability to construct the prayer in good liturgical language.

Heinemann's understanding is coherent with the continuation of the Mishnah, which objects to fixed prayer as not sufficiently supplicatory.[44] It was only Babylonian rabbis of later generations who insisted on fixed prayer because of fear of error, effectively reinterpreting this Mishnah. Fleischer, apparently, read the Mishnah through their lens, a problematic move.

Certainly by the time of the redaction of the Mishnah, by the early third century, Rabban Gamliel was an authoritative voice within rabbinic circles. But even according to remembered stories about him, his own colleagues challenged his authority and deposed him.[45] Who might have been listening to him in the late first century, and how would they have learned of this instruction? The earliest preserved evidence that rabbinic Jews wrote down their prayers dates from centuries later, so could a tightly scripted ritual have been successfully promulgated? Even if the prayers were written, in this world scribes copied scrolls one by one, writing materials were expensive, and transporting books was not a trivial undertaking. What might have brought nonrabbis to agree to participate in this complex verbal ritual? There are texts that suggest that some, perhaps many, resisted rabbinic encouragement maybe even a century or more later. Rabbinic texts record a not insignificant number of teachings seeking to persuade people to comply, promising them rewards in the afterlife, for instance.[46] This suggests that success was far from immediate.

Let us return to the story of the person rebuked by Rabbi Ḥanina for praying effusively. Obviously, this unnamed person leading the prayers was participating in the rabbinic system but felt free to innovate and elaborate on the prayer's biblical language with additional divine attributes. Yet the point of the Talmud's story seems to be that his prayer text deviated from an authorized one. Does this suggest that he accepted or rejected rabbinic authority? Was he free to compose his own language or not? How do we assess the historicity of this narrative and the reality behind it? Here, we can beneficially apply some newer methods for interpreting rabbinic literature.

As we have seen, the Babylonian Talmud places this story in the presence of Rabbi Ḥanina, presumably Rabbi Ḥanina bar Ḥama, a first-generation Amora active in the Land of Israel in the first half of the third century. However, when we look at the Jerusalem Talmud's parallel narrative, we find Rabbis Yoḥanan and Yonatan, sages of about the same time, visiting some place in the south where they found the *ḥazzan*, presumably the official prayer leader of the synagogue, expanding similarly at this same point in the prayer. Where the later Babylonian Talmud records that Rabbi Ḥanina waited for the prayer leader to finish before rebuking him, the Jerusalem Talmud tells us that these rabbis jumped right in and immediately silenced the *ḥazzan* for deviating from the established text of the prayer. Rabbi Ḥanina's rebuke was theological: any praise of God is necessarily insufficient, so we rely on that authorized by Moses. Rabbis Yoḥanan and Yonatan's rebuke is more procedural and *halakhic*: this *ḥazzan* was refusing to accept the rabbinic authority that had fixed at least this phrase of the prayer.

Why these differences? Jeffrey Rubenstein has fruitfully examined how the Babylonian Talmud reworks traditions from the Land of Israel to its own purposes.[47] If this is a single story, the setting has obviously been reworked in ways that go beyond the different attributions. The itinerant rabbis of the Land of Israel, visiting services led by a designated, perhaps professional liturgical leader, have become a single settled rabbi holding court, before whom someone unnamed and untitled is incidentally leading prayer. This fits Rubenstein's observations about developments in the nature of the rabbinate and the Babylonian Talmud's reworking narratives to reflect its own more settled academies. The changed nature of the rebuke apparently also reflects a development in the liturgical reality. In the Land of Israel these rabbis seem insecure of their authority, so they respond with exceeding strictness, silencing the leader of the local services at which they are just visitors. In contrast, Rabbi Ḥanina, remade in the Babylonian model, calls for theological thoughtfulness next time. Error still occurs, but it has a different tenor entirely.[48] Nonetheless, we do note that the Jerusalem Talmud's *ḥazzan* is already complying with at least the outline of the rabbinic prayer system, even if he is changing the words. By the time of our story in the third century, or the redaction of the Jerusalem Talmud in the fifth century, at least some synagogues in some places have partially adopted the rabbinic prayer structure. Yet in neither setting has fixed language successfully become an accepted expectation.

Indeed, our question about the acceptance of rabbinic authority and with it rabbinic prayer is one of "when" and "where," but not "whether."

As this story would seem to indicate, the process was gradual and un-even, even in the heart of the rabbis' own territory. Various other scat-tered clues help us to unpack this picture further. What was the nature of the locus in which this *hazzan* was leading prayer? Was it a synagogue? Whose? We tend to evaluate archaeological finds of synagogues primar-ily in light of their conformity to rabbinic norms. Think, for instance, of the now-debunked assumption that there was a women's gallery in early synagogues, of interpreting synagogue art, like mosaic floors or the paintings from Dura Europos, in dialogue only with known mi-drashic traditions, or of understanding the location and orientation of synagogues through rabbinic *halakhah*.[49] Instead, the synagogue likely originated as a civic institution with no necessary connection to the rab-bis or their predecessors. Reading early remains as necessarily rabbinic can thus be erroneous. If the rabbis only gradually became influential, then their particular ways of using this space might have become nor-mative only gradually as well; some, but not all, synagogues were likely rabbinic. The material evidence of synagogue remains in the Land of Israel becomes much richer from the fourth century, precisely the point where scholars posit a more established rabbinic leadership. Though we should be cautious of too facile a parallel, we do find that synagogues in this period are increasingly built in ways that are consistent with rab-binic teachings and theology. This is particularly marked in their ori-entation toward Jerusalem and their decoration with iconography that memorializes the Temple.

Stronger evidence for rabbinic liturgy comes from *piyyut*, because this liturgical poetry, at least that which survived, was composed to elab-orate upon the regular rabbinic prayers. The sixth-century poet Yannai composed cycles for every Sabbath morning, creating extended compo-sitions that replaced the body of the texts of the first three blessings of the *amidah* with content reflecting on the week's Torah reading. Yannai's context was clearly rabbinic, as is evidenced both by the structure of his poetry and by his allusions to familiar rabbinic interpretations of the biblical texts on which he elaborated poetically.[50] However, in his time, in the Land of Israel, at least the leader's repetition of the *amidah* did not need to include more than the basic structure of the rabbinic prayer.

It would be erroneous to presume that all synagogues had a resident gifted poet. Others instead imitated his poetry or performed his compositions themselves, to the point that Yannai's compositions eventually found their way to the Cairo Geniza for modern scholars to rediscover. Relatively speaking, we know of only a tiny handful of such poets, those whose works were preserved. Were there others? Did some write for some other sort of worship situations, but because their context was lost their works were not preserved?[51] Were it not for the Geniza this would be the fate of Yannai and his immediate colleagues, for the triennial cycle of Torah readings for which they wrote according to the Land of Israel's rite itself gave way to the Babylonian annual cycle, lasting long enough in this one Cairo synagogue for these texts to survive. The Babylonian insistence on fixed prayer texts also challenged the incorporation of *piyyut*.

Another critical step in fully understanding the emergence of Jewish liturgy is to move beyond the boundaries of the Land of Israel. Scholars of rabbinic history, particularly, tended for a long while to ignore the broader Jewish world. Here there are at least two areas of growing concern: the Babylonian rabbinic culture as influenced by its local context; and the rest of the diaspora. I have already invoked Jeffrey Rubenstein's method in investigating how the Babylonian Talmud's redactors reshaped texts from the Land of Israel to function according to the social and cultural norms of the Babylonian rabbinic academies. This sensitivity to the processes of redaction throws another huge wrench in Jewish liturgical history. Any tradition recorded only in the Babylonian Talmud as taking place in the Land of Israel becomes potentially suspect, particularly if it lacks parallels in texts from the Land of Israel that can confirm its details.

An example of this problem is the "institution narrative" of the *Birkat Ha-Minim*, the curse of heretics. This text appears only in the Babylonian Talmud (*b. Ber.* 28b), cited as a tannaitic source (*baraita*), but narrated as taking place in a setting that fits the social structure of a Babylonian academy. In addition, we know that Jews in the Land of Israel prayed an eighteen-benediction *amidah* while Jews in Babylonia expanded the prayer to nineteen. The Talmud begins by asking how the eighteen of the Mishnah became the nineteen they know; it answers by telling about the addition of the *Birkat Ha-Minim* under Rabban Gamliel. The narrative thus serves a Babylonian purpose, incorporates the mode in which the Babylonian rabbinic academy functioned, and has no parallels to the Land of Israel. Does it represent a first-century Land of

Israel reality (with the consequent possibility that the prayer responds to early Christianity) or something later and Babylonian? I have suggested the latter.[52] The entire rabbinic corpus of narratives about prayer needs to be reevaluated with these sorts of criteria in mind.[53]

If we need to ask when rabbinic authority became real in the Land of Israel, the question is even more pressing for the diaspora. Is the Babylonian rabbinic suspicion of Jews outside their immediate environs a sign that many Jews in the Sassanian Empire in which they lived were not falling into line?[54] Certainly, the emergence of groups like the Karaites, with their insistence on the normativity only of the written Bible, even for prayer, points to increasingly organized resistance to rabbinic power in the post-talmudic period. But was this resistance a new phenomenon or something older asserting its validity?

Jews already lived throughout the Mediterranean world by the time of the destruction of the Temple in 70 CE, but we know relatively little about how they expressed their Judaism. We know they had synagogues, but what happened in them? Evidence suggests that reading of scripture, often in Greek, was part of it, but did they pray fixed prayers communally? What is the source of the prayer texts preserved in Greek that have been identified as Jewish? While these all participate in the Second Temple heritage of liturgical rhetorical norms, none of the prayers are obviously rabbinic. At what points did the different diaspora communities of Jews begin worshipping according to rabbinic norms?[55] Descriptions of Judaism and Jewish practice by non-Jews are helpful, especially Christian critiques, because of their desire to differentiate themselves and construct communal boundaries. It seems pretty clear that diaspora Jewish communities adhered to *a* Jewish calendar dependent on sighting the new moon, but for the most part this may have been a biblically driven cycle determined locally. In other words, these communities may not actually have received sufficiently efficient calendrical notifications from the rabbinic court; but did they want to? We know about this from the Christian struggle to unify the date of Easter, resolved only at the Council of Nicaea in 325. The church fathers deemed heretical the practice, common in Asia Minor and parts of Syria, of consulting with Jews to determine the date of the paschal celebration. These Jewish communities did not themselves all celebrate Passover in the same month, meaning that they were setting their calendars locally.[56]

Various church fathers make (disparaging) comments about Jewish practices, including in the synagogues. Most infamous are John Chrysostom's eight *adversos iudaeos* sermons, occasioned by members of his community's apparent preference for attending the synagogue over coming to church. Chrysostom's tirades teach us striking things about the nature of this synagogue community in northern Syria. Apparently, the entertainment value of the synagogue service was high; it must have been accessible to non-Jews and fun to be there. This suggests that its language was the vernacular, likely Greek, and that it likely included good music, good preaching, or both. Antiochians considered the synagogue a place of religious power, particularly because of the presence of the Torah scrolls. Nothing in Chrysostom's rants should lead us to presume a liturgy structured according to rabbinic norms or a rabbinic presence.[57]

Evidence *for* penetration of rabbinic liturgy to the diaspora as something accomplished reaches us only much later. Around 800 CE, Pirqoy ben Baboy, a polemicist on behalf of the heads of the Babylonian rabbinic academies, wrote to the Jewish communities in North Africa and Spain, criticizing them for adhering to the teachings of the rabbinical academies in the Land of Israel, including on some matters of liturgy. Thus, his recipients presumably did use rabbinic liturgy, albeit with some "wrong" details.[58] Similarly, the Jews of (sometimes Byzantine) Italy wrote *piyyutim* from the ninth or tenth centuries, and the eleventh-century *Megillat Ahima'atz* narrates how one member of the community was able to lead prayers in the rabbinic academy in the Land of Israel.[59] However, there is a counternarrative: in the late ninth century, two Spanish communities, probably Lucena and Barcelona, independently wrote to the Babylonian geonim, asking for basic instruction on how to pray. The answers, Rav Natronai Gaon's list of the hundred benedictions one should recite daily, and the first Jewish prayer book, by Rav Amram Gaon, form the model for all subsequent European liturgical books. If the Jews of Spain or elsewhere in Europe had a prior liturgical system, it seems to have been radically transformed after this point, leaving no trace of what went before. The need for such a volume suggests not only that these Jews previously were not following Babylonian direction; it may well be that they had not been looking for rabbinic direction at all.

Nothing earlier than this prayer book, known as the *Seder Rav Amram Gaon*, has yet been published.[60] Prior to this, if prayers were written down, they were written for private use. For the most part, prayer, like all of rabbinic learning, was orally performed and transmitted. This makes it impossible for us to reconstruct most of its details in earlier periods and to confine a discussion of Jewish liturgical origins to the early rabbinic world.

The Geniza and Medieval Manuscripts

From Solomon Schechter's first publication of the findings from the Geniza, which contained our first evidence for the rite of the Land of Israel, until today, the information it contains has challenged scholarly thinking about the nature and origins of Jewish liturgy.[61] How can we account for the diversity that appears in the Geniza manuscripts? These are the earliest texts we have of Jewish prayers, and yet they present a greater diversity than we find among Jewish rites about a millennium later! Presumably, if the prayers began as authored texts, diversity might have entered through error, but to this degree? Answers to this question have been shaped largely by one's understanding of rabbinic history and the degree of effective authority one understands the rabbis to have had at any one point. Thus, Ezra Fleischer adamantly expressed the conviction that this later variation resulted from deliberate changes to the original compositions or from error.[62] I have already discussed in some detail two problems with his claims: both his diminishment of the significance of the liturgical heritage of the Second Temple period and his uncritical reading of received rabbinic literature as an accurate historical record. His presumptions also have implications, though, for how we deal with the Geniza manuscripts.

The primary focus of Fleischer's scholarly career was unpacking and making sense of the myriads of liturgical fragments found in the storage rooms for worn-out Hebrew documents in Cairo. The city's desert climate created a unique situation in which many of the texts survived, mostly in the Ben Ezra synagogue's attic, although in increasingly fragile and fragmentary condition as they aged. Solomon Schechter had for the most part packed up the fragments and transported them to England, eventually distributing some to major scholarly Judaica libraries around the world.[63] Most of the surviving texts date approximately to the tenth to eleventh centuries, meaning that the manuscripts themselves date about a full millennium after the apparent origins of rabbinic liturgy at Yavneh. In this period, there were Jews in Cairo following the Babylonian rabbis and their *halakhic* norms and others following the rabbis from the Land of Israel. The Ben Ezra synagogue was that of the Jews of the Land of Israel. This allowed for the preservation in manuscript of this rite, which otherwise shortly ceased to exist with the devastation caused by the First Crusade in its homeland.[64]

Prior to the last decades, publications of Geniza materials have been fairly hit or miss, depending on what a scholar happened to locate. Beginning in the 1960s, the fragments were microfilmed. Today, digitized images can be accessed and manipulated through the Friedberg Jewish Manuscript Society's portal.[65] Fleischer's main interest was not the prayers, but liturgical poetry. In the course of cataloging this corpus, he paid attention to the prayer texts interspersed, leading to his 1988 Hebrew volume on the rite of the Land of Israel.[66] It was in the wake of writing this volume that Fleischer turned to questions of the origins of the prayers. However, the initial sorting of the Geniza's contents had also generated multiple boxes of mostly fragmentary manuscripts of normal prayer texts. These Fleischer neither catalogued nor considered. Thus, his articles on the origins of prayer, while heavily dependent on the Geniza, were written without a systematic study of the most relevant Geniza manuscripts. Uri Ehrlich has been working to fill this lacuna, publishing his first book of results in 2013.[67] Here, he carefully organizes the variety within the Geniza evidence for individual blessings and then seeks to explain at least elements of it as chronological development of the text. In other words, he seeks to work back toward the original formulation of the rabbinic prayers. In this, he largely accepts Fleischer's theory but also tests it. Ultimately, he does not claim to date the characteristics he identifies as belonging to the earliest texts, but he suggests paths of diachronic development toward the versions found in the Geniza. Although impossible to determine, given the state of the evidence, it is possible that the variety in the Geniza represents not just change over time, but a more complex geographic network of very local rites than Ehrlich and others have suggested.[68]

Conclusion

The modern study of Jewish liturgy has proposed a series of theories, one overturning the last, about how the rabbinic liturgical system came into existence. Many scholars recognize that the latest proposal, that of Ezra Fleischer first published in 1990, remains significantly problematic, but no one has yet set forth a method that answers its challenges and goes beyond them, setting forth a new methodology for reading the available evidence. Until this is done, no discussion of the origins of Jewish liturgy will be adequate.[69]

A new, better-nuanced understanding of the origins of rabbinic liturgy will integrate carefully the various sources of information and methods discussed here, many of which were not available in earlier generations. We know much more now about the nature of liturgical language and the varieties of religious expression in the pre-rabbinic period. We know much more about the variety of forms in which rabbinic liturgy manifested itself in the early medieval period, many centuries after its emergence. Between these bookends, we also have learned much more about the emergence of the rabbinic movement and especially about the formation of the texts that it generated and how to read them as sources of history. Finally, we know that not all Jews worshiped God according to rabbinic norms even as late as the first millennium CE. A new theory of the origins of rabbinic prayer—one that is not yet written—will interweave all these factors, producing a clearer picture of how rabbinic prayer evolved to the mature state documented in the Cairo Geniza.

NOTES

1 With the exception of the Karaites; but even their liturgy, at least in the published forms, demonstrates either shared presuppositions of the norms and structures of worship or rabbinic influence. There are a few published articles on Karaite liturgy. See, most recently, Daniel Frank, "Karaite Prayer and Liturgy," in *Karaite Judaism: A Guide to Its History and Literary Sources*, ed. Meira Polliack (Leiden: Brill, 2003), pp. 559–589; and Friedmann Eissler, "Die karäische Liturgie: Strukturelle Fragen in Horizont von Polemik und Anpassung," in *Orient als Grenzbereich? Rabbinisches und ausserrabbinisches Judentum*, ed. Annelies Kuyt and Gerold Necker (Wiesbaden: Harrassowitz, 2007), pp. 65–75.

2 For short introductions to the history of Jewish liturgy and its components, see my annotated bibliography of sources in the field, *Jewish Liturgy: A Guide to Research* (Lanham, MD: Rowman and Littlefield, 2015).

3 Ruth Langer, "Jewish Liturgy: A Field on the Move Again," *AJS Perspectives* 3.1 (2001): 6–7.

4 For an up-to-date bibliography of publications about the Dead Sea Scrolls and a link to the digitized images of the scrolls themselves, see Orion Center, "The Orion Center for the Study of the Dead Sea Scrolls and Associated Literature," orion.mscc.huji.ac.il. A Geniza is a storage space for worn Hebrew texts that have too much sanctity to be discarded. On the Cairo Geniza and its discovery and importance, see Adina Hoffman and Peter Cole, *Sacred Trash: The Lost and Found World of the Cairo Geniza* (New York: Schocken, 2011).

5 While the basic structure of the liturgy mandated by the rabbis was eventually accepted universally, regional rites marked by different wordings of these prayers emerged early in the two major rabbinic centers of the Land of Israel and Babylonia. The second became dominant and shaped today's Ashkenazi, Sephardi, Italian, and Yemenite rites, while the first died out in its homeland with the Crusades, surviving briefly in the Cairo synagogue that housed the Geniza.

6 Leopold Zunz, *Die gottesdienstliche Vortraege der Juden historisch Entwickelt* (Berlin: A. Asher, 1832), pp. 366–381. In the Hebrew translation, *HaDerashot BiYisrael*, Hanoch Albeck significantly expanded the notes, not always in ways coherent with Zunz's own writing.

7 Developed for the study of the Bible to discern the documents that some editor(s) had later combined into the received text. The original intent of these documents could then be placed in their historical contexts and better understood.

8 S. Schechter, "Geniza Specimens," *Jewish Quarterly Review* 10 (1898): 654–659.

9 Ismar Elbogen, *Jewish Liturgy: A Comprehensive History*, trans. Raymond P. Scheindlin (Philadelphia, Jerusalem, New York: Jewish Publication Society, Jewish Theological Seminary of America, 1993 [German original, 1913; Hebrew translation with updates, 1972]). The updates, by leading liturgists of the time, are clearly indicated in this edition. Scheindlin does not further update the work.

10 For an overview of the scholarship according to this method, see Richard S. Sarason, "On the Use of Method in the Modern Study of Jewish Liturgy," in *Approaches to Ancient Judaism: Theory and Practice*, ed. William Scott Green (Missoula, MT: Scholars Press, 1978), pp. 97–172. For an example of Finkelstein's studies, see his most quoted article, "The Development of the Amidah," *Jewish Quarterly Review* ns 16 (1925): 1–43 and 127–170. He also published on the Passover Seder, the Grace after Meals, the *Qedushah*, and *Hallel*.

11 Published in English, updated by the author, as Joseph Heinemann, *Prayer in the Talmud: Forms and Patterns*, trans. Richard S. Sarason (Berlin: Walter de Gruyter, 1977).

12 This is a necessarily unfair summary of Fleischer's arguments, as his relevant publications cover hundreds of pages. The articles are now collected and repub-

lished as *Statutory Prayers: Their Emergence and Development* (Hebrew), 2 vols., ed. Shulamit Elizur and Tova Beeri (Jerusalem: Magnes Press, 2012). For my summary and review of most of them, see "Revisiting Early Rabbinic Liturgy: The Recent Contributions of Ezra Fleischer," *Prooftexts* 19 (1999): 179–194; and the subsequent rejoinders, Ezra Fleischer, "Controversy, on the Origins of the 'Amidah: Response to Ruth Langer," *Prooftexts* 20 (2000): 380–384; and Ruth Langer, "Controversy, Considerations of Method: A Response to Ezra Fleischer," *Prooftexts* 20 (2000): 384–387.

13 There have been some attempts to address this, most notably a research group convened at the Institute for Advanced Studies at Hebrew University in 1997. Papers generated in that context have been published as *From Qumran to Cairo: Studies in the History of Prayer*, ed. Joseph Tabory (Jerusalem: Orhot Press, 1999). They are individually important but do not result in any clear conclusions.

14 The most up-to-date and academically credible presentation, that of Lee I. Levine in his encyclopedic *The Ancient Synagogue: The First Thousand Years*, 2nd ed. (New Haven, CT: Yale University Press, 2005), chapter 13, "The Sages and the Synagogue," and chapter 16, "Liturgy," nuances Fleischer's findings and reads the sources more carefully, but it is far from comprehensive.

15 Mark J. Boda, *Praying the Tradition: The Origin and Use of Tradition in Nehemiah 9* (Berlin: Walter de Gruyter, 1999); Judith H. Newman, *Praying by the Book: The Scripturalization of Prayer in Second Temple Judaism* (Atlanta, GA: Scholars Press, 1999); and Rodney Alan Werline, *Penitential Prayer in Second Temple Judaism: The Development of a Religious Institution* (Atlanta, GA: Scholars Press, 1998). While I reviewed Newman's book soon after it appeared, its significance for the larger picture of Jewish liturgical studies is something that has become more evident to me in light of the larger discussion here.

16 Following James Kugel. See Newman, *Praying by the Book*, pp. 12–13.

17 Ibid., pp. 101–102.

18 *B. Berakhot* 33b; *b. Megillah* 25a. The Jerusalem Talmud's parallel discussions, *y. Bererakhot* 7:3, 11c, and *y. Megillah* 3:7, 74c, invoke the biblical parallels, seeking to explain why Jeremiah, Daniel, and Nehemiah 1 abbreviate the adjectives. There, the Men of the Great Assembly, and apparently in the Babylonian recensions here as well, refers to the Nehemiah 9 passage.

19 *The Origins of Penitential Prayer in Second Temple Judaism* (vol. 1), *The Development of Penitential Prayer in Second Temple Judaism* (vol. 2), *The Impact of Penitential Prayer Beyond Second Temple Judaism* (vol. 3), ed. Mark J. Boda, Daniel K. Falk, and Rodney A. Werline (Atlanta, GA: Society for Biblical Literature, 2006–2008).

20 For a comprehensive presentation with good introductions of what is known about early Jewish prayers in Greek, some reused and adapted by Christians, but some found in manuscripts likely used by Jews, see Pieter W. van der Horst and Judith H. Newman, *Early Jewish Prayers in Greek* (Commentaries on Early Jewish Literature; Berlin: Walter de Gruyter, 2008).

21 *M. Soṭah* 7:1–2 establishes the permission for recitation of the central prayers in any language in contradistinction to various other rituals whose exact language is prescribed in the biblical text. *T. Soṭah* 7:7 cites Rabbi's objection to allowing the *Shema* to be recited in other languages, because it commands internally "these words . . . shall be upon your heart" (Deut 6:6), that is, the *Shema* itself is biblical text. However, the *gemara* presents the majority position as overruling him (*b. Soṭah* 32b–33a, *b. Berakhot* 13a). *B. Ber.* 40b debates the legitimacy of an Aramaic blessing that does not even translate the mandated rabbinic prayer, at least by someone who cannot do better. *Soferim* 18:5 presents teaching prayers to women and children in other languages as a concession to their educational level. A full discussion of this should also consider the status of translated written biblical texts used for liturgical purposes, either for scripture readings or in *tefillin* and *mezuzot*. However, even though arguably liturgical objects, these remain biblical texts, not newly composed prayer texts.

22 For an English one-volume presentation of these texts with the author's own translation and references to the discussions available at the point of his publication, see James R. Davila, *Liturgical Works* (Eerdmans Commentaries on the Dead Sea Scrolls; Grand Rapids, MI: William B. Eerdmans, 2000). Daniel Falk proposes that significant elements of these prayer texts reflect verbal liturgies connected to the Jerusalem Temple (*Daily Sabbath and Festival Prayers in the Dead Sea Scrolls* [Leiden: Brill, 1998]). This is a difficult claim to prove.

23 For a transcription and translation, see Florentino Garcia Martínez and Eibert J. C. Tigchelaar, eds., *The Dead Sea Scrolls Study Edition* (Leiden: Brill, 1997), vol. 2, pp. 1044–1047. The language of Psalm 146 appears in Frag. 2, col. II, line 8. There are multiple references to resurrection throughout. For the text of Dead Sea Scroll 4Q521 itself, see the Leon Levy Dead Sea Scrolls Digital Library, www.deadseascrolls.org.il/explore-the-archive/manuscript/4Q521-1 (accessed February 2, 2014).

24 Most recently, Stephen Hultgren, "4Q521, the Second Benediction of the *Tefilla*, the *Ḥăsîdîm*, and the Development of Royal Messianism," *Revue de Qumran* 23 (2008): 313–340; but see also David Flusser, "A Qumran Fragment and the Second Blessing of the 'Amidah,'" in *Judaism of the Second Temple Period, Vol. 1 Qumran and Apocalypticism*, trans. Azzan Yadin (Grand Rapids, MI: Eerdmans, 2007), pp. 66–69 (Hebrew publication *Tarbiz* 64 [1995]: 331–334).

25 The authoritative publication on the texts of the *amidah* from the Geniza is Uri Ehrlich, *The Weekday Amidah in Cairo Genizah Prayerbooks: Roots and Transmission* (Hebrew; Jerusalem: Yad Ben-Zvi, 2013), pp. 44–61.

26 For a discussion of this and bibliography, see my *Cursing the Christians? A History of the Birkat Haminim* (Oxford: Oxford University Press, 2012), pp. 36–38.

27 This tendency to see precursors of rabbinic prayers in Qumran texts is particularly characteristic of the work of Moshe Weinfeld. See part I of his collected articles: *Normative and Sectarian Judaism in the Second Temple Period* (London: T&T Clark, 2005).

28 For examples of Second Temple-period Jewish prayers in definitely or perhaps originally in Greek, see *Prayer from Alexander to Constantine: A Critical Anthology*, ed. Mark Kiley et al. (London: Routledge, 1997), especially chapters 9, 10, 12, 14, 16, and 17. The most comprehensive work on Jewish Greek prayers, including those from late antiquity, is van der Horst and Newman, *Early Jewish Prayers in Greek*.

29 Respectively, *b. Berakhot* 26a; *b. Pesaḥim* 56a (and its midrashic sources); *b. Megillah* 17b–18a.

30 *B. Berakhot* 28b; *b. Megillah* 17b–18a; *y. Berakhot* 2:4, 4d.

31 *B. Berakhot* 48b.

32 *Y. Megillah* 4:1, 75a. Curiously, this tradition does not appear in the Babylonian Talmud at all.

33 See, for instance, chapters 3, 5, and 8 in Heather A. McKay, *Sabbath and Synagogue: The Question of Sabbath Worship in Ancient Judaism* (Religions in the Graeco-Roman World, vol. 122; Leiden: Brill, 1994). Her discussions are stronger on non-Hebrew sources.

34 *Sifrei Deuteronomy* 31.

35 Mark 12:29–30. Matt 22:37 and Luke 10:27 omit Deut 6:4, the *Shema* itself. None indicate a liturgical setting.

36 *M. Berakhot* 1:4; named *emet veyatziv* as in *m. Tamid*.

37 Reuven Hammer, "What Did They Bless? A Study of Mishnah Tamid 5:1," *Jewish Quarterly Review* 81 (1991): 305–324.

38 *The Memory of the Temple and the Making of the Rabbis* (Philadelphia: University of Pennsylvania Press, 2013), 3 and passim.

39 *M. Soṭah* 7:7–8.

40 The list of relevant studies is long. See, for example, Lee I. Levine, *The Rabbinic Class of Roman Palestine in Late Antiquity* (Jerusalem: Yad Izhak Ben-Zvi / Jewish Theological Seminary of America, 1989); Seth Schwartz, *Imperialism and Jewish Society 200 B.C.E. to 640 C.E.* (Princeton, NJ: Princeton University Press, 2001); or Sacha Stern, *Calendar and Community: A History of the Jewish Calendar Second Century BCE–Tenth Century CE* (New York: Oxford University Press, 2001).

41 *M. Berakhot* 4:3.

42 "On the Beginnings of Obligatory Jewish Prayer" (Hebrew), *Tarbiz* 59 (1990): 425–439.

43 Ibid. He elaborates on this discussion in a second article, building on the presumptions established in the first: Ezra Fleischer, "The Shemoneh Esreh: Its Internal Order, Content and Goals," *Tarbiz* 62 (1993): 179–223 (Hebrew).

44 *M. Berakhot* 4:4.

45 *B. Berakhot* 27b–28a; *y. Berakhot* 4:1, 7d; *y. Taʾanit* 4:1, 67d.

46 For sources, see the discussion in my *To Worship God Properly: Tensions between Liturgical Custom and Halakhah in Judaism* (Cincinnati, OH: Hebrew Union College Press, 1998), pp. 14–19.

47 Jeffrey L. Rubenstein, *The Culture of the Babylonian Talmud* (Baltimore, MD: Johns Hopkins University Press, 2003), chapter 1, "The Rabbinic Academy," is particularly relevant here.

48 B. *Berakhot* 33b; b. *Megakhot* 25a; y. *Berakhot* 9:1, 12d.

49 Hannah Safrai, "Women and the Ancient Synagogue," in *Daughters of the King: Women and the Synagogue, a Survey of History, Halakhah, and Contemporary Realities*, ed. Susan Grossman and Rivka Haut (Philadelphia: Jewish Publication Society, 1992), p. 41, citing an article later republished in English as Shmuel Safrai, "Were Women Segregated in the Ancient Synagogue?" *Jerusalem Perspective* 52 (1997): 24–36. Also see Steven Fine's discussion in this volume.

50 The best English-language discussion of *piyyut* with rich introductory essays and translations of poetry is Laura S. Lieber, *Yannai on Genesis: An Invitation to Piyyut* (Cincinnati, OH: Hebrew Union College Press, 2010).

51 Hints of this appear in prayers embedded in early mystical texts, some of which have parallels in rabbinic liturgy. See, on this, Meir Bar-Ilan, *The Mysteries of Jewish Prayer and Hekhalot* (Hebrew; Ramat Gan: Bar-Ilan University Press, 1987); and Michael D. Swartz, *Mystical Prayer in Ancient Judaism: An Analysis of Maʿaseh Merkavah* (Tübingen: J. C. B. Mohr [Paul Siebeck], 1992).

52 See chapter 1 of my *Cursing the Christians?*; for the possible link to Christianity, see Adele Reinhartz's chapter in this volume.

53 An additional consideration is that it is often likely that, in the instances where rabbinic literature transmits prayer language, those transmitting the prayer, whether orally or in writing, have "corrected" its language to reflect their own practice. This is demonstrable in medieval liturgical manuscripts. Of course, a rejected text is more likely to have been transmitted without deliberate change.

54 See the final chapter of b. *Qiddushin*.

55 On the development of rabbinic authority, see Christine Hayes's chapter in this volume.

56 See Paul F. Bradshaw and Maxwell E. Johnson, *The Origins of Feasts, Fasts, and Seasons in Early Christianity* (Collegeville, MN: Liturgical Press, 2011), chapter 5, "The Quartodeciman Celebration." For the history of the Jewish calendar, see S. Stern, *Calendar and Community*, who demonstrates the fallacy of accepting the presumption embedded in rabbinic texts that theirs was the only Jewish calendar (p. 156, referring to the previous three chapters). He also reviews the evidence for observance of Jewish festivals in the diaspora, including new moons and Christian reflections on Jewish calendation as this affected the Easter debates (pp. 62–70). Timothy C. G. Thornton, "Problematical Passovers: Difficulties for Diaspora Jews and Early Christians in Determining Passover Dates during the First Three Centuries A.D.," *Studia Patristica* 20 (1989): 405n13, points to m. *Yevamot* 16:7, b. *Megillah* 18b, and b. *Sanhedrin* 26a as sources describing rabbis traveling to sort out diaspora calendation issues. These obviously require evaluation as to their historical value as sources.

57 On this issue in general, see Tessa Rajak, *Translation and Survival: The Greek Bible of the Ancient Jewish Diaspora* (New York: Oxford University Press, 2009), "Religious Practice in the Diaspora," pp. 107–112.

58 For a discussion of this letter, see Robert Brody, *The Geonim of Babylonia and the Shaping of Medieval Jewish Culture* (New Haven, CT: Yale University Press, 1998), pp. 113–117, 129, and the sources he cites.

59 Peter Sh. Lehnardt, "Redactions of the Prayer Book according to the Italian Rite: First Reconsiderations on the Basis of the Different Outlines of the Liturgical Poetry," *Italia* 20 (2010): 38–39, 42.

60 A slightly earlier manuscript was sold in 2013 to a private collector, and a scholarly publication about it by a Bible, not a liturgical, scholar was announced for 2015. As of 2017, nothing has been published, but I have been able to verify that the manuscript is being studied. See Menachem Wecker, "1,200-Year-Old Jewish Prayer Book Is Unveiled," *Forward* (September 27, 2013), www.forward.com.

61 "Geniza Specimens," *Jewish Quarterly Review* 10 (1898): 654–659.

62 For his own exposition of this in English, see Fleischer, "Controversy, on the Origins of the 'Amidah.'" In his collected essays, he expands this claim to other prayers as well.

63 See Hoffman and Cole, *Sacred Trash.*

64 The Geniza apparently served both communities, as can be judged from its contents.

65 Visit the home page of the Friedberg Jewish Manuscript Society at https://fjms. genizah.org.

66 Ezra Fleischer, *Eretz-Israel Prayer and Prayer Rituals as Portrayed in the Geniza Documents* (Hebrew; Jerusalem: Magnes Press, 1988).

67 Ehrlich, *Weekday Amidah*. Because of its comprehensive nature, this volume makes all previous publications and analyses of the Geniza data on this prayer obsolete.

68 See my development of this theory with regard to medieval European rites in "Mapping Medieval Rites: A Methodological Proposal," in *Jewish Prayer: New Perspectives*, ed. Uri Ehrlich (Beer Sheva: Ben Gurion University, 2016), pp. 31–70.

69 Hence, readers of Raymond Scheindlin's 1994 translation of Elbogen should be aware that this is a 1913 text. Reuven Hammer's more popularly oriented text, *Entering Jewish Prayer: A Guide to Personal Devotion and the Worship Service* (New York: Schocken, 1994), is better, but still presents a somewhat misleading historical picture. Stefan C. Reif's *Judaism and Hebrew Prayer: New Perspectives on Jewish Liturgical History* (Cambridge: Cambridge University Press, 1993) is a more complex text that asks many necessary questions but does not provide a clear set of answers. For now, I recommend turning to Levine, *Ancient Synagogue.*

8

Ancient Jewish Gender

ELIZABETH SHANKS ALEXANDER

All forms of contemporary Judaism, from the most liberal to the most conservative, inherit a framework for thinking about gender from classical rabbinic sources. Whether Jews embrace or repudiate so-called traditional gender roles, these sources establish the parameters for contemporary gender identities. As feminism, with its concern for gender equality, developed in Western culture, it drew attention to arenas of life where traditional Jewish practice falls short of egalitarian ideals. In the early to mid-1970s, Jewish feminists argued that legal sources (*halakhah*) disregard the full personhood of women and called for new legal developments to enfranchise them.[1] Traditionalists countered that Jewish law has the highest regard for women and, though it admittedly crafts the lives of men and women differently, each set of contributions is vital and precious.[2]

The parties to this debate more or less agreed on which *halakhic* sources were relevant to the discussion. What they disagreed about was whether these sources configure gender identities in a way that is appropriate today. Traditionalists' priority was to preserve an ancient and authoritative vision of gender. Feminists, on the other hand, wanted to break with the past; for them, the priority was to bring their Jewish lives in sync with other domains of modern society where women were empowering themselves on equal terms with men.

These cultural debates set an agenda for critical scholarship by drawing attention to the sources that impact gender. But scholars recognize that these sources have a different relationship to the social world where gender is lived in the ancient and modern worlds. In the modern world, rabbinic sources are authoritative and set the norms for behavior. Gender is constructed when the sources direct men and women to do different things and we attach social significance to the different patterns of behavior. In the ancient world, however, the sources were not yet authoritative; they were in the process of being composed. The issues that were contested in the rabbis' day, and to which the rabbis responded, are not the same as the issues that are at stake in the contemporary cultural debates. Critical scholarship, then, focuses on what sources tell us about the social aspirations of the rabbis who composed them in antiquity, stressing that their work responds to social conditions that are very different from those of today.

This chapter focuses on three areas of Jewish life—ritual commandments, rituals connected with menstruation, and home/domesticity—that attract scholarly attention because of their relevance to contemporary cultural debates. The chapter demonstrates that the gender that the ancient rabbis performed when composing their texts is quite different from the gender that contemporary Jews perform when patterning their lives after the template of rabbinic sources.

Gender in Ritual

Joan Scott offers a useful definition of gender at the outset of her book *Gender and the Politics of History*: "Gender, in these essays, means *knowledge about sexual difference.* I use knowledge, following Michel Foucault, to mean the understanding . . . of human relationships, in this case of those between men and women. . . . Knowledge refers not only to ideas, but to institutions and structures, everyday practices as well as specialized rituals, all of which constitute social relationships."[3] One comes to know the difference between men and women, then, not only in the ideas we have about who men and women are, but also in the social practices whereby we perform and encounter those differences.

Perhaps the most visible social context in which contemporary Jews have learned what it means to be "man" versus "woman" is public ritual. Until the 1950s (and still today in Orthodox settings) the synagogue was (and is) a place where gender is prominently visible. One concrete marker of male-female difference is the physical barrier (*mehitzah*) that separates men from women while praying. Male-female difference is also constituted by the fact that men and women engage in different ritual activities on their respective sides of the *mehitzah*. To list only the most well-known examples: men wear phylacteries (*tefillin*) and prayer shawls (*tallit*) with the biblically commanded fringes (*tzitzit*), they publicly declaim the week's Torah verses from a podium, they lead prayers, they shake the palm branch (*lulav*) on the holiday of Sukkot, and they blow the ram's horn (*shofar*) on Rosh Hashanah. In the traditional synagogue, women do none of these things. Gender is vividly manifest for all to see.

As feminists and traditionalists debated whether this way of performing gender is appropriate today, scholars turned to the sources that gave rise to it. They wanted to understand what the rabbis who distinguished male from female ritual participation sought to achieve.

Two kinds of sources determine the patterns of ritual performance observable in synagogues today. One set of texts exempts women (often along with slaves and minors) from specific rituals. For example,

> Women, slaves and minors are exempt from recitation of the *Shema* [a prayer affirming Israel's devotion to the one God] and from *tefillin* (phylacteries). (*m. Berakhot* 3:3)

> Rabbi Shimon exempts women from *tzitzit* (fringes). (*t. Qiddushin* 1:10, *Sifre* Numbers 115)

> Women, slaves, and minors are exempt [from blowing the *shofar* (ram's horn)] and [if they do blow the *shofar*] they do not absolve others of their obligation. (*t. Rosh Hashanah* 2:5)

> Women, slaves and minors are exempt from [dwelling in] a *sukkah* (booth) [on the holiday of Sukkot]. (*m. Sukkah* 2:8)

Another set of texts exempts women from entire categories of ritual. For example,

> Every commandment pertaining to the son, [and performed by] the father [*kol mitzvat ha-av al-ha-ben*]—men are obligated [to observe], but women are exempt [from observing] . . .

> Every positive commandment occasioned by time (*kol mitzvat 'aseh she-ha-zman gramah*)—men are obligated [to observe], but women are exempt [from observing]. (*m. Qiddushin* 1:7)

These traditions do not explain why women are exempt from certain rituals or groups of ritual. One goal of scholarship has been to identify the rationale for these legal rulings.

The last of these traditions, women's exemption from the category of "positive commandment[s] occasioned by time," has received more scholarly attention than any of the other exemptions. Scholars and laypeople alike have seen it as key to understanding the entirety of women's ritual exemptions. In common parlance, the category is known as "timebound, positive commandments," or even just "timebound commandments." They are "positive" because they are ritual acts that must be actively performed rather than passively refrained from (the "thou shalts" as opposed to the "thou shalt nots"), and they are "timebound" because they must be performed at, by, or during a specified time frame.

The complete version of the timebound exemption reads as follows:

1. Every positive commandment occasioned by time (*kol mitzvat 'aseh she-ha-zman gramah*)—men are obligated [to observe], but women are exempt [from observing].
2. Every positive commandment not occasioned by time—men and women are equally obligated [to observe].
3. Every negative commandment, whether occasioned by time or not—men and women are equally obligated [to observe]. (*m. Qiddushin* 1:7)

This expanded version appears to be a comprehensive statement of how female obligation differs from male. Commandments are divided into four categories: (1) timebound positive; (2) non-timebound positive; (3) timebound negative; and (4) non-timebound negative. Since every commandment is either "positive" or "negative" and either "timebound" or "not timebound," the four categories account for all commandments. The fact that women are exempt from only one of the four categories suggests that timebound commandments are the only set of rituals from which women are exempt.

Scholars have directed their efforts toward understanding the relevance of *time* to female exemption. Several explanations have been proposed:[4]

- Timebound commandments *take* time. Women do not have expendable time because of their responsibilities to home and children. The conclusion was that the rabbis thought that women's lives revolve around domestic tasks and childcare.[5] Contemporary Jews across the ideological spectrum have generally accepted this explanation of the timebound exemption. Much of the contemporary debate on gender and ritual arose because feminists did not want their religious life to be circumscribed by the traditional preoccupations of wife and mother.
- Timebound commandments *mark* time. The responsibility for marking such occasions falls to those in the social order most like the priests (i.e., men). The conclusion was that the rabbis thought that men occupy a position of greater responsibility in the social order and while women are full citizens, they occupy a lesser rank.[6]
- Timebound commandments need to be performed "*on time.*" Women lack the self-control to do so. The conclusion was that the rabbis thought that men are characterized by cultured self-control, while women are wild, untamed creatures of nature.[7]

Each of these theories imagines rabbinic gender in light of the timebound exemption. How are we to arbitrate among them? Which one accurately reflects rabbinic views on the differences between men and women? One difficulty with using the timebound exemption as our main evidence for rabbinic gender is that the text does not provide any clues as to how—or even if—time and gender are causally connected.

There is another difficulty with using the timebound exemption as key evidence for rabbinic gender: it is contradicted by a number of specific rulings.[8] In violation of line 1 ("women are exempt from timebound commandments"), there are a number of timebound rituals that women are obligated to perform, such as *hakhel*, *simchah* offering, eating *matzah* on Passover, *kiddush hayom*, lighting Hanukkah candles, drinking four cups of wine on Passover, and reading the *megillah* on Purim.[9] And in violation of line 2 ("women are obligated to perform non-timebound commandments"), there are a number of non-timebound rituals from which women are exempt, such as Torah study, redemption of one's firstborn son, circumcising one's son, and "be fruitful and multiply" on the view of all except Yoḥanan b. Baroka.[10]

Women's Exemption from Specific Rituals

It appears that the quality of "timeboundness" cannot teach us as much about women's ritual exemptions as we might have hoped. Another strategy is to try to determine the rationale for exempting women from the individual rituals that are named as members of the timebound category. If gender is enacted when ritual is performed, we can ask how gender is constituted by the male performance of, and female exemption from, *specific* timebound rituals.

The earliest rabbinic sources name three rituals as timebound commandments, and there is disagreement about a fourth: "What is a positive commandment occasioned by time? For example, *sukkah, lulav, tefillin*. . . . Rabbi Shimon exempts women from *tzitzit* because they are a positive commandment occasioned by time" (*t. Qiddushin* 1:10). Two of these rituals (*sukkah* and *lulav*) are performed during the fall harvest festival of Sukkot. The other two (*tefillin* and *tzitzit*) are connected to the rabbinic prayer known as the *Shema*.

Sukkot Rituals (Sukkah and Lulav)

The Bible instructs the people of Israel to dwell in booths (*sukkah* sing., *sukkot* pl.) throughout the seven days of the festival in order to recall the booths that provided shelter during their desert journeys (Lev 23:42–43). Additionally, they are told to "take" fruit and branches from several types of trees (one of which is a palm, *lulav*) on the first day (v. 40). The rabbis interpreted these instructions in very specific ways.

They envisioned the *sukkah* as an insubstantial structure with a porous roof and a minimum of three walls. For the duration of the holiday, the fragile *sukkah* replaces one's solidly built house, becoming one's "surrogate home."[11] Marjorie Lehman examines the exemption of women from the *sukkah* in light of its dual character as both "home" and "not-home."[12] The *sukkah* is home insofar as one engages in all the ordinary, daily activities that one regularly performs in the home (e.g., eating, drinking, lounging, and sleeping). But it is unlike a home in that its architectural requirements create vulnerability rather than security. Lehman argues that the female exemption further differentiates the ritual "*sukkah*-as-home" from the permanent home. In the permanent home, a male householder presides over a domestic community consisting of his wife, servants, and children. During Sukkot the householder presides over a different kind of home, one that has been "masculinized" and emptied of his extended domestic community.[13] The exemption of women from *sukkah* highlights the centrality of the male householder in the rabbinic gender economy. Each man stands at the center of his domestic community, but each also has the capacity to convene a ritual domicile independent of his dependents.

The second Sukkot ritual named as a timebound commandment is *lulav*. The rabbinic ritual derives from a biblical verse that instructs Israel to take a bouquet of flora as an expression of festal joy. In the late Second Temple period, the ritual had been performed by lay Israelite men who made the pilgrimage to the Jerusalem Temple. At the Temple, they held the *lulav* while the Levites recited verses of divine praise (*hallel*) and the priests marched around the altar with willow branches. After the Temple was destroyed, the setting for the *lulav* ritual shifted to the synagogue and the rabbinic house of study. In the synagogue, the *lulav* was shaken during the recitation of *hallel* and following the recitation of a blessing.[14] The rabbis never explicitly state their reason for exempting women from *lulav*. Shevah Yalon suggests, compellingly I think, that the exemption derives from the ritual's origins at the Jerusalem Temple, a domain in which men, and not women, were ritual actors.[15] On this view, the rabbis exempted women in order to connect the new rabbinic ritual to that of their predecessors. As Lehman notes, the rabbis often used gender to think about their relationship to the now-defunct Temple.[16]

Shema Rituals (Tefillin, Shema, Torah Study, and Tzitzit)

The final ritual that is listed unequivocally as a timebound commandment in the text cited above is *tefillin*. As practiced by the rabbis, the *tefillin* ritual entails attaching two small, black leather boxes containing parchment inscribed with four biblical passages to one's arm and head with black leather straps. In contrast to contemporary observance, in antiquity the leather boxes were quite small (archaeological evidence suggests the size of a thumbnail) and were worn throughout daylight hours.

The rationale for this exemption is best understood by turning to the ritual's biblical sources, which became the central text of a rabbinic prayer known as the *Shema*. It consists of three biblical passages that are framed by introductory and concluding blessings.[17] In general terms, these passages affirm Israel's commitment to a covenantal relationship with God. They also direct Israel to embody its commitment to this relationship through several ritual practices.

A list of four rituals is repeated in the first and second paragraphs of the *Shema* (the same four in each paragraph). First, the practitioner is told to transmit membership in the covenantal relationship to the next generation. The rabbis interpreted this instruction as an obligation for fathers to teach Torah to their sons and, by extension, to engage in Torah study themselves. Second, the practitioner is instructed to speak regularly of the covenantal relationship, which the rabbis interpreted as an obligation to recite the three paragraphs of the *Shema* twice daily. Third, the practitioner is told to mark his body with signs of the relationship. The rabbis interpreted this instruction as the obligation to wear *tefillin* containing the first two paragraphs of the *Shema* and two additional paragraphs.[18] Fourth, the practitioner is told to inscribe words declaring Israel's commitment to God on the doorpost (*mezuzah*). The rabbis performed this ritual by affixing the first two paragraphs of the *Shema* on their doorposts.[19] Note that the first two paragraphs of the *Shema* play a role in the performance of *Shema, tefillin,* and *mezuzah*; note also that they are the very paragraphs that prescribe these rituals. In addition, the third paragraph of the *Shema* instructs Israel to wear fringes (*tzitzit*) on the corners of their garments to remind them of their covenantal obligations.

The four rituals mentioned in the first two paragraphs (Torah study, *Shema, tefillin,* and *mezuzah*) are performed by engaging biblical scripture. Teaching Torah to one's sons and studying Torah oneself involve free-form intellectual interaction with scripture. The *Shema* involves recitation of three important scriptural passages. *Tefillin* attaches two of the *Shema* scriptural passages (along with two others) to one's body, and the *mezuzah* posts them at the entrance to one's home. These similarities notwithstanding, the *Shema* rituals were evaluated differently when it came to women's participation. The rabbis exempted women from three of these rituals (*tefillin*, Torah study, and *Shema*) and obligated women in only one (*mezuzah*). If all of these rituals derive from the *Shema* and if three (*Shema*, *tefillin*, and *mezuzah*) are performed by *using* the *Shema* passages, why did the rabbis treat *mezuzah* as an exception? Or, put differently, what did *tefillin*, Torah study, and *Shema* have in common that warranted the exemption of women in each case?

Interestingly, the rabbis characterize both *Shema* and *tefillin* as types of Torah study.[20] As different ways of enacting Torah study, the three rituals (Torah study, *Shema*, and *tefillin*) are of a piece. I have elsewhere argued that women's exemption from all three follows from the fact that all are forms of Torah study.[21] Rabbinic sources are unequivocal in their exemption—and even exclusion—of women from this most central of rabbinic practices.[22]

Women's exemption from *tefillin* makes the most sense, then, when we see it as an extension of their exemption from Torah study. Women's exemption from Torah study, in turn, is best understood in the context of the "commandments pertaining to the son, [and performed by] the father."[23] As we saw above, this is a category of commandments from which women are exempt. Torah study is one of the "father-to-son" commandments because the father must teach Torah to his son. Other father-to-son commandments include the requirement that a father circumcise his son and, provided the son is a firstborn, that the father redeem him from a priest. Like Torah study, these rituals induct the son into and perform his membership within the covenantal community. Other father-to-son obligations are more practical. A father must set up his son as a householder in his own right by teaching him a trade and marrying him off. Taken as a group, the father-to-son obligations enable a father to reproduce his cultural/religious identity (within the covenantal community) and social identity (as householder) in the next generation.[24]

We now have all the pieces in place to understand the rationale for women's exemption from *tefillin*. Like Torah study, *tefillin* ensures intergenerational continuity. Both rituals help to reproduce the father's cultural, religious, and social identity in the next generation. Why were women exempt from rituals that supported that goal? Daughters were structurally prevented from reproducing their fathers' identity. Daughters would marry someone else's son and help continue *that* man's line. Since continuing her father's line was not something that daughters could do, women (insofar as they were always someone's daughter) were exempt from the rituals (*tefillin*, *Shema* and Torah study) that sustained their father's line in the next generation.

The Dispute about Women and Tzitzit

The final *Shema* ritual, *tzitzit*, is the only ritual derived from the third paragraph of the *Shema*. It is also the only ritual that does not directly employ biblical scripture (recall that *tzitzit* are the fringes attached to the corners of one's garment). *Tzitzit* is also the only *Shema* ritual to provoke rabbinic disagreement on the matter of women. These three features of *tzitzit* are not unrelated.

The rabbis had clarity about women's obligation when it concerned rituals from the first two paragraphs of the *Shema*. Those rituals were evaluated on the basis of their similarity (or dissimilarity) to Torah study, from which the rabbis already knew women to be exempt. *Tefillin* and *Shema*, which were like Torah study, were not relevant for women. *Mezuzah*, which was not like Torah study, was relevant for women. As the only ritual from the *Shema*'s third paragraph, *tzitzit* was also the only *Shema* ritual that did not require the use of scripture when performing it. As such, the criterion of being like (or unlike) Torah study was not an appropriate way to determine women's obligation. Though *tzitzit* and Torah study were not comparable, *tzitzit* could be compared to other rituals from the first two paragraphs of the *Shema*. *Tzitzit* might be like *tefillin* and/or *Shema*, in which case women should be exempt. Or *tzitzit* might be more like *mezuzah*, in which case women should be obligated.

In the text cited above (*t. Qiddushin* 1:10), R. Shimon exempts women from *tzitzit* on account of their timebound status. What might R. Shimon have had in mind when calling *tzitzit* timebound and invoking the timebound exemption? One possibility is that he wished to emphasize the commonality between *tzitzit* and *tefillin*, both of which are worn during daylight hours but not at night. We know that *tefillin*'s status as timebound was not the reason for women's exemption. Perhaps it was not the reason for women's exemption from *tzitzit* either. *Tzitzit* and *tefillin* share other qualities that might have been more determinative of the exemption. Like *tefillin*, *tzitzit* encompasses the body. And like *tefillin*, *tzitzit* marks membership within the covenantal community on one's person. And so (according to R. Shimon) it made sense that, as with *tefillin*, the body encompassed by *tzitzit* should be that of the male householder.

* * *

Having now surveyed various rituals (*sukkah, lulav, tefillin, Shema,* Torah study, and *tzitzit*) linked to the timebound exemption, we see several recurring themes. First is the prominence of the householder in the rituals from which women are exempt. Women's exemption from dwelling in the *sukkah* emphasizes that the male householder, unlike his dependents, can make a home with or without them. Torah study, along with the other father-to-son obligations, likewise features the male householder, who seeks to replicate himself in the next generation. Insofar as *tefillin* and *Shema* are the functional equivalents of Torah study, they also showcase the male householder. From the general rubric of father-to-son rituals, we learn that fathers (and sons when they eventually become fathers) constitute the household, while wives (and daughters when they become wives) merely populate it. Another theme that emerges from the ritual exemptions is that they at times reflect anxiety about how the covenantal community will endure over time. Women's exemption from *lulav* forges a link between past and present by connecting the new rabbinic synagogue ritual to earlier Temple ritual. And Torah study as a father-to-son obligation constructs the male householder as an agent of continuity. And, finally, we see a link between gender and rituals that are performed on the body, as in *tefillin* and *tzitzit*. The more central the body is to performance, the more likely the rabbis were to distinguish male from female obligation.

Revisiting the Category of Timebound Commandments

Thus far we have focused on understanding the rationale of exempting women from particular rituals. We found that the "timebound" label cannot tell us much about why the rabbis thought it appropriate to exempt women from individual rituals. But we learned a lot when we examined the specific rituals encompassed by the category, which leads us to ask whether we can learn anything about the rabbinic understanding of gender from texts that cite the category as a whole. Or have scholars been misguided in their attention to the timebound exemption?

The key is to recognize that rabbinic texts can be read in different ways. Up to this point, we have read rabbinic texts as *legal sources* and tried to understand the motivation behind their legal stipulations (e.g., why are women exempt from *lulav* or *tefillin*?). But we can also read rabbinic texts as *discourse*, that is, *as a record of how the rabbis talk about matters of interest to them*. When reading the texts in this manner, we ask what is accomplished when the rabbis talk about a given subject as they do.

How, then, do the rabbis talk about the timebound exemption as a categorical imperative? In what contexts do they invoke it, and to what ends? It turns out that the timebound exemption appears on several lists of male-female difference. One such list reads as follows:

What are some legal rulings that distinguish between [*mah bein*] man and woman?

A man [leper] uncovers [his hair] and tears [his garment], but a woman [leper] does not uncover [her hair] or tear [her garment].

A man may submit his son to a Nazirite vow, but a woman may not submit her son to a Nazirite vow . . .

A man may betrothe his daughter, but a woman may not betrothe her daughter.

A man is stoned naked, but a woman is not stoned naked . . .

A man is sold [as a slave] to repay what he stole, but a woman is not sold [as a slave] to repay what she stole. (*m. Soṭah* 3:8)

One need not be familiar with the intricacies of Jewish law to observe several things about this list. First, the items are drawn from diverse areas of law (leprosy, Nazirite vows, betrothal, capital punishment, and debt slavery). Second, each item references a very specific ruling. What purpose is served by bringing these diverse rulings together?

The question that introduces the list ("What are some legal rulings that distinguish between man and woman?") makes clear that the list functions to construct knowledge about the difference between men and women. Interestingly, this social knowledge emerges not from attributing certain qualities to men and women respectively (e.g., "women are emotional and men are rational"). It also does not result from making legal decrees that require men and women to do different things. After all, the decision to treat men and women differently *precedes* the lists. List making as the rabbis perform it is an *academic* way to construct social knowledge. It involves reviewing a large number of legal traditions, identifying those that treat men and women differently, and organizing them according to a new principle. No longer is the stipulation that "men, but not women, are stoned naked" set alongside other traditions about capital punishment where its main function is to inform readers of proper procedure. The stipulation is now set alongside stipulations from other areas of law that conform to a pattern. The collected traditions accomplish something together that none can accomplish alone—they confirm that the law treats men and women differently. Men and women are different kinds of legal subjects.

It is noteworthy that the timebound exemption appears on three lists of male-female difference.[25] In the context of the lists, the timebound exemption helps stabilize gender identities—but not by virtue of prescribing different patterns of ritual performance to men and women. Like other items on the lists, the timebound exemption is a specific ruling from a particular area of law. It contributes to the construction of gender by being one piece in a larger patchwork of individual rulings. As with the other items on the lists, its significance lies in the fact that it conforms to the pattern. It reinforces the lists' impact by adding one more example.

Gender in the Rabbinic House of Study

There is an interesting irony in the fact that the rabbis construct knowledge of sexual difference while engaged in the academic work of list making. Even though this knowledge is about differences between men and women, women are not involved in its production. Gender that emerges when rabbis compile a list is notably different from gender that emerges when people perform ritual. In the case of ritual, gender arises from the fact that men and women do different things with their bodies. In the case of list making, gender emerges in a social setting that is exclusively male; there are no women in the rabbinic house of study (*beit midrash*) where the lists are produced.

And here we reach a conclusion that is repeated in much scholarship on ancient rabbinic gender: though scholars often begin their inquiries with a desire to find "real, live" women, the preponderance of evidence reaches us through rabbinic texts that were produced in the all-male *beit midrash*. Rabbinic texts may mention women, but discussions of women always reflect rabbinic (male) points of view.

The limitations of this evidence are clear if we think about a modern analogy. Imagine trying to learn about the differences between contemporary men and women while relying exclusively on a transcript of conversations from a men's locker room. You would certainly learn something about how contemporary gender operates, but your insights about society as a whole would be limited. You might speculate that men talk about women in particular ways in the locker room in order to assert their maleness to one another. But you likely would not accept the claims made there as accurate representations of social reality. In like manner, scholars recognize that rabbinic texts tell us more about gender in the *beit midrash* than elsewhere. The texts give us access to rabbinic conversations about matters of interest to them. Conversations in the *beit midrash* were, for the most part, self-referential; they pointed back to earlier conversations rather than to the social world beyond its walls. Though scholars might wish to use rabbinic texts to reconstruct ancient gender in diverse social settings, they often find that the most they can do is watch the rabbis negotiate gender in the all-male house of study.

Gender and the Female Body

Another area of Jewish life that sparked debate between feminists and traditionalists is the rituals and practices connected with menstruation, commonly known as the laws of *niddah*. The Bible stipulates that a man and a woman should not have conjugal relations during "the time of her impurity" (Leviticus 18:20; see also 20:19), that is, while she is menstruating. In the rabbinic version of this practice, sexual contact is to be avoided when the female partner has menstrual bleeding and during a "buffer zone" of seven additional days. Throughout this time, the couple abstains from not only sexual touching, but also more prosaic physical contact (like passing a dish) on the chance that it might lead to sexual intimacy. The period of separation ends when the female partner immerses in a ritual bath (*miqveh*), at which point the couple may resume sexual relations and regular physical contact.

The laws of *niddah* drew the ire of feminists who felt that they evince disgust for the female body with its regular bloody secretions.[26] This assessment was exacerbated by the fact that the Bible characterizes the menstruating woman as "impure." To feminists, the Bible's language implied that women, but not men, are a locus of impurity in the family. For their part, traditionalists countered that the laws of *niddah* sanctify a couple's marital relations. The required periods of abstention promote sexual tension over the course of a couple's life as husband and wife eagerly await the monthly reunion.[27] Again, the contemporary debate revolved around whether gender identities orchestrated by this ritual regimen are compelling today. And again, both parties to the debate assumed that the practices reflect an ancient social code. Feminists and traditionalists simply differed on whether they wanted to maintain a connection or break ties with social norms of the past.

Scholarly interest in the laws of *niddah* is undoubtedly stimulated by contemporary cultural debates. But scholars ask *how* rabbinic texts produced gendered identities in antiquity, rather than assuming that it happened then the way it does today. Charlotte Fonrobert observes that the contemporary debates generally focus on how the social identities of men and women are shaped by the practice of menstrual rituals. When analyzing the ancient texts, she directs attention to rabbinic discourse about the practice, that is, to rabbinic ways of speaking about *niddah*.[28]

Recognizing that the texts available to us were produced in the *beit midrash*, Fonrobert "listens in" as the rabbis discuss the laws of *niddah*. She finds that rabbinic conversations are driven by a key problem. The period of separation between husband and wife is established by the onset of menstruation, an event that takes place deep within the recesses of a woman's body. How are the rabbis to regulate the laws of *niddah* when they lack access to the central experience around which the practice revolves?

Female Body as Inanimate Object

Fonrobert argues that the rabbinic solution is to displace the woman as the natural interpreter of what is happening in her body. Rabbinic texts envision the inside of a woman's body, especially her sexual and reproductive organs, as a series of rooms. Architectural metaphors are especially prominent in discussions about the onset of menstruation.[29] Consider the following texts:

> The sages crafted a metaphor concerning the woman: [there is in her] *a chamber, a vestibule, and an upper chamber.* Blood from the *chamber* is in the status of impurity. If it [the blood] is located in the *vestibule,* it is in the status of doubtful impurity, since the assumption is that it derives from the source. (*m. Niddah* 2:5)[30]

> The blood in the *chamber* is in the status of impurity, but the blood of the *upper chamber* is in the status of purity. (*y. Niddah* 2:4, 50a)[31]

According to Fonrobert, the effect of using architectural metaphors is to imagine the woman's body as both an empty space and an inanimate object. As an empty space, the chambers of the woman-as-house can be otherwise occupied. Sources unrelated to menstruation make clear that the appropriate occupant is her husband. He alone may "open the door" and "tear away the bolt."[32] (This is a clear reference to the expectation that his bride be a virgin.) Alternatively, if the woman's body is an inanimate object, she is not uniquely positioned to determine what is happening within it. The onset of menstruation becomes something that an outsider can critically evaluate and establish.

Rabbis as Expert Interpreters of the Female Body

Fashioning the woman's body as an inanimate object lays the groundwork for establishing the rabbis as experts in menstruation. The second step involves developing a "science of blood" to determine when vaginal bleeding is menstrual.[33] The rabbis focus on aspects of female bleeding that are accessible to an outside observer, often a bloodstain (*ketem*) on the woman's undergarments or bedsheets. Unlike internal sensations, external evidence can be analyzed according to objective criteria (color, location, other attributable causes) to determine its status. For example,

> Five [types or colors of] blood are impure in a woman: the [color of] red, the [color of] black, the [the color of] saffron, the [color of] muddy water, and the [color of] diluted wine. (*m. Niddah* 2:6)[34]

If a woman saw a stain on her flesh near her private parts, she is impure;
if not near her private parts, she is pure.

If on her heel or her big toe, she is impure.

If on the inner side of her thigh or feet, she is impure;

If on the outer side, she is pure.

If on the flanks, on either side, she is pure. (*m. Niddah* 8:1)

These texts provide a taxonomy of blood, outlining the attributes that distinguish impure (menstrual) from pure (nonmenstrual) bleeding. For example, if the bleeding is the color of muddy water, it is impure (i.e., menstrual); if the bloodstain appears proximate to her private parts, it is impure (i.e., menstrual). While the rabbis may not have access to a woman's internal sensations, they surely know what muddy water looks like or where on a garment the stain appears.

We cannot know how, or even whether, the rabbis implemented these measures outside the *beit midrash*. To what extent did women use this taxonomy of colors to decide if they had begun menstruating? For Fonrobert, that is not the point. She argues that the rabbinic "science of blood" is first and foremost a *way of talking* about women's bodies. The effect is to make the female body into an object, one that rabbis are uniquely positioned to interpret by virtue of their extensive training in scripture and legal traditions.

What Did Women Think?

Even as the rabbis position themselves as expert interpreters of the female body, they appear anxious about the legitimacy of their endeavor. Perhaps women will have their own ideas about when menstruation begins? Will they (women) recognize rabbinic interpretations of the female body as authoritative? Fonrobert hears these anxieties as she eavesdrops on another conversation in the *beit midrash*.[35] One text features the rabbinic sage Shmu'el claiming that the onset of menstruation should be determined by a woman's internal sensations.[36] After introducing Shmu'el's position, the text provides three counterarguments when one would have sufficed. The energy that the text invests in suppressing Shmu'el's position reveals just how powerful the rabbis find it to be. It is not a position to be dismissed lightly. We cannot know how the women of antiquity felt about rabbinic ways of talking about the female body, but we see that *the rabbis* felt the watchful eye of contemporary women upon them.

Fonrobert's approach strikes an interesting balance between two competing scholarly *desiderata*. She takes the limits of our evidence seriously. Rabbinic texts offer information first and foremost about the rabbis. The literature reflects their preoccupations, their questions, and their answers. Their concern is to regulate the practice of *niddah* without firsthand experience of the bodily event around which it revolves. Their solution? To use metaphors that imagine the woman's body as an inanimate object and to establish external criteria by which to determine what is happening inside the woman's body. But Fonrobert has another scholarly impulse. She also wants to move beyond what the rabbis say "about women." She wants to hear from women themselves. She comes to see that the rabbis acknowledged that women might not appreciate how they (the rabbis) positioned themselves as expert interpreters of their (women's) bodies. The women's point of view, indeed *that there is such a thing*, comes to light when the rabbis react to it (albeit among themselves). Fonrobert focuses on men because it is their voices that are preserved. History's women emerge when she notices the tension between the dominant discourse about the female body and the anxious concern that women might not agree.

Gender in the Public and Private Spheres

One final area of scholarly interest has been stimulated by contemporary cultural debates. American feminism of the late 1960s and early 1970s was in many ways a repudiation of the prevailing social norms from the previous decade. The 1950s feminine ideal had been the homemaker whose social prestige was linked to her domestic accomplishments. Feminists wanted to break away from what they saw as the confining strictures of the home and home-related tasks. For Jewish feminists, these concerns translated into a mission to bring women into the public life of Judaism (largely at the synagogue). At the same time, feminists deemphasized women's contributions at home. Traditionalists, on the other hand, valorized the Jewish housewife for all that she did in the home; they affirmed the importance of the home as a central institution of Jewish life, where, among other things, Jewish values were transmitted to the next generation.

This debate is grounded in certain assumptions about how gender is expressed in space. The public sphere is marked as male and the home as female, and the two are conceived in binary terms, that is, according to a set of opposing, paired attributes. The public sphere is where people meet to conduct economic, political, cultural, and religious business; the home is where people go to recuperate from the activities of the public sphere. The public sphere is characterized by movement and social interaction, the private sphere by rest and social isolation. And while feminists and traditionalists disagree about the appropriateness of this way of arranging gender in space today, both parties assume that this series of binaries accurately reflects ancient Jewish ways of arranging men and women in space.

Until recently, scholars also assumed that men and women inhabited distinct spatial spheres in the villages, towns, and urban centers of Roman Palestine. With increasingly sophisticated archaeological methods, scholars tried to locate the isolated quarters that kept women out of the public eye. Cynthia Baker has demonstrated, however, that the search for women's quarters is destined to fail because it is misguided.[37] The sharp distinction between public and private space that scholars and laypeople alike attribute to Jewish antiquity is simply not warranted.

No Ancient Evidence for a Sharp Distinction between Public and Private Spheres

Unlike today's homes, domestic dwellings in ancient Palestine were not set off from other dwellings and centers of commerce. Baker observes that "houses throughout . . . ancient Galilee were frequently built in clusters or blocks."[38] Multiresidence complexes were usually arranged around a shared courtyard. Members of different households would encounter each other there engaged in various household and commercial activities. Furthermore, commercial goods were both produced in and sold in domestic settings. Summarizing a survey of shops in small cities, towns, and villages, Yizhar Hirschfeld notes that "most shops were part of domestic dwellings."[39] In some cases, the courtyard was open at two ends and served as a thoroughfare for people who had no connection at all to the residents. In all of these ways, domestic structures were places where both residents and nonresidents could be found; they were characterized by social interaction and movement, rather than isolation and rest.

Just as dwelling structures were not cordoned off from outsiders, so, too, domestic tasks were not confined to the dwelling structure. Baker explains that "houses . . . rarely encompassed architecturally all of the activities essential to household functioning."[40] In many cases, water was carried from a cistern, well, or river, laundry was taken to running water, people relieved themselves in nature, and food preparation involved the use of shared tools and equipment (e.g., ovens and grindstones). Just as the household members had no privacy from the outside world while at home, it was also not possible to manage household affairs within the confines of the dwelling structure.

Given these findings, it simply makes no sense to envision gendered spaces in the manner described above, with women confined to the privacy of the home and men engaged in public affairs elsewhere. Men and women could be found both within dwelling structures and in communal spaces like the courtyard and marketplace. If we want to understand how space was linked to gender, it is futile to ask which spaces were occupied by men and which by women. Baker's observations point us to a different set of questions. How did men and women negotiate the shared spaces? And how did men's and women's movements through the shared spaces differ?

Performing Gender by Manipulating Visibility and Invisibility

Baker finds an important clue in the helter-skelter and asymmetrical arrangement of adjoining rooms within dwelling structures. The floorplans of domestic dwellings reveal that "doorways on opposing walls are seldom set directly opposite each other; as a result, sight lines only occasionally pass uninterrupted through more than one room."[41] Privacy here is achieved by limiting *visual* access and imposing circuitous movement patterns. It is achieved not by restricting the movement of certain people, but by redirecting sight. Though dwelling structures typically feature a central courtyard, very few of the surrounding rooms are immediately accessible to the courtyard. Baker summarizes her conclusions as follows: "these built structures convey a sense of constant negotiation of visibility/invisibility, both within enclosures and between enclosed and unenclosed spaces. This architecture seems to be about not seeing, as well as not being seen, from one space to another."[42] In this way of configuring space, gender was stabilized *by manipulating visibility and invisibility* within spaces that were traversed by both men and women.

Rabbinic texts from the same period corroborate these conclusions. Like the architecture, the texts deal with the fact that men and women occupy the same spaces by manipulating visibility and invisibility. The following text assumes that both men and women pass through communal spaces, but it also offers a strategy for maintaining women's invisibility, regardless of where she is: "A woman who has a husband: whether she adorns herself or not, nobody stares at her. . . . A woman who has no husband: whether she adorns herself or not, everybody stares at her" (*t. Qiddushin* 1:11). In this source, a woman's visibility in public space is tied to her having a husband. If she is married, she passes through anonymously and unseen ("nobody stares"); if she is unmarried, she is seen by all ("everybody stares"). One way, then, for a woman to maintain invisibility while traversing spaces inhabited by both men and women is to be someone's wife. How will people know if she is married? Baker suggests that married women were recognizable by their headgear. Hats were an essential component of the married woman's wardrobe, as the husband had to provide his wife with a hat.[43] Also, the wife had to wear the hat: leaving the house with an uncovered head could be grounds for divorce.[44]

Linking Wives to Their Husbands—Wherever They May Be

The practice of married women covering their heads was merely one way that women carried their relationship with a husband wherever they went. Rabbinic ways of talking about men, women, and the dwelling structure additionally linked wives to their husbands. For example, the title "householder" assumes a man's supervisory role over his wife, children, and servants. The wife plays an especially important role in establishing her husband as householder. Her primacy is reflected in the fact that she is sometimes called "his house," as in "I called my wife 'my house.'"[45]

A wife's obligations to her husband as householder are additionally encoded in a euphemism for her genital area (which is called "her house" or simply "the house"). Her wifely responsibilities include keeping both herself-as-house and her sexual-organs-as-house in a state of purity readiness for him, the householder.

Twice [a day] she makes an examination [for evidence of menstrual bleeding]: in the morning and in the evening; also when she prepares to "serve her house" ['overet l'shamesh 'et beitah]. (m. Niddah 1:7)

The pious prepare for themselves [an examination cloth] with which to set in order "the house" [l'hatkin 'et ha-bayit]. (m. Niddah 2:1)

These texts discuss the wife's obligation to check for menstrual bleeding, a task that is described as "setting the house in order." An ordered house is needed so the couple can freely engage in sexual relations, a consummation referred to as "serving her house."[46] "The house" that the wife checks, then, is one where the "householder" is shortly expected. This set of usages bind the wife to her husband at the site of the house. These usages do this, however, without restricting the wife's movement. The linguistic enmeshment of husband, wife, and house was necessary precisely because women did traverse all manner of domains.

According to Baker, linguistic and embodied practices work together to craft gendered identities in space. Inside the home, a woman becomes a wife by "setting her house in order" for "the householder." Outside the home, she marks her status as someone's "house" with her headgear. In the rabbinically imagined world, a woman internalizes her social invisibility so that she could inhabit spaces (whether public or domestic) characterized by movement and social interaction.

As we remarked with respect to the niddah ritual, we cannot know whether women participated (willingly or resentfully) in the rabbinic discourse that linked husbands, wives, and houses. Even if women did use this language, cover their heads, and check themselves before sexual relations, we cannot know whether they internalized the social invisibility that the rabbis assumed they would. At most, we can conclude that this language and these practices were an effective means *for the rabbis* to manage their anxiety as men and women occupied and moved through the same spaces.

Conclusion

It should not come as much of a surprise that gender was not acted out in antiquity in the same ways that it is today. Though the contemporary cultural debates bring energy and interest to the task of scholarship, they are most useful to scholarship when they do that—and *only* that. They draw attention to domains of life where gender is prominently on display, but they do not tell us what it looked like in antiquity.

Perhaps the most interesting of our findings concerns the extent to which our conclusions are at their strongest when they focus on the institutional setting of the rabbis, the *beit midrash* or house of study. Scholars are increasingly skeptical about the extent of rabbinic influence beyond their own small disciple circles.[47] More than anything, rabbinic texts tells us about the hopes and aspirations, concerns and anxieties of the sages. When the rabbis speak about various spheres of life, they tell us about the world they wanted to bring about—and about themselves as its architects—rather than the world as it was. The texts that have survived from the *beit midrash* tell us how the rabbis hoped to structure the lives of men and women in relation to each other. Was their vision accepted and internalized by ancient Jewish women? It is hard to know. From the surviving rabbinic texts, it seems that the most we can learn is that at times the rabbis suspected there might be resistance to their program. But that is a far cry from having direct access to women's voices.

NOTES

1 For a classic expression of this position from the 1970s, see Rachel Adler, "The Jew Who Wasn't There: Halakha and the Jewish Woman," in *Contemporary Jewish Ethics*, ed. Menachem Marc Kellner (New York: Sanhedrin Press, 1978), pp. 348–354.

2 See Moshe Meiselman, *Jewish Woman in Jewish Law* (New York: Ktav, 1978).

3 Joan Wallach Scott, *Gender and the Politics of History* (New York: Columbia University Press, 1988), p. 2 (emphasis added).

4 This summary is adapted from Elizabeth Shanks Alexander, *Gender and Time-bound Commandments in Judaism* (New York: Cambridge University Press, 2013), pp. 5–6.

5 Shmuel Safrai, "The *Mitzva* Obligation of Women in Tannaitic Thought," *Bar Ilan Annual* 26–27 (1995): 233 (Hebrew).

6 Judith Hauptman, *Rereading the Rabbis: A Woman's Voice* (Boulder, CO: Westview Press, 1998), pp. 226–227; see also Natan Margalit, "Priestly Men and Invisible Women: Male Appropriation of the Feminine and the Exemption of Women from Positive Time-Bound Commandments," *Association for Jewish Studies Review* 28 (2004): 305–306.

7 Lawrence A. Hoffman, *Covenant of Blood: Circumcision and Gender in Rabbinic Judaism* (Chicago: University of Chicago Press, 1996), pp. 164–167.

8 See Alexander, *Gender and Timebound Commandments*, 8–9, and works cited in n. 23.

9 Deut 31:12 and 15:14; *t. Ḥagigah* 1:4; *t. Pesaḥim* 1:34; *b. Berakhot* 20b; *b. Shabbat.* 23a; *b. Pesaḥim* 108a–b; and *b. Megillah* 4a.

10 *Sifre* Deut 46; *t. Qiddushin* 1:11; *t. Qiddushin* 1:11; and *m. Yevamot* 6.

11 Jeffrey L. Rubenstein, *The History of Sukkot in the Second Temple and Rabbinic Periods* (Atlanta, GA: Scholars Press, 1995), pp. 226–228.

12 Marjorie Lehman, "The Gendered Rhetoric of Sukkah Observance," *Jewish Quarterly Review* 96 (2006): 309–335.

13 See ibid., p. 335, and Elizabeth Shanks Alexander, "Ritual on the Threshold: Mezuzah and the Crafting of Domestic and Civic Space," *Jewish Social Studies* 20 (2015): 117–120.

14 See Rubenstein, *History of Sukkot*, pp. 198–199.

15 Shevah Yalon, "'Women Are Exempted from All Positive Ordinances That Are Bound up with a Stated Time': A Study in Tannaitic and Amoraic Sources" (MA thesis, Bar Ilan University, 1989), pp. 66–71 (Hebrew).

16 See Marjorie Lehman, "Imagining the Priesthood in Tractate Yoma: Mishnah Yoma 2:1–2 and Bt Yoma 23a," *Nashim: A Journal of Jewish Women's Studies and Gender Issues* 28 (2015): 88–105; see also her "The Gendered Rhetoric of Sukkah Observance," 329–332.

17 The three biblical passages that form the core of the *Shema* are Deut 6:4–9, Deut 11:13–21, and Num 15:37–41.

18 The four passages included in *tefillin* are Deut 6:4–9, Deut 11:13–21, Exod 13:1–10, and Exod 13:11–16.

19 The two passages included in the *mezuzah* are Deut 6:4–9 and 11:13–21.

20 On *Shema* as Torah study, see *m. Berakhot* 2:1, which regards recitation of the *Shema* as a subset of the larger category of Torah study. See also *t. Berakhot* 2:12–13, which appears to consider recitation of *Shema* and Torah study as parallel phenomena. On *tefillin* as Torah study, see *Mekhilta Bo* 17 (ed. Horowitz-Rabin, p. 68).

21 See Elizabeth Shanks Alexander, "Women's Exemption from Shema and Tefillin and How These Rituals Came to Be Viewed as Torah Study," *Journal for the Study of Judaism in the Persian, Hellenistic, and Roman Periods* 42 (2011): 531–579.

22 See *Sifre* Deut 46 and *t. Qiddushin* 1:11 in conjunction with *m. Qiddushin* 1:7.

23 See *m. Qiddushin* 1:7 and *t. Qiddushin* 1:11.

24 See Alexander, *Gender and Timebound Commandments*, 178–210.

25 *T. Soṭah* 2:7–9; *t. Bikkurim* 2:3–7; *m. Qiddushin* 1:7–8.

26 For example, see Rachel Adler, "In Your Blood, Live: Re-visions of a Theology of Purity," *Tikkun* 8.1 (January 1993): 38–41.

27 For example, see Blu Greenberg, *On Women and Judaism: A View from Tradition* (Philadelphia: Jewish Publication Society of America, 1981), pp. 105–124.

28 Charlotte Elisheva Fonrobert, *Menstrual Purity: Rabbinic and Christian Reconstructions of Biblical Gender* (Stanford, CA: Stanford University Press, 2000), especially p. 16.

29 See the discussion in ibid., pp. 40–67; also Gail Susan Labovitz, *Marriage and Metaphor: Constructions of Gender in Rabbinic Literature* (Lanham, MD: Lexington, 2009), pp. 122–128.

30 Translation following Fonrobert, *Menstrual Purity*, p. 50.

31 Translation following ibid.

32 *B. Ketubot* 10a, discussed in Fonrobert, *Menstrual Purity*, pp. 59–60; see also discussion in Labovitz, *Marriage and Metaphor*, pp. 125–128.

33 See Fonrobert, *Menstrual Purity*, pp. 102–127.

34 Translation following ibid., p. 106.

35 Ibid., pp. 68–102.

36 *B. Niddah* 57a.

37 The following discussion is based on Cynthia M. Baker, *Rebuilding the House of Israel: Architectures of Gender in Jewish Antiquity* (Stanford, CA: Stanford University Press, 2002), pp. 1–76.

38 Ibid., p. 36.

39 Yizhar Hirschfeld, *The Palestinian Dwelling in the Roman-Byzantine Period* (Jerusalem: Franciscan Printing Press and Israel Exploration Society, 1995), p. 99; cited in Baker, *Rebuilding the House of Israel*, p. 40.

40 Baker, *Rebuilding the House of Israel*, p. 38.

41 Ibid., p. 43.

42 Ibid., p. 44.

43 *M. Ketubot* 5:8.

44 *T. Soṭah* 5:9; see also *t. Ketubot* 7:6 and *m. Ketubot* 7:6.

45 Lit. "My wife I called 'my house'" (*b. Shabbat* 118b). For a complete list of sources that equate wife with "house," see Labovitz, *Marriage and Metaphor*, pp. 115–122.

46 See the discussion of this phrase in Labovitz, *Marriage and Metaphor*, pp. 132–138.

47 See Lee I. Levine, *The Rabbinic Class of Roman Palestine in Late Antiquity* (Jerusalem: Yad Izhak Ben-Zvi, 1989); and Seth Schwartz, *Imperialism and Jewish Society, 200 B.C.E. to 640 C.E.* (Princeton, NJ: Princeton University Press, 2001).

9

Inventing Rabbis

CHRISTINE HAYES

As we have seen, Second Temple Judaism was very diverse. It was the rabbis who were responsible for the forms that are familiar today. This chapter explores the origins of rabbinic Judaism, which crystallized in the centuries following the destruction of the Second Temple in 70 CE and reached its full and classical formulation by the early seventh century CE.

In so doing, it is important to recognize the partial nature of our sources—partial in the sense that they are incomplete and partial in the sense that they represent and favor a particular point of view. This understanding is important if we hope to distinguish rhetoric from reality. Much of our information about this period comes from texts composed by the rabbis themselves and from later medieval works defending rabbinic Judaism from Karaite attack. The stories the rabbis tell about their own emergence and significance (stories echoed by their medieval defenders and apologists) are understandably rabbino-centric. Moreover, because "who we are" is often assumed to be a function of "where we came from," the rabbis' reflections on their past represent an attempt to invent their present and secure their place in Jewish society.

This chapter examines the "myth of origins" by which the rabbis invented themselves in their own day and asks whether it is possible to uncover the rather messy reality beyond the rhetoric. The evidence of nonrabbinic sources from antiquity is important, but only insofar as it is realized that such sources, too, are partial, both in the sense of being incomplete and also in the sense of representing and favoring a particular point of view.

Complicating our task is the fact that the activity of "inventing the rabbis" is engaged in not only by the ancient rabbis themselves but also by modern scholars. Over the course of the last century, modern scholars have invented and reinvented both the rabbis and rabbinic Judaism in various ways—some negative and some positive. This chapter also reviews the shifting representations of rabbinic Judaism in modern scholarship and asks again whether it is possible to uncover the complicated reality beyond the rhetoric.

From Biblical Israel to Rabbinic Judaism

It is helpful to begin with some facts. What do we know? We know that by the early seventh century CE there existed a cultural formation that is now designated "rabbinic Judaism" and that this cultural formation differed from biblical Israel in radical ways. How did biblical Israel become seventh-century rabbinic Judaism?

The people of Israel underwent enormous changes across the nearly two millennia that constitute the biblical, Second Temple, and rabbinic periods (approx. 1300 BCE–700 CE). The six hundred years of Jewish history referred to as the Second Temple period (520 BCE–70 CE) saw dramatic changes in the politics, society, culture, and religion of Judea and the Jewish communities of the diaspora. Certainly, as Shaye J. D. Cohen notes, biblical Israel to the time of the Restoration and rebuilding of the Second Temple (late sixth century BCE) and Second Temple-period Judaism (520 BCE–70 CE) shared many commonalities—the belief in a creator God who chose and entered into a covenant with Israel; an attachment to the land of Israel, the city of Jerusalem and the Temple; observance of a sacred calendar; and various ritual and legal practices.[1] Nevertheless, as Cohen also points out, the two were markedly different. Biblical Israel was a tribal society led by kings and prophets, dwelling on its ancestral land. Membership in this society was determined largely by birth or a simple process of "naturalization," often through intermarriage. Biblical-period Israelites engaged in communal sacrifices and worship of Yahweh at a Temple controlled by priests. The principal institutions of this period were the priesthood, the monarchy, the Temple, and the land of Israel itself. Most important, in biblical times there was no Bible.

By contrast, the tribal structure had all but disappeared in the Second Temple period; those Judeans who returned from the Babylonian exile were organized by clans. Many Judeans did not live in the ancestral land at all but dwelled in diaspora communities such as Alexandria. During this period, Judaism came to be defined in religious rather than national terms. As Cohen rightly notes, intermarriage with non-Jews became prohibited in Second Temple times; nevertheless, a process of conversion was created, enabling foreigners to gain membership in the community. There were other discontinuities: the sacred writings that would form the Hebrew Bible were being assembled and gaining authority— not all at once, but in stages and alongside many other important texts that would ultimately be excluded from the central national-religious corpus we refer to today as the Hebrew Bible; while the Temple and its sacrificial service continued alongside prayer and the recitation of scripture, Torah study became increasingly important. Additionally, the community was no longer headed by kings; instead priests held power and, in the time of the Maccabees, even claimed the title of king despite a lack of Davidic lineage. Prophets were less prominent in Second Temple Jewish society, although apocalyptic visionaries and charismatic healers were active. Persons skilled in the transmission and interpretation of sacred writings (scribes) began to emerge. Finally, new ideas and beliefs began to find expression in Second Temple Jewish texts. Some of these texts show the influence of platonic dualism, some adopt a belief in a multitude of angels and other intermediaries, and some espouse the idea of reward and punishment after death or contain eschatological visions of an end-time resurrection of the dead and restoration of the nation under an anointed king or messiah.

Most important, Jewish society in the Second Temple period was riven by various sects, the most well known of which were the Pharisees, the Sadducees, and the Essenes. Our ancient sources differ from one another in their identification of the issues dividing Jews in the Second Temple period. Cohen notes that the evidence in rabbinic sources suggests that the central foci of sectarian polemics were the Temple, law, and scripture. The legitimacy of the Second Temple and of the priests officiating there was a contentious matter.[2] As descendants of Zadok, a priest under David, the Sadducees believed they held exclusive claim to the high priesthood. They likely formed as an opposition to the non-Zadokite Hasmoneans who appointed themselves high priests in the second century BCE.[3] The Essenes' rejection of what they believed was an illegitimate and profane Temple and priesthood led them to withdraw from society to live in small communities according to a rigorous discipline that emphasized ritual purity and religious purification, including—many scholars maintain—a desert community at Qumran near the Dead Sea. Legal matters were a second source of contention that encouraged the formation of sects in ancient Jewish society. The Pharisees, comprising laity and priests skilled in law and jurisprudence, possessed ancestral traditions that they viewed as binding. These Pharisees, who by the early first century CE appear to have divided into two schools of thought, referred to as the House (i.e., students) of Hillel and the House (i.e., students) of Shammai, emphasized laws of purity, tithing, Sabbath, and marriage. Rabbinic sources depict them as engaging in legal disputes with Sadducees; moreover, writings associated with the (probably Essene) community living at Qumran reveal legal positions at odds with positions attributed to Pharisees. These Dead Sea Scrolls also contain works of biblical exegesis in accordance with the ideology of the sect, suggesting that interpretation of scripture was a third area of contention that fueled sectarian division.[4] To the evidence from rabbinic sources we must add the evidence of Josephus, according to whom the major sects were distinguished from one another by philosophy, social standing, politics, and general way of life.[5] Philosophically, they disagreed on such topics as fate, immortality of the soul, and resurrection. Socially, the Sadducees were aristocratic and valued hereditary privilege and the authority of priests; the Pharisees were popular with the masses and valued leadership based on learning, knowledge, and wisdom; and the Essenes were religious virtuosi separate from the community.[6] There were still other groups that added to the ferment of Jewish society in the Second Temple period—zealots, apocalyptic visionaries, *sicarii* (lit. "dagger men," a reference to some kind of violent rebel), and Christians.

The differences between biblical Israel and Second Temple Judaism outlined here are difference enough, but if we shift our gaze to the classical rabbinic period (second–seventh centuries CE) we stand at an even greater distance from biblical Israel. In the rabbinic period, there was no longer a Temple or sacrificial service and priests no longer played a central role, or anything more than a purely ceremonial role, in the life of the community. Prayer and the study of Torah took center stage in the religious lives of both the community and individuals. Indeed, piety on the whole became more individualistic, and study of Torah became the supreme religious deed. Prophets and kings had disappeared as well as the sects known from the Second Temple period, and by the late third century rabbis had emerged as the new leaders of the community, headed by a Patriarch (a rabbinic scholar recognized as political head of the Jewish community in Roman Palestine) who, to be sure, claimed descent from the house of David (as did the exilarch, the lay head of the Jewish community in Babylonia). The authority of the rabbis was not based on heredity (like that of priests and kings) or divine charisma (like that of prophets) but on their mastery of the sacred scriptures and the ancestral tradition. Instead of the Temple, the synagogue and the *beit midrash* (study house) were the central institutions for the transmission of religious culture. Scripture was still important, but it shared its central position with another text—the Mishnah, a set of legal traditions and disputes produced and studied by the rabbis and declared to be the Oral Torah given at Sinai. In short, in the rabbinic period there was no Temple, no sacrificial system, no functioning priesthood, prophecy, or monarchy—all staple features of biblical Israel. The Israelite heritage had turned in a new direction.

Rabbis Inventing Rabbis

How did rabbinic Judaism emerge from both biblical Israel and the Second Temple Judaism that preceded it? Is this a story of continuity and natural evolution or a story of discontinuity and rupture?

We begin by asking how the rabbis themselves answered the question. How did they present the story of their emergence and their relationship to Israel's past? When examining the rabbinic evidence, it is important to remember that the question of origins is deeply implicated in the question of identity. In view of the popular belief that the past leads inevitably to the present, a group's construction of its past is simultaneously an attempt at constructing its present. When the rabbis told stories about their origins, they were not merely seeking to *understand* or *explain* themselves; they were in fact *inventing* themselves. Moreover, they were justifying a certain role for themselves in Jewish society of the first six centuries of the Common Era.

The following selections from chapters 1 and 2 of Mishnah *Avot* draw a direct line of cultural transmission from the biblical past to the rabbinic present:

> Moses received the Torah at Sinai and handed it down to Joshua, and Joshua to the elders, and the elders to the prophets, and the prophets to the men of the great assembly.
>
> The latter used to say three things: "Be deliberate in judgment, raise up many disciples, and make a (protective) fence around the Torah."
>
> Simeon the Righteous was one of the last of the Men of the Great Assembly.
>
> He used to say, "The world is based upon three things: The Torah, divine service and acts of loving kindness."
>
> Antigonus of Sokho received from Simeon the Righteous.
>
> He used to say, "Do not be like servants who serve the master in the expectation of receiving a reward, but be like servants who serve the master without the expectation of receiving a reward, and let the fear of heaven be upon you."
>
> Yosi b. Yo'ezer of Zeredah and Yosi b. Yoḥanan of Jerusalem received from them [Simeon the Righteous and Antigonus of Sokho].
>
> Yosi b. Yo'ezer used to say: Let your house be a meeting house for the sages and let yourself be covered by the dust of their feet and drink in their words with thirst.
>
> Yosi b. Yoḥanan of Jerusalem used to say . . .
>
> Joshua b. Peraḥiah and Nittai the Arbelite received from them [the foregoing pair].
>
> Joshua b. Peraḥiah used to say . . .
>
> Nittai the Arbelite used to say . . .
>
> Judah b. Tabbai and Shimeon b. Shetaḥ received from them [the foregoing pair].
>
> Judah b. Tabbai used to say . . .
>
> Shimeon b. Shetaḥ used to say . . .
>
> Shemayah and Avtalion received from them [the foregoing pair].
>
> Shemayah used to say . . .
>
> Avtalion used to say . . .
>
> Hillel and Shammai received from them [the foregoing pair].

Hillel used to say, "Be one of the disciples of Aaron, loving peace and pursuing peace, loving one's fellow beings and bringing them near to Torah . . ."

. . . He also used to say, "If I am not for myself, who is for me; but if I am for myself alone, what am I; and if not now, when? . . ."

Shammai used to say, "Make your Torah [study] a regular habit. Speak little but do much, and receive all men with a pleasant countenance."

Hillel also used to say . . .

R. Yoḥanan b. Zakkai received from Hillel and Shammai.

He used to say, "If you have learned much Torah, do not claim credit for yourself, because it was for this purpose that you were created."

R. Yoḥanan b. Zakkai had five disciples and they were these R. Eliezer b. Hyrcanus, R. Joshua b. Ḥananiah, R. Yosi the priest, R. Simeon b. Netana'el, and R. Eleazar b. Arakh . . .

They each said three things . . .

Tractate *Avot*, one of the sixty-three tractates of the third-century rabbinic compilation known as the Mishnah, thus opens with a clear assertion of continuity across the centuries.[7] The text states that Moses received Torah at Sinai and transmitted it to Joshua, beginning a sequence of reception and transmission that continued through the Elders to the Prophets, to the men of the Great Assembly (in the time of Ezra), among whom was Simeon the Righteous (third century CE). The transmission continued from Simeon the Righteous and his disciple Antigonus of Sokho through five pairs of teachers—the last being the famous pair Hillel and Shammai. Hillel and Shammai transmitted Torah to R. Yoḥanan b. Zakkai, who lived at the time of the destruction of the Second Temple (70 CE) and who, in turn, transmitted Torah to five disciples.

Each "link" in this chain of transmission is reported to have said three things—generally pithy aphorisms, which are then cited (though omitted here for brevity). Additional teachings are reported in some instances, and the teachings of R. Yoḥanan's five disciples (first to second century CE) as well as those of later sages (second century CE) continue in the ensuing paragraphs. It is not only the Written Torah but also additional oral teachings that are transmitted from master to disciple.

In this text, the rabbis position themselves as the sole legitimate recipients and guardians of the nation's ancient heritage. Their Oral Torah—a massive collection of teachings, traditions, and laws that elaborate and interpret the Written Torah—is represented as continuous with God's revelation to Moses at Sinai. Other rabbinic texts make the same claim in different ways. According to a few accounts, the Oral Torah—Mishnah, Talmuds, and midrash—was revealed in full at Sinai and relayed orally alongside the Written Torah.[8] Other rabbinic texts represent the Oral Torah as immanent within the Written Torah and developing gradually from it over the course of centuries, particularly through the application of divinely revealed interpretative rules.[9] Despite local differences, these rabbinic accounts of the origin of the Oral Torah agree on two points: first, the Oral Torah is rooted directly or indirectly in God's revelation to Moses at Sinai; second, because the Oral Torah develops and completes the Written Torah it is essential to a full and proper understanding of God's will as expressed in the Written Torah.

The paradoxical idea that the Torah revealed at Sinai is both divine and yet completed through human elaboration and interpretation is expressed by the following pair of rabbinic assertions: on the one hand "the Torah is from heaven," but on the other hand it is "not in heaven" any longer.[10] In other words, because the Torah is from heaven, it expresses the divine will; but because it is no longer in heaven, the task of interpreting the Torah and elaborating the divine will is an ongoing task that has been given over to humankind or, to be specific, to the rabbis.

The rabbis maintain that the task of accessing and articulating God's will for Israel falls to them because prophecy has ceased: "R. Abdimi from Haifa said: Since the day when the Temple was destroyed, prophecy has been taken from the prophets and given to the wise."[11] In the biblical past and in the Second Temple period, they asserted, God sent prophets to announce His will to Israel, but no more. Since the destruction of the Second Temple, God's will for His people is revealed through interpretation of the Written Torah revealed at Sinai, and interpretation is the task of scribes and sages—the rabbis themselves. Seeking to secure their position as the authoritative interpreters of God's written revelation, the rabbis read themselves into Deuteronomy 17's procedure for adjudicating difficult legal cases. Deuteronomy 17:8–13 states that when a case is too difficult to decide it is to be presented to the Levitical priests or the judge (*shofet*) in charge at the time, and the verdict is to be followed scrupulously. The rabbis understood themselves to be the "judge" in charge at the time. Not only, however, did Deuteronomy 17 provide scriptural warrant for the rabbis to serve as authoritative judges and interpreters of God's will for their community in their view, but it also served to disable any recourse to charismatic figures who might claim oracular or prophetic knowledge of the divine will. There was one legitimate path to knowledge of God's will, and that path passed through the rabbis.

This rabbino-centric construction of the means by which God communicates His will to Israel is matched by a rabbino-centric account of the Jewish community's recovery following the destruction in 70 CE. Many late rabbinic stories depict the rabbis (or sages) as playing a central leadership role in the immediate postdestruction period. According to these stories, it was *they*, under the leadership of R. Yoḥanan ben Zakkai, who busied themselves with the reconstruction of Jewish life in the nation's darkest hour. According to a rather fantastic rabbinic legend, R. Yoḥanan anticipated the destruction of Jerusalem. He escaped the Roman siege by having himself smuggled out of Jerusalem in a coffin and, after impressing the Roman emperor Vespasian, obtaining the latter's permission to assemble a group of sages and disciples at Yavneh (near modern-day Tel Aviv).[12] Rabbinic tradition credits the sages of Yavneh with beginning the process of transforming Temple-centered biblical Israel into Torah-centered rabbinic Judaism by collecting and sorting traditional teachings that might otherwise have been confused or forgotten.[13]

R. Yoḥanan ben Zakkai is portrayed in rabbinic sources as forward-looking, refusing to dwell on the grief engendered by the destruction. In *Avot deRabbi Natan*, as R. Joshua weeps over the Temple ruins because Israel has lost its means of atonement, R. Yoḥanan b. Zakkai comforts him with the following words: "My son, be not grieved. We have another atonement as effective as this. And what is it? It is acts of mercy, as it is said, 'For I desire mercy and not sacrifice' (Hos 6:6)."[14] This legend encapsulates the rabbinic message: Jews are no less capable of obtaining atonement for their sins, of attracting and maintaining the divine presence, in the absence of the Temple than they were when the Temple stood. Reconstructing a life of Torah means developing practices, concepts, and institutions that could nourish Jewish life without a temple and in the midst of communal devastation. R. Yohanan b. Zakkai's pupil R. Joshua learns this lesson well. In a story from the Babylonian Talmud, R. Joshua encounters a group of ascetics who refuse to eat meat or drink wine after the destruction of the Temple. But R. Joshua counters that one must not give in to nihilism despite the recent national trauma.[15] This tale conveys the message that fixating on destruction paralyzes the community and brings life to a halt. Life goes on, and one must move forward—remembering *without* despairing.

These and other stories redacted in rabbinic works of a later date (fourth to seventh centuries) portray the rise of rabbinic Judaism as the work of noble (though not flawless) and determined sages acting with foresight and purpose on a large scale to renew and sustain Jewish life in the immediate postdestruction period (late first century CE). Thus, the sources describe Yohanan ben Zakkai and later Gamliel II as reconstituting the Sanhedrin and undertaking a series of *taqqanot* (rabbinic enactments) that transformed and preserved Judaism as a post-Temple, nonpriestly creation.[16] These *tannaim* (a term that refers to sages up to approximately 220 CE) are credited with drawing together the legal traditions and teachings of preceding generations and establishing normative practice (or *halakhah*) in accordance with the Pharisaic school of Hillel.[17] While early rabbinic sources suggest an emphasis in the postwar period on laws of purity, tithing, and calendar-setting, later texts credit the Yavneh generation with composing obligatory daily prayers in commemoration of the daily sacrifices in the Temple as well as prayers and blessings for a variety of occasions and adapting or transferring to the home and/or synagogue certain Temple observances—especially the ceremonies associated with the pilgrimage festivals.[18] Thus, even though the Passover lamb could no longer be sacrificed, a family observance of the Passover was possible, and the non-Temple elements of the ceremony—the eating of unleavened bread and of bitter herbs—took on a heightened importance. The basic framework of the Passover *haggadah* (the liturgy accompanying the Passover meal in the home) is believed to have been composed in the early rabbinic period. These "reconstruction" texts, with their depiction of the rabbis as innovators who met the challenges of a new era, stand in tension with Mishnah

Avot 1 and its depiction of the rabbis as adding their own teachings to an unchanging core tradition.

An important aspect of the rabbis' self-fashioning was their rejection of the zealotry that exacted so high a price in the war with Rome and the Bar Kokhba revolt (132–135 CE). Although it is clear from rabbinic sources that the rabbis had no great love for Rome, they did not seek to inflame zealous nationalism or rebellion against the hated regime. In the eyes of the rabbis, the disastrous Bar Kokhba revolt and the persecutions that followed in its wake only confirmed the dangers of political messianism and nationalism.[19] The rabbinic program was one that focused inward on the quest for piety and sanctity in the belief that God will bring an end to the dominion of the idolaters when He sees fit. God's hand cannot be forced. The Jews will be restored, the Temple will be rebuilt—but in God's own time. The task of the community until that time is dedication to God's Torah, which offers a blueprint for the life of *imitatio dei*. Torah was seen as the source of life, and to abandon it was to live without divine protection and blessing.[20]

The idealized and streamlined picture of a chain of tradition as well as the rabbinic role in reconstruction after 70 found in some rabbinic texts was magnified in post-talmudic accounts of the origin of rabbinic Judaism. Enormously influential in this regard was the *Iggeret*, or letter, of Rav Sherira Gaon. Written in 987 by the head of the Pumbeditha *yeshiva* in Babylonia to Jacob ben Nissim of Kairouan (in Tunisia), the letter addresses a series of questions concerning the history of the Oral Law and the formation and compilation of the Mishnah, Talmuds, and other works of rabbinic literature. The community in Kairouan was troubled by the charges and attacks of Karaites, an antirabbinic group that rejected the authority of the Oral Law as reflected in talmudic tradition. The Karaites cited the presence of controversy and multiple opinions as proof that the Oral Law was not a faithful transmission of divinely revealed teaching but a human invention. Against this, Sherira asserts the unity of the content of the Oral Torah and the unbroken chain of transmission from the time of Moses to its formulation in the Mishnah that was edited by Rabbi Judah ha-Nasi.[21] Relying on Mishnah *Avot* and an array of talmudic texts—many clearly legendary in character—Sherira provides an idealized history of the Oral Law and the rabbinic movement that emphasizes the unity and reliability of the former and the integrity and authority of the latter. The early sages were brilliant, knew the tradition by memory, and taught the law, though each in his own way. Despite differences in formulation, the content and explanation of the Oral Law were known to all sages. Eventually, R. Judah ha-Nasi gathered earlier traditions, formulated them in a fixed language, and produced the authoritative Mishnah, which was immediately and universally accepted.[22]

Dissonant Voices

While it is true that by the fourth century CE the main contours of rabbinic Judaism were in place and the rabbis, backed by the patriarch, were found in local communities serving as adjudicators, teachers, and advisors, the process of their emergence was not as smoothly continuous and unified as some rabbinic and early medieval sources would suggest. Indeed, a closer look at Mishnah *Avot* itself hints at discontinuities and disjunctions.

We noted earlier that the themes of uniformity, stability, and continuity are front and center in Mishnah *Avot*; and yet, if one scratches beneath the surface, these themes are quickly destabilized by markers of difference and discontinuity. First, the content of the tradition that is transmitted is not constant, but grows continually through the addition of new teachings. Second, the chain of transmission of Torah presented in this mishnah omits the one group biblically appointed to teach Torah to Israel—the priestly class (Lev 10:11)—and includes another group, the rabbis, who appear nowhere in biblical tradition. These features raise the suspicion that the text's portrait of a seamless transmission of a stable tradition masks a radical discontinuity. This suspicion is strengthened by thematic and textual elements that resonate with the text's Greco-Roman milieu as distinct from its biblical past. Specifically, the pedagogical ideal of oral transmission from master to disciple is consonant with the master-disciple relationship at the heart of Greco-Roman *paideia* (education). In addition, the list of sages may be compared to the *diadoche* texts of Greco-Roman philosophical schools—succession lists of recognized teachers of a particular school beginning with its founder. Such succession lists were also composed by early Christian writers from the second century CE on (e.g., Justin, Irenaeus, and Athanasius) as an authority-conferring strategy.

Thus, while the theme of continuity is predominant in Mishnah *Avot*, markers of discontinuity are not entirely effaced. Discontinuity comes to the fore in another very famous passage from the Babylonian Talmud—a multigenerational rabbinic compilation that reached completion in the sixth or early seventh century CE. In this fanciful story, a rabbinic author imagines a time-travel encounter between Moses and the second-century CE rabbinic master R. Akiva and conveys a sense of tremendous distance and difference from the world of biblical Israel:

> Rav Judah said in the name of Rav: "When Moses ascended to heaven [to receive the Torah] he found the Holy One, blessed be He, engaged in affixing [decorative] crownlets to the letters." Moses said, "Lord of the Universe, why do you bother with this?" He answered, "There will arise a man at the end of many generations, Akiva b. Joseph by name, who will expound upon each crownlet heaps and heaps of laws." "Lord of the Universe," said Moses, "allow me to see him." He replied, "Turn around." Moses went and sat down behind eight rows [and listened to the discussions]. Not being able to follow their arguments, he was depressed; but when they came to a certain topic and the disciples said to the master, "Whence do you know it?" and the latter [R. Akiva] replied, "It is a law given unto Moses at Sinai," Moses was comforted. Thereupon he returned to the Holy One, blessed be He, and said, "Lord of the Universe, You have such a man, and You give your Torah by me!" He replied, "Be silent, for such is My decree." Then Moses said, "Lord of the Universe, You have shown me his Torah, now show me his reward." "Turn around," said He, and Moses turned around and saw them weighing out his flesh at the market-stalls. "Lord of the Universe," cried Moses, "such Torah, and such a reward!" He replied, "Be silent, for such is My decree." (*b. Menaḥot* 29b)

According to the story, Moses ascends to heaven to bring the Torah to Israel and finds God attaching final calligraphic flourishes to the text. When God explains that a man will later derive numerous laws from these seemingly meaningless squiggles, Moses asks to see the man. Transported to the second-century CE schoolhouse of R. Akiva, he sits in the back with the least skilled students where he is at a complete loss to understand the proceedings. Moses, the very one to whom God entrusted His Torah and the first to teach Torah to Israel, does not recognize that Torah in the hands of a rabbinic sage, a midrashic virtuoso, some 1,500 years later. The story signals a rabbinic awareness of the yawning gulf that separates the rabbis' world from the Torah of Moses and the world of biblical Israel. That this discontinuity is a cause of some anxiety is reflected in the sense of alienation and depression experienced by Moses, relieved only when R. Akiva comes upon a law he is unable to derive by means of his complex exegesis of scripture. The law must be accepted, independent of scriptural authority, as a law stretching back to Moses at Sinai, a fact that comforts Moses. Despite an overwhelming impression of radical discontinuity, the story assures the reader of some degree of continuity, however attenuated. And yet the tragic fate that meets R. Akiva, who was martyred by the Romans during the Bar Kokhba revolt, raises the possibility that the rabbinic enterprise, even if divinely underwritten, is a dangerous one.[23]

The theme of discontinuity is openly acknowledged in some rabbinic sources (as in b. Menaḥot 29b) and denied in others. Open acknowledgment may be seen in Mishnah Ḥagigah 1:8, which likens certain rabbinically elaborated laws to mountains hanging by a thread (because they are voluminous but have little scriptural support) while others simply float in the air and have no scriptural support whatsoever. By contrast, there are entire works of halakhic midrash (legal exegesis) that seek to show the biblical basis for rabbinic laws. In other words, rabbinic literature see-saws between disclosing the discontinuous and innovative character of rabbinic law and concealing it.

This very tension highlights the extent to which the rabbis' account of their own origins requires critical investigation. This investigation, carried out by modern scholars for nearly two centuries, has resulted in a radically different account of the origins of rabbinic Judaism from that found in the classical sources.

Modern Scholarship: Inventions and Reinventions

The ancient rabbis were not the only ones to engage in the activity of "inventing the origins of rabbinic Judaism." Modern scholars have also

labored to reconstruct the origins of rabbinic Judaism, with widely varying results. As we investigate the invention and reinvention of rabbinic
Judaism in the modern period, we will consider whether it is possible to
uncover the complicated reality beyond rabbinic rhetoric, which is the
task that modern scholarship often sets for itself. To the extent that such
a thing is possible (and there are those who would deny that it is ever
possible), it would seem to require a comparative methodology.

One of the characteristic features of modern scholarly inventions of
rabbinic Judaism is the comparative method. Nonrabbinic sources of
various kinds are brought into conversation with rabbinic sources to
serve as a kind of check. If a number of nonrabbinic sources make an assertion that corresponds to something in rabbinic materials, then there
is a good chance that we have uncovered some kind of historical reality,
even if it is only a shared ideology or perception. However, nonrabbinic
sources, no less than rabbinic sources, have their biases and problems,
making the work of comparison particularly challenging.

We see this plainly in the work of scholars in the nineteenth and early
twentieth centuries who sought to understand the origins and nature of
rabbinic Judaism in the light of New Testament and Christian sources. E.
P. Sanders has pointed out that much of the New Testament scholarship
has been marred by distorted views of Judaism that have taken at face
value the polemical representations of First and Second Temple Judaism
found in the Gospels and the writings of Paul.[24] The New Testament
contains polemical descriptions of Pharisaism as a legalistic works-
righteousness or equally degenerate form of religion, which Ferdinand
Wilhelm Weber described as one in which "one must earn salvation by
compiling more good works ('merits') whether on his own or from the
excess of someone else, than he has transgressions."[25] Influenced by Weber's views and equating the distorted image of first-century Pharisaism
with rabbinic Judaism and rabbinic Judaism with Judaism writ large,
New Testament scholars portrayed ancient Judaism in the first centuries
CE and beyond as at best an inadequate and nonfunctional religion, with
regrettable elements of nationalism, and, at worst, one that destroys any
hope of forgiveness or a proper relationship between God and man.[26]
New Testament scholars referred to Judaism in this time as "late Judaism," implying that it was approaching its natural end and would soon
relinquish the stage to Christianity. Sanders sums up: "The supposed

legalistic Judaism of scholars . . . serves a very obvious function. It acts as the foil against which superior forms of religion are described. It permits . . . the writing of theology as if it were history."[27]

The negative portrayal of ancient Judaism by New Testament scholars prompted responses by scholars of Judaica, who tried to paint a different portrait of rabbinic Judaism. These apologetic offerings were often based on a selective reading of rabbinic sources and were romantic and idealized. The modern scholarly invention of rabbinic Judaism in the middle of the twentieth century was caught, it would seem, between polemics and apologetics.

Breaking the Impasse

In the 1980s, two historians, Isaiah Gafni and Shaye J. D. Cohen, produced accounts of the rise of rabbinic Judaism that attempted to steer a middle course by adopting two simple strategies. First, they strove to understand ancient Judaism and rabbinic Judaism *on their own terms* and not as a foil (whether negative or positive) for Christianity. To this end, they avoided a common methodological problem found in much New Testament scholarship: the tendency to extract from rabbinic sources information about topics important to the study of the New Testament but of marginal or no interest to the authors of rabbinic texts and, conversely, to ignore the issues of primary importance in rabbinic texts. The result of these tendencies was seen as a distorted picture of rabbinic Judaism. Gafni and Cohen approached rabbinic sources with a greater awareness of their unique character and concerns as well as the special challenge they pose for the historian.[28] Because rabbinic texts are anthologies of often-conflicting traditions of various genres produced over the course of centuries, a comprehensive assessment of the available sources on a given topic is a desideratum. This assessment must be attentive to differences of time and place, but sorting out what is early and what is late, what represents an individual teaching or a broader consensus, is a difficult matter. Moreover, rabbinic sources are almost uniformly uninterested in historiography, and the historical reflections they contain serve ideological purposes. The historian must proceed cautiously.

Second, to varying degrees, these scholars like others in the latter part of the twentieth century, sought to understand rabbinic Judaism *in its proper context.* Much prior scholarship, especially New Testament scholarship, had assumed that rabbinic Judaism and ancient Judaism were one and the same thing, but this assumption faded as evidence of nonrabbinic forms of Judaism came to light. In the latter part of the twentieth century, scholars acknowledged the great complexity of ancient Jewish society and arrived at radically new conclusions regarding the rabbis' place within Jewish society of the first three centuries of the Common Era. Ironically, it was precisely as the rabbis were decentered and marginalized that they came into sharper focus.

In an effort to understand the origins of the rabbis, Gafni and Cohen focused on identifying the rabbis' predecessors in the Second Temple period and on determining how and why a class of rabbi-sages should have crystallized in the wake of the destruction. What relationship did this new class have to the various groups or sects in existence on the eve of the destruction? Or did the rabbis emerge from a coalition of surviving groups? Why is it that after the destruction we do not hear of Sadducees, Pharisees, and Essenes, but only sages and the disciples of the sages? Did the rabbis emerge from one group because that group alone survived and the others did not?

In an essay entitled "The Historical Background of Rabbinic Literature," Isaiah Gafni set himself the task of testing the reasonableness of the rabbinic account of the rabbis' emergence and role in Jewish society against what we know about Roman-period Palestine both socially and politically.[29] He acknowledged the difficulty of identifying the Second Temple forerunners of the later rabbinic movement because of the rabbinic tendency to rabbinize earlier Jewish history; nevertheless, he cited evidence of a fairly linear progression from the Pharisaic movement of the Second Temple period to the rabbinic circles of the second and third centuries. Certainly, rabbinic sources seem to know little about their ancestors other than Hillel and Shammai; in addition, they do not refer to themselves as Pharisees. Nevertheless there are some clear affinities between the rabbis and the earlier Pharisees as described in Josephus, the New Testament, and rabbinic sources themselves. For example, important rabbinic leaders are from the house of Gamliel, and Gamliel is identified as a Pharisee in the New Testament. Thus, Gafni, like many other scholars, assumed some kind of connection, though not necessarily identity, between Second Temple Pharisees and later rabbis.

Weighing the traditional rabbinic account against our knowledge of the social and political realities of Roman Palestine, Gafni sketched the following picture. (1) Hillel was likely an important sage, though the designation of him as a *nasi* (patriarch) and the assertion of a Hillelite dynasty are anachronistic. We may, however, accept the claim that Hillel was responsible for a number of ordinances and a new system of exegesis that produced new biblical interpretations and *halakhic* solutions. (2) The Gamalielides had a revered status but no official bureaucratically recognized role. (3) Jewish society in the predestruction period was quite variegated, with groups adhering to Pharisaic ideas but behaving differently. (4) In the postdestruction period the Essenes and Sadducees disappear. (5) Although the rabbinic accounts of Yavneh are shrouded in legend, it is reasonable to attribute to R. Yoḥanan b. Zakkai and the sages of Yavneh a clear policy of rebuilding the religious foundations of the community. (6) The project of R. Yoḥanan b. Zakkai was carried on by R. Gamliel II, who established a religious framework for Jewish life and an authority structure, including a new Sanhedrin at Yavneh, understood to be a continuation of the Jerusalem Sanhedrin. (7) The sages slowly took on more formal roles and became a definite social class that created a normative type of Judaism. (8) A giant of the generation after R. Gamliel was R. Akiva, who features prominently with his disciples in the period leading up to the final redaction of the Mishnah by R. Judah ha-Nasi (180–220). (9) When the patriarchate reached a peak under Judah ha-Nasi, the rabbinic movement was centered in Sepphoris and Tiberias. (10) R. Judah ha-Nasi was quite wealthy, attracted messianic speculation, enjoyed imperial support, and, at the time of his death, was recognized as the Jewish leader. (11) An ideological rift developed, however, between the patriarchs and the rabbis, and the patriarch's prestige was enhanced by the support of diaspora Jewish communities.

In constructing this account, Gafni moved cautiously and acknowledged evidence to the contrary. While recognizing that one cannot posit a direct line from scribes to Hasidim to Pharisees without qualification, he connected Second Temple Pharisees to the early rabbis in a fairly linear way, with other groups fading from the scene. He created a strong and purposeful Yavneh and rabbis with clear policies and (eventually) the power to actualize them. All of this is consistent with his clearly articulated and modest goal: not to describe Judaism writ large (he recognized that Jewish society contained elements other than the rabbis), but simply to assess the reasonableness of the rabbis' account of themselves in light of what our knowledge of the era tells us was possible.

Gafni broke with the traditional account of the emergence of rabbinic Judaism as exemplified in the *Iggeret* of Rav Sherira Gaon, which posited a single uniform tradition transmitted from Sinai to the sages. According to this traditional medieval account, the destruction of the Second Temple effected a rupture, a break that led to a loss of knowledge and the rise of legal controversy. However, the rabbis undertook a rescue effort, beginning at Yavneh and leading eventually to a unified and authoritative formulation of the tradition—the Mishnah of R. Judah ha-Nasi. Gafni's account, like many modern accounts, pushed against this older narrative by positing a *lack* of unity prior to the Second Temple period and a later invention of unity—what would eventually become normative Judaism—by rabbis following the destruction. But how were the rabbis able to create a unified tradition after the destruction? This is where Shaye Cohen made a significant contribution.

For Cohen, Yavneh was not a site of Pharisaic triumphalism and of the formation of a uniform orthodoxy that expelled non-Pharisees, Christians, and other heretics and purged the canon of nonorthodox writings. In his 1984 article "The Significance of Yavneh: Pharisees, Rabbis and the End of Jewish Sectarianism," Cohen objected to representations of Yavneh as a Jewish version of the fourth-century council of Nicaea in which one party triumphed and defined Christian orthodoxy and the Christian canon and expelled heretics.[30] This model is simplistic and ignores the fact that the rabbis refused to describe themselves as Pharisees. The rabbis' lack of a sectarian consciousness was deliberate, said Cohen. The sages who gathered in Yavneh renounced sectarianism and exclusivism and absorbed many elements of Second Temple Jewish society within their ranks. The Temple had been a focal point of sectarian dispute, and its destruction provided the impetus for the creation of a pluralistic society in which all groups were welcome, and dispute and controversy were tolerated. Rather than the work of a sect triumphant, Yavneh was a grand coalition characterized not by uniformity and monism but by diversity and pluralism and the recognition that truth is many, not one. According to Cohen, only those who insisted on a sectarian identity were excluded—Christians and *minim* (heretics of various descriptions). Thus, the Pharisaic leadership that emerged after the destruction was an amalgam of elements drawn from the many groups in Jewish society—from the priests, an emphasis on the sacred though expanded now well beyond the Temple; from the sages, a commitment to the study of Torah and its application to community life; from the zealots, apocalyptic visionaries and messianic separatists, the idea that Israel has a unique destiny of cosmic significance.

Cohen's invention of rabbinic Judaism reversed the classical and medieval rabbinic account entirely. That account posited a basic predestruction unity that was disrupted by the destruction and only eventually reestablished with the publication of the Mishnah. It is a model of unity, followed by diversity, followed by a restored and relatively monistic unity. By contrast, Cohen posited a basic predestruction disunity and sectarianism that was brought to an end by the destruction and replaced by a "big-tent" coalition that absorbed diverse elements to create a pluralistic but unified rabbinic Judaism. It is a model of diversity followed by relatively pluralistic unity.

Cohen's invention of Yavneh and the rabbinic Judaism drew a response from Daniel Boyarin in his 2000 article "A Tale of Two Synods: Nicaea, Yavneh, and Rabbinic Ecclesiology."[31] Boyarin accepted Cohen's claim that a certain sectarianism centered on the Temple disappeared after 70 and yet, following Martin Goodman, he maintained that there is evidence for the view that Second Temple sectarianism gave way to Jewish orthodoxy as one group achieved hegemony and found it possible to plausibly portray itself as Judaism writ large.[32]

So which is it? Are we to imagine with Boyarin that Yavneh was like Nicaea and saw the establishment of orthodoxy by a triumphant sect that filled a power vacuum following the destruction and secured its authority by adopting a policy of exclusion and monism rather than inclusion and pluralism? Or are we to imagine with Cohen that Yavneh was unlike Nicaea and saw the formation of a kind of nonexclusive, pluralistic, big-tent coalition of diverse groups?

Boyarin himself notes that rabbinic literature contains both views of Yavneh—an exclusivist Yavneh that rejects difference and an inclusivist Yavneh that valorizes difference and sanctifies controversy. He resolves the tension between these two contradictory portraits by emplotting them chronologically. The inclusivist Yavneh in which both disputants in a controversy may be said to be advancing the words of the living God is a product of later talmudic myth making.[33] By contrast, the earlier traditions of Yavneh do not represent it as a grand coalition. It was not until the fourth or fifth century that rabbinic culture saw a shift in the status of dissent and the Talmud began to perceive and to portray Yavneh as a kind of ecumenical council, transmitting the continually evolving and pluriform Oral Torah.

For Boyarin, Yavneh is a foundation legend, or more precisely a sequence of two foundation legends—an earlier exclusivist version and a second inclusivist revision—by which the rabbis were able to invent themselves and their distinctive textual and literary culture. Comparison with the council of Nicaea is particularly apt because this foundation legend of orthodox Christianity also underwent revision, from an earlier more inclusivist version to a later version emphasizing an exclusivist orthodoxy. The direction of the revision is reversed, however, because the myth of the gathering at Yavneh was revised from an earlier version of exclusivism to a later version emphasizing divinely sanctioned heterodoxy and pluralism. Thus, the rabbis and the church fathers invent themselves through foundation legends, but these legends pull in opposite directions to explain each of these very different cultural systems.

An entirely different invention of rabbinic Judaism may be found in Seth Schwartz's 2001 volume *Imperialism and Jewish Society, 200 BCE to 640 CE*.[34] The fundamental tenet of Schwartz's revisionist account is that Second Temple Judaism was not in fact fragmented by sectarianism but was fundamentally a cohesive entity prior to the destruction. Histories of the period have focused on the diverse elements constituting Jewish society in the Second Temple period and have lost sight of the fact that Jewish society was actually an integrated society with an overarching centralizing ideology. According to Schwartz, imperial support for the Temple and the Torah established them as the chief symbols of Jewish corporate identity. Jewish society was certainly loosely centralized and ideologically complex, but the various sects that have garnered so much scholarly attention did not play a central role in Jewish society. Schwartz endorses Albert Baumgarten's claim that the sects were an essentially unitary and mainstream phenomenon that valued Torah and the proper conduct of the Temple cult.[35] Their disagreements were disagreements over a core integrating ideology.

The destruction in 70 and the Bar Kokhba revolt in 132–135 CE shattered this integrated society; Jewish society was all but destroyed. Schwartz rejects accounts that posit a continuity between pre- and post-war Jewish society, such as the claim that leadership passed from the Pharisees before the war to their spiritual descendants, the rabbis, after the war. Roman annexation after the war entailed the concentration of all legal and political power in the hands of the Roman governor and local city councils. No rabbi or patriarch would have possessed official status, and the rabbis would have been powerless to compete with the Roman courts and the Jewish landowners and councilors who followed the legal, religious, cultural, and social norms of Greco-Roman elites. Life in Palestine was pervaded by pagan norms as indicated by archaeological remains. Judaism was a vestigial identity; most Jews incorporated themselves into an essentially Greco-Roman and pagan cultural system.

The intermediaries of Torah—the rabbis—lost all authority and status. Utterly marginal, with little residual prestige and few supporters, they turned inward. The account of rabbinic origins found in rabbinic sources in its minimalist version is, according to Schwartz, unobjectionable as a description of this small group—that is, as an account of rabbinic Judaism and rabbinic history—but not as a history of the general Jewish community. The story of the general Jewish community in the period following the destruction is one in which the rabbis played virtually no part according to Schwartz. In the face of an influential, authoritative, and religiously compelling Greco-Roman cultural norm, most Jews chose to participate in the pagan public life of the city and to maintain a minimal sense of their identity as Jews, if they maintained it at all. Thus, the movement of former Pharisaic and/or priestly scribes, judges, and teachers that took shape after 70 CE around R. Yoḥanan b. Zakkai and R. Gamliel and especially after 135 had the cohesion and internal focus of a sect. Only in the third century CE did the rabbis gain some prestige and visibility as a result of preaching, legal advising, and even miracle working and healing; but they did not control anything in rural Palestine, including the synagogues. Existing on the margins, the rabbis preserved an altered but recognizable version of Judaism. Into the fourth century they still had only a small number of followers and very limited and informal authority; and yet in this century, probably in response to the spread and increasing success of Christianity, Judaism underwent something of a revival centered on Torah and synagogue that spread to villages. Judaism in this period experienced an explosion of literary production and synagogue construction.

In some respects, Schwartz's invention of rabbinic Judaism revives the classical and medieval account reversed by Cohen. That account posited a basic predestruction unity that was disrupted by the destruction and only eventually reestablished with the publication of the Mishnah: unity, diversity, restored unity. Similarly, Schwartz posits a basic predestruction unity that was brought to a crashing halt by the destruction of the Second Temple. The integrating and unifying ideology, Judaism, was revived in modified form only in the fourth century.

Schwartz's work was important in distinguishing the history of rabbinic Judaism from the history of Judaism generally. In addition, his insistence on the utter marginality of the rabbis did more than force scholars to revise their assessment of the rabbis' role and influence in the postwar period; it changed the very nature of scholarly research into the period. Earlier scholarly effort had often been devoted to the task of confirming or falsifying the main contours of the rabbinic account. As we have seen, this account described the heroic restoration of Jewish life in the wake of the destruction led by forward-thinking rabbis widely recognized as authoritative leaders and commanding the loyalty of the masses. Scholars wanted to know how much of this account was supported by ancient sources and by our knowledge of Roman provincial society. For Schwartz, the stories the rabbis told about themselves are more rhetorical than real, the product of a small and insular group of religious virtuosi with little influence and few supporters. Renouncing the effort to confirm the various elements of these stories, contemporary scholars now focus attention on understanding more precisely the nature of this small and insular movement.

Hayim Lapin, for example, insists that the small rabbinic movement is best understood as a product of the provincial context of Roman Palestine rather than a natural development of Jewish national practices. He describes the rabbinic movement as "an association of religious experts claiming ancestral knowledge, employing a rhetoric of self-representation with affinities to Greco-Roman associations and especially to philosophical schools, and capable of using wider cultural motifs to their own ends."[36] As such, he writes, their development tracked the transformation of the Palestinian provincial landscape.

* * *

Over the last one hundred years, modern scholars have invented and reinvented the origins of rabbinic Judaism in opposing ways: rabbinic Judaism was continuous with Second Temple Judaism or it was discontinuous; the rabbis were central to Jewish society after the destruction or they were utterly marginal; the rabbis enjoyed legal authority and the loyalty of the masses, enabling them to reconstruct Jewish life after the destruction, or they were powerless and practically invisible; Yavneh saw the rabbinic imposition of orthodoxy and uniformity or a celebration of heterodoxy and difference. The fact is, like the texts with which we began, rabbinic sources in general pull in opposite directions.

Taking note of the conflicting evidence in the sources, Catherine Heszer asserts that they are all authentic reflections of a complex reality.[37] She argues that throughout the tannaitic (first–early third centuries CE) and amoraic (third–fifth centuries CE) periods the rabbis did not form a unified organization—they were socially fragmented and lacked formal institutions for legal discussion. Their contacts were informal and episodic, and most rabbis had direct contacts with a very limited number of colleagues. The rabbinic estate was thus not an organized corporate group but a loose network, making it impossible to fix the *halakhah* or achieve a majority opinion on any matter. To the extent that they might consult the rabbis as legal advisors, some individuals would follow the advice of one rabbi and others would follow the advice of another. The later editors of rabbinic tradition employed two distinct strategies to cope with the existing diversity. On the one hand they created anonymous views to fix the *halakhah* and delegitimize dissenting views; on the other hand they accepted disputes and controversy and legitimated them with a theory of Torah as containing multiple possible meanings and interpretations (polysemy). Both the effort to establish unity and the effort to legitimate diversity, she argues, are textual fictions operating simultaneously in response to a fundamental social fragmentation. This, we might say, is the reality behind the rhetoric.

The erosion of rabbino-centrism in twentieth-century research on ancient Judaism led to a scholarly emphasis on the discontinuity that exists between rabbinic Judaism and other expressions of ancient Judaism—both earlier (a vertical discontinuity) and contemporary (a horizontal discontinuity). Increasingly, scholars came to view the rabbinic movement as small, fractured, and insular in the late first century. It was increasingly argued that it would be some time before rabbinic Judaism would acquire a sizable degree of prestige and authority among the general Jewish populace and even more time before a normative Judaism centered on the synagogue and the Torah would arise, largely in response to the Christianization of the empire.

The invention and reinvention of the rabbis and rabbinic Judaism have not ended, and the reassertion of a greater continuity between Second Temple and rabbinic Judaism as well as a more central role for the rabbis in Palestinian Jewish society in the early centuries CE are likely, as evidenced by the papers delivered at a recent symposium entitled "In the Wake of the Destruction: Was Rabbinic Judaism Normative?"[38] On the other hand, other recent scholarship relying on archaeological evidence points to a continuity between Second Temple Judaism and postdestruction Judaism *as distinct from rabbinic Judaism.*[39] The collected papers in the 2014 volume *Was 70 CE a Watershed in Jewish History: On Jews and Judaism before and after the Destruction of the Second Temple* add nuance to the question by recognizing that different aspects of Second Temple Judaism ceased, continued, or were transformed for different segments of the population, providing insight into the transition from diverse "Judaisms" and the rise of rabbinic Judaism.[40] We conclude then with the observation of Hillel Newman who, after considering scholarly claims and counterclaims regarding rabbinic Judaism, noted that "revisionism is a salutary process, which inevitably proceeds dialectically and in which overstatement and excess are to be expected. These excesses should not be canonized into a new fundamentalism."[41]

NOTES

1 See Shaye J. D. Cohen, *From the Maccabees to the Mishnah*, 3rd ed. (Louisville, KY: Westminster John Knox Press, 2014), chapter 1.

2 *B. Pesaḥim* 57a.

3 *B. Qiddushin* 66a.

4 For more on the philosophical issues dividing ancient Jewish sects, see Jonathan Klawans, *Josephus and the Theologies of Ancient Judaism* (New York: Oxford University Press, 2012).

5 Cohen, *From the Maccabees to the Mishnah*, pp. 142–146.

6 *B. Yoma* 71b. Rabbinic sources increasingly speak of knowledge of Torah as the true crown (i.e., basis for authority) in an attempt to legitimize their own claim to authority over considerations of lineage (*Midrash Psalms* on Ps 146:8; *Sifre Numbers; Koraḥ* 119; *m. 'Avot* 6:6; *b. Ta'anit* 7a).

7 For a discussion of the date and structure of tractate *Avot*, see Amram Tropper, *Wisdom, Politics, and Historiography: Tractate Avot in the Context of the Graeco-Roman Near East* (Oxford: Oxford University Press, 2004), chapter 3 and references provided there.

8 *Y. Ḥagigah* 1, 76d; *b. Berakhot* 5a.

9 *Sifre* Deuteronomy 313; *m. 'Avot* 5:22; *b. Megillah* 19b.

10 *B. Sanhedrin* 99a; *B. B. Meṣi'a* 59b.

11 *B. B. Batra* 12a.

12 *'Avot R. Natan* 4.

13 *T. 'Eduyot* 1'.

14 *Avot R. Natan* 4.

15 *B. B. Batra* 60b.

16 See, for example, *m. Rosh Hashanah* 4:1–4; *m. Pesaḥim* 10:5; *t. Shevi'it* 1:1; *b. Berakhot* 48b; *b. Soṭah* 40a, 47a; *b. Keritot* 9a.

17 *B. 'Eruvin* 13b.

18 *B. Megillah* 17b–18a; *b. Berakhot* 28b; *M. Rosh Hashanah* 4:1–4.

19 Rabbinic literature contains derogatory references to Bar Kokhba as well as graphic descriptions of the terrors and tortures of the revolt; see *y. Ta'anit* 4:5, 24a; *b. Giṭṭin* 57a–b; *b. Berakhot* 61b; *Lamentations Rabbah* ii. 2 and 5.

20 See *b. Berakhot* 61b.

21 For a discussion of the elaboration of the "chain of tradition" theme in early medieval sources such as *Seder Tannaim ve-Amoraim*, the *Iggeret*, and *Sefer ha-Qabbalah*, see Fred Astren, *Karaite Judaism and Historical Understanding* (Columbia: University of South Carolina Press, 2004), chapter 1 and especially pp. 57–60.

22 Varying accounts are provided by Rav Saadya Gaon, R. Shimshon of Sens, and others; but despite differences in detail and emphasis, the underlying purpose of these medieval writers is apologetic and the perspective is rabbino-centric. For a summary of several medieval accounts of the history of the Oral Law, see Ḥanokh Albeck, *Mavo la-Mishnah* (Jerusalem: Bialik Institute, 1966–1967), chapter 4 (Hebrew).

23 Though the author makes it clear that R. Akiva's death is not a punishment for any sin.

24 E. P. Sanders, *Paul and Palestinian Judaism* (Philadelphia: Fortress Press, 1977), p. 4 and passim.

25 Ibid., p. 38.

26 Sanders attributes these views to Wilhelm Bousset, Justus Köberle, and R. H. Charles (in ibid., pp. 38–41).

27 Ibid., p. 57.

28 Mention must be made of Jacob Neusner, a vocal proponent of the view that, as selective compositions shaped by the ideologies of their tradents and redactors, rabbinic texts are of limited use to the historian. According to Seth Schwartz in *Imperialism and Jewish Society, 200 BCE to 640 CE* (Princeton, NJ: Princeton University Press, 2001), Neusner effected a revolution in the study of ancient Judaism in his insistence on understanding rabbinic literature as a historical artifact of a society in which the rabbis themselves were marginal (p. 8). However, as Schwartz himself notes (ibid.), beginning in the 1980s, Neusner went on to adopt extreme and counterintuitive views regarding the unreliability of rabbinic attributions and the insusceptibility of rabbinic texts to analysis beyond the level of redaction.

29 Published in *The Literature of the Sages*, section 2, vol. 3 of *Compendia Rerum Iudaicarum Ad Novum Testamentum*, ed. Samuel Safrai (Assen, Netherlands / Philadelphia: Van Gorcum / Fortress Press, 1987), pp. 1–34.

30 *Hebrew Union College Annual* 55 (1984): 27–53. Many of the insights from this article are incorporated in Cohen's later work, *From the Maccabees to the Mishnah*.

31 *Exemplaria* 12 (2000): 21–62.

32 Martin Goodman, "The Function of Minim in Early Rabbinic Judaism," in *Geschichte-Tradition-Reflexion: Festschrift für Martin Hengel zum 70. Geburtstag*, ed. H. Cancik, H. Lichtenberger, and P. Schäfer (Tübingen: Mohr Siebeck, 1996), vol. 1, pp. 501–519.

33 B. 'Eruvin 13b.

34 Schwartz, *Imperialism and Jewish Society*.

35 Ibid., p. 91.

36 Hayim Lapin, "The Origins and Development of the Rabbinic Movement in the Land of Israel," in *The Cambridge History of Judaism*, ed. Steven T. Katz (Cambridge: Cambridge University Press, 2006), vol. 4, p. 225. These ideas find full development and exposition in Lapin's recent excellent book, *Rabbis as Romans: The Rabbinic Movement in Palestine, 100–400 C.E.* (New York: Oxford University Press, 2012).

37 Catherine Heszer, "Social Fragmentation, Plurality of Opinion, and Nonobservance of Halacha: Rabbis and Community in Late Roman Palestine," *Jewish Studies Quarterly* 1 (1993–1994): 234–251.

38 The proceedings were published in *Jewish Identities in Antiquity: Studies in Memory of Menahem Stern*, ed. Lee I. Levine and Daniel R. Schwartz (Tübingen: Mohr Siebeck, 2009), pp. 163–266.

39 See, for example, Joshua Schwartz, "Yavneh Revisited: Jewish 'Survival' in the Wake of the War of Destruction," in *Jews and Christians in the First and Second Centuries: How to Write Their History*, ed. Peter J. Tomson and Joshua Schwartz (Leiden: Brill, 2014), pp. 238–252. In addition, papers employing a wide range of methodologies to investigate Yavneh as both a historical reality and a concept

will be included in the conference volume *Yavne Revisited: The Historical Rabbis and the Rabbis of History*, ed. Peter J. Tomson and Joshua Schwartz (Leiden: Brill, forthcoming).

40 Edited by Daniel R. Schwartz and Zeev Weiss, in collaboration with Ruth A. Clements (Leiden: Brill, 2014).

41 Hillel Newman, "The Normativity of Rabbinic Judaism," in Levine and Schwartz, *Jewish Identities in Antiquity*, p. 171.

Conclusion

"In My Beginning Is My End"

ROBERT GOLDENBERG

This volume has focused on early Judaism, but it is interesting to note that there is no chapter devoted to the Bible, a book in which the earliest form of Judaism can seemingly be located. There is a reason for this, other than the merely practical consideration that a previous volume in this series was entirely devoted to the Hebrew scriptures. The more important reason is that the Jews, and for that matter Judaism as well, are essentially postbiblical phenomena. The Bible gave rise to the Jews and to Judaism, but neither is to be found there in any simple way.[1]

The Bible speaks of a nation called the Children of Israel, one subdivision of which (a tribe, they would have said) was called Judah. Judah was only one part of this larger whole and for a long time was politically split off from the larger portion of it; it would be meaningless to speak of "the Jews" as a clearly defined entity as long as that was the case. Then, by sheer historical chance as it were, the rest was swept away and only Judah was left. The people of Judah were now heirs to the heritage of the Children of Israel.

As heirs will do, they conceived of this prehistory as though it had been leading up to them the whole time. It is the rump Kingdom of Judah, not the larger and apparently wealthier Kingdom of Israel, that has the biblical authors' attention overall. Of the twelve sons of the eponymous Jacob, it is Judah who rescues the family from unspeakable tragedy, and it is from his putative descendants that the only successful kings of united Israel, namely David and Solomon, emerged.

Later a reconstituted remnant of the conquered rump kingdom returned to the old homeland. They rebuilt the national shrine in the old capital of Jerusalem and tried to construct a way of life that restored some of what had been lost over years of exile and foreign rule. It is among those people that the earliest forms of Judaism can be found.

They called themselves *yehudim*, that is, people of Judah, and their foreign rulers (for they remained under foreign rule) let that be their name, first in Aramaic, then in Greek, and finally in Latin.[2] The country was small: so many *yehudim* emigrated while others, it seems, were carried off; still, they called themselves *yehudim* or the equivalent wherever they settled, and they preserved—to the degree they could—a Judaean way of life.

Their foreign rulers tolerated and sometimes even encouraged and assisted this project. When the *yehuda'ei* in far-off Upper Egypt ran afoul of their neighbors and their temple to the Judaean god was destroyed, they appealed to the Persian authorities for help in restoring it, and those authorities gave more support (partial support to be sure, but more) than the *yehudi* authorities in Jerusalem to whom they had also appealed.

There is an important lesson in this early episode. A temple in which the ancestral god of Israel was honored had been destroyed, and those who had worshiped in this temple naturally wanted it back. Equally naturally, they thought that others who worshiped the same god in a similar temple (as they supposed) would support them in this desire, but about that they were wrong. Those who worshiped the god of Israel were united in some respects but not, it turns out, in all. Not even in all respects of that worship.

This pattern repeated itself throughout ancient Jewish history. People who called themselves *yehudim* (Hebrew) or *ioudaioi* (Greek) or *iudaei* (Latin) held many things in common, and about these things they could grow very passionate, but then, at surprising moments or in surprising ways, their unity broke down.

Several quick examples will shed light on this phenomenon. Under the Seleucid King Antiochus IV (175–165 BCE) a struggle broke out among aspirants to the high priesthood in Jerusalem. Two of these aspirants were brothers. To a degree the struggle was simply a matter of ambition and perhaps even greed, but the rivals also disagreed about the proper way to worship the God whose Temple they wished to govern. The issue, briefly, was whether it was incumbent upon *ioudaioi* to worship their God in a manner that distinguished him from all other gods and themselves from all other peoples. One rival thought such distinctiveness was (to use a modern term) the essence of Judaism, but his brother thought that was just a silly notion; in his view this attitude merely kept the Jews apart from the mainstream of modern life (then known as Hellenism). Not only did he think this silly; more significantly, he also thought it made other people dislike them and so was actually dangerous.[3]

Matters got out of hand. The struggle collapsed into all-out civil war until finally the king stepped in out of an understandable desire to maintain royal authority. Of course he threw his weight behind the faction that wanted Jews to be more like Greeks (because why not?), but other Jews kept up the struggle until the king gave in. These Jews really cared about their Temple, but they could not find a way to express that care to which they all could subscribe. They were willing to kill each other to express their care, but they could not agree.

Two hundred years later, when the Roman emperor Caligula wanted to put a statue of himself in every temple where Romans ruled, Jews, not only in Jerusalem, but in the capital city Rome as well, let it be known that he could kill them all but they would never yield to such a demand.[4] Thirty years after that, however, when the great rebellion against Rome broke out, Jews were divided. Some supported the revolution, some fought on the side of the Romans, some just laid low and hoped to survive. The great Jewish philosopher Philo had a nephew who used the name Tiberius Julius Alexander; he became a general in the Roman army and took part in the destruction of Jerusalem. Of him the Jewish historian Josephus mildly says that he had abandoned the ways of his ancestors.[5] The Roman historian Tacitus variously calls him an Egyptian or a Roman but never mentions his ancestors at all.[6]

This is the world we have seen examined in this book. Some contributors have tried to capture the wild diversity over centuries of the people called *ioudaioi*. Some have singled out one version from the many for closer inspection. Particular attention has been devoted to the rabbinic version of Judaism that ultimately captured the field and drove alternative conceptions underground, or out of the world of *ioudaioi*, or indeed out of existence altogether.[7]

Given this background, what are we talking about when we talk about the early forms of Judaism?[8] If we mean the group called *yehudim* or its cognates, then we can locate that group in the pre-exilic Kingdom of Judah, or more particularly among the returned exiles who appear in the biblical books of Ezra and Nehemiah. But in this book something more complicated seems in question: the contributors to this volume have been looking for the roots of a way of life that was then called *ioudaismos* and is now called Judaism. The group called *yehudim* had existed for quite a while already when the contours of that way of life first began to emerge.

Most of the salient elements of that way of life trace their origins in some way to that book, which is not discussed here, but that book repeatedly offers concepts without clarifying them. That is why the diversity seen here was not only possible but unavoidable. Again, some examples follow.

The Bible emphasizes keeping the Sabbath. It works the Sabbath into the very origins of the cosmos, and it condemns to death those who violate its rest. But it says remarkably little about how to keep the Sabbath: what are the prohibited acts of labor that must be avoided, and what (other than sacrificing a couple of sheep) should the people do with the leisure that is generated when they cannot engage in all those prohibited activities? It does not say, and for much of ancient Jewry we do not know how they answered that question. There were synagogues all over the diaspora—Professor Fine talks about a couple of them—but we hardly know what was done in them. No doubt those in attendance said some prayers—Dr. Langer talks about that—but we rarely can say what these were. Surely someone read from the Torah and probably someone expounded on it, but how did the worshipers decide what to read, and how did they decide who should expound? Again, we have no idea. Indeed, there is no reason to think they all were doing the same things—it seems clear that the Pharisees and the followers of Jesus had very different ideas about proper Sabbath observance—but they all were convinced that they were doing what the Torah (that is, God) wanted them to do. And the Dead Sea Scrolls give an idea of what some Jews had to say about other Jews who were doing things differently.

A more basic question brings us closer to the question raised by Schwartz in his chapter: who and what is the Israel whom the Torah (again, that is, God, so to speak) was addressing in the first place? One is tempted to oversimplify that question and answer "Why, of course, the people, the nation of Israel; it says so itself, repeatedly." But then what can it mean that the Christian Church, most of whose members were not and never had been *ioudaioi*, called itself the true Israel? And what can it mean that the Qumran scrolls refer to the people of Jerusalem of all places as the Children of Darkness? It is clear that scripture distinguishes between a certain group of people and the rest of humanity, but later interpretations differed drastically as to who was who.

This question leads to another, because each self-declared Israel had its own way of reading the Torah. Most Jews read the Torah as a book of behavioral rules, though Philo saw that it might be more as well. But Christians did not; as early as Paul they distinguished between the letter and the spirit and thought the other *ioudaioi* were blind to scripture's true meaning and enslaved to a bunch of meaningless laws. The Rabbis did not either; in rabbinic eyes, Jews who tried to base their lives directly on scripture were ignorant or heretical: without the rabbis' Oral Torah, the Written Torah could not possibly be fulfilled.

So what indeed are we talking about when we talk about early Judaism? The origins of various groups or practices? The rabbis, whose approach is simply called *yiddishkeit* two thousand years later? Or perhaps an ethnic consciousness that many, though not all, of these groups did seem to share? Such questions have haunted every page of this book.

* * *

So much for the beginning. What about the end?

The Jewish end, of course, is not quite the counterpart to the Jewish beginning: the Jews did have a beginning, but they have not yet come to an end. However, as the title of this chapter suggests, it is useful to examine the Jewish present—neither end nor beginning—and inquire whether this volume sheds any light on the Jews and their situation today.

With respect to recent Jewish history, the two overwhelming events of the last century were the Shoah and the establishment of the State of Israel. In the course of ancient history, something like each of those events took place, and it is instructive to have a brief look at similarities and differences.

There was no systematic attempt in antiquity to eradicate the Jews, though there were local attempts, best known to us from Alexandria, which came close.[9] Why would anyone have been so hostile to the Jews as to behave in this way? Perhaps the most useful point to make in this connection is that in the ancient world groups massacred each other with some frequency. In order to maintain their empire, the citizens of Athens were ready to obliterate cities inhabited by other Greeks.[10] When Mithridates VI, King of Pontus, wanted to get the Romans out of Asia Minor, he arranged that on a certain day in 88 BCE all Italians in his kingdom should be killed. The number of dead reached the tens of thousands.[11] Jews and Greeks lived side by side in many Mediterranean cities and did not always get along; ethnic groups in modern American cities do not always do much better. At a later time one could speak of anti-Semitism as a chronic disease of Western civilization (sometimes latent, sometimes not), but that term is not very useful when discussing interethnic tensions in the ancient city.

Nor was hostility the only attitude of others toward the Jews; Erich Gruen made this point at greater length in his chapter, and it is important. Jews have almost always constituted a minority in the places where they lived, and even where things might have seemed otherwise—Judah before the exile or Judaea under the Maccabees—they saw themselves as a beleaguered minority surrounded by alien peoples, alien gods, alien ways of life. In fact, however, and the occasional quite spectacular breakdowns notwithstanding, Jews were pretty much left alone to preserve their own heritage; mostly, the Jews just lived their lives. That is a major implication of this book.[12]

Another similarity between ancient and more recent Jewish history has to do with trauma. The ancient Jewish trauma was the destruction of the Temple. One might say that outside Judaea this event was only of theological significance, but that is to underestimate the bond between diaspora Jews and the ancient homeland. I have already mentioned the widespread dismay when Caligula proposed to defile (as the Jews saw it) the Temple. Now the whole basis of the Jews' covenant with their God had been taken away.

The modern equivalent developed in two forms. The Shoah was a horror, but outside the war zone the formal arrangements of diaspora Jewish life seemingly remained as they had been, with only a vague sense of mourning and ever-present danger that lingers everywhere in Jewish life. But the other major trauma concerns the complex changes that we call the Emancipation. As in antiquity, the whole previous basis of the Jews' collective life was demolished. In exchange for receiving citizenship in the countries where they lived (no small thing to be sure), the Jews lost the legally protected right to live according to the Torah, and their rabbis lost the dominant authority that they had enjoyed for a thousand years. The early rabbis had figured out how to rescue Judaism from the effects of the ancient disaster. It is not clear who outside the Orthodox world is even listening as modern rabbis try to repeat that accomplishment. What the rabbis were given, the rabbis have had taken away.

In one important respect the collapse of rabbinic authority has returned the Jews to a situation rather like the one reflected early in this book, that is, the vigorous diversity in ways of life that different groups of Jews have adopted. With respect to ancient Jewry, several chapters in this volume discuss religious diversity, but they could have talked about political diversity as well: I have already mentioned that the Jews could not achieve unity in 66 CE when the war against Rome broke out. Perhaps we can learn from this that plurality, not consensus, is the natural Jewish configuration. We often receive the message that the Jewish people was tightly united until (pick your villain: Reform? socialism?) blew things apart, but this book suggests something different: the medieval consensus around rabbinic leadership (itself never perfect) was the anomaly, not the disorientation and division that mark Jewish life today.

For a while it seemed that the Jews might unite instead around a new set of would-be leaders called Zionists, and this brings us to the other major event of modern Jewish history. Zionism, at least secular Zionism, frankly offered itself as the successor to rabbinic Judaism, a new, modern basis for organized Jewish life.

The creation of the State of Israel brought about a situation surprisingly like the situation at the turn of the eras: most Jews lived outside the Land of Israel but cared about what was happening there. Many of those Jews, then as now, could have moved back to the Land but did not; they visited, but then they went home. They watched from afar and sent lots of money—most of it back then to the Temple in the form of the annual half-shekel—and they got upset when bad things happened there, but they went on with their lives wherever they were. This is one of the most striking continuities in all of Jewish history.

A related similarity (not quite a continuity, after so long a break) is the restoration of Jewish sovereignty, under the Maccabees then and now again through Zionism. In the case of ancient Judaea, the great diversity that has been reflected in this book initially flourished under conditions of sovereignty, though it survived into the period of Roman domination. In modern times the diversity came first, and one might say it has been a thorn in the side of Israeli governments since 1948; today it is no less luxuriant in the diaspora than in the Jewish state. The point again seems to be that Jewish life does not naturally tend toward consensus: contention seems built into the Jewish collective psyche.

* * *

I wish in closing to return from the end to the beginning. The Jewish people have returned to a situation rather like the one in which they found themselves at the time of their origins. The homeland is surrounded by enemies and wrought with faction. The diaspora is holding its own, but largely on terms that are not of their own designing. Indeed, it is sometimes forgotten that even the Bible is the product of a minority, indeed a minority that saw itself as embattled and in danger. Deuteronomy reflects the mood of a society fighting for its integrity while surrounded by other societies who embodied deeply inimical values. The prophets, speaking to their own people, represented a monotheist (or henotheist) faction surrounded by fellow Israelites who saw nothing wrong with a polytheistic way of life. The prophets' frantic entreaties are those of would-be leaders who cannot get other people to listen to them. There are leaders today who sound like that as well. The long interlude of the Middle Ages teaches us that things can always be different, but meanwhile the end and the beginning turn out to have a lot in common. *Plus ça change, plus c'est la même chose.*

NOTES

1 By "the Bible," I always mean the Hebrew scriptures (Old Testament).

2 This name appears in biblical writings starting during the time of the Exile; it appears prominently in the narrative portions of Jeremiah as well as in the Books of Nehemiah and Esther.

3 For a classical statement of this point of view, admittedly as expressed by its opponents, see 1 Maccabees 1:11.

4 In Book 18 of his *Jewish Antiquities* (18.vii.2–9 §§261–304, Loeb Classical Library [LCL] vol. 12, pp. 154–179), Josephus tells the story in great detail.

5 *Jewish Antiquities* 20.v.2 §100 (LCL vol. 13, pp. 54–55).

6 An Egyptian in *Histories* 1.11.1 (LCL vol. 1, pp. 20–21); a Roman knight in *Annals* 15.28.3 (LCL vol. 4, pp. 258–259).

7 The Christians are the most important example here, though they were happy enough to go.

8 The only chapter in this book that is headed by a question is the one by Seth Schwartz, and this is his question as well.

9 Philo describes these events in some detail. See his two memoirs, *Against Flaccus* and *The Embassy to Gaius*.

10 Melos (Thucydides, 5.116, LCL vol. 3, pp. 176–179). The people of Mytilene narrowly escaped a similar fate (Thucydides, 3.36, LCL vol. 2, pp. 54–59).

11 Plutarch's figure of 150,000 (*Sulla* 24.4, LCL vol. 4, pp. 404–405) is probably exaggerated, but see Appian, *Roman History* XII (*Mithridatic Wars*) iv.22–23 (LCL vol. 2, pp. 278–281), and Valerius Maximus, *Memorable Doings and Sayings* ix.2 ext. 3 (LCL vol. 2, pp. 314–315), for the still remarkable figure of 80,000 killed in one day.

12 This was the case even in the Middle Ages, which are often depicted in dramatically different terms, and it is the case today. If Jewish life in our time sometimes appears to be falling apart, the cause is not hostility but the opposite.

Elizabeth Shanks Alexander is Professor of Talmud and Rabbinics in the Department of Religious Studies at the University of Virginia. She is the author of *Transmitting Mishnah: The Shaping Influence of Oral Tradition* and *Gender and Timebound Commandments in Judaism* and coeditor of *Religious Studies and Rabbinics: A Conversation.*

Steven Fine is the Dean Pinkhos Churgin Professor of Jewish History and director of the Center for Israel Studies at Yeshiva University. His recent books include *The Menorah: From the Bible to Modern Israel*; *Art, History and the Historiography of Judaism in Roman Antiquity*; and *Art and Judaism in the Greco-Roman World.*

Robert Goldenberg is Emeritus Professor of History and Judaic Studies at Stony Brook University. A former editor of the *AJS Review*, his most recent book is *The Emergence of Judaism.*

Erich S. Gruen is Gladys Rehard Wood Professor of History and Classics, Emeritus, at the University of California, Berkeley. He is the author of *Heritage and Hellenism: The Reinvention of Jewish Tradition, Diaspora: Jews amidst Greeks and Romans,* and *Rethinking the Other in Antiquity.*

Christine Hayes is Weis Professor of Classical Judaica at Yale University and author of several works on biblical and rabbinic Judaism, including *Gentile Impurities and Jewish Identities* and *What's Divine about Divine Law? Early Perspectives*, winner of the 2015 National Jewish Book Award and the 2016 Jordan Schnitzer Award.

Martha Himmelfarb is the William H. Danforth Professor of Religion and director of the Program in Judaic Studies at Princeton University.

Her most recent book is *Jewish Messiahs in a Christian Empire: A History of the Book of Zerubbabel.*

Ruth Langer is Professor of Jewish Studies and Associate Director of the Center for Christian-Jewish Learning at Boston College. Her recent books include *Cursing the Christians? A History of the Birkat HaMinim* and *Jewish Liturgy: A Guide to Research.* She is currently working on a history of Jewish liturgy.

Adele Reinhartz is Professor of Classics and Religious Studies at the University of Ottawa and was elected to the Royal Society of Canada and the American Academy of Jewish Research. Her books include *Befriending the Beloved Disciple: A Jewish Reading of the Gospel of John; Scripture on the Silver Screen;* and *Casting out the Withered Branch: The Gospel of John and the Parting of the Ways.*

Seth Schwartz is the Lucius N. Littauer Professor of Classical Jewish Civilization and chair of the Department of History at Columbia University. He is the author of *Imperialism and Jewish Society, 200 BCE–640 CE* and *Were the Jews a Mediterranean Society? Reciprocity and Solidarity in Ancient Judaism.*

James VanderKam is the John A. O'Brien Professor of Hebrew Scriptures, Emeritus, at the University of Notre Dame. He has been a member of the committee charged with publishing the Dead Sea Scrolls and has written *The Dead Sea Scrolls Today* and coauthored *The Meaning of the Dead Sea Scrolls.*

INDEX